EPIC TINY VICTORIES

A Hopeful Memoir about Depression, Anxiety, and Reframing Your Life

Colin Ryan

Published by Haver Press

Copyright © 2026 by Colin Ryan

978-0-9997168-2-3 Paperback | 978-0-9997168-3-0 Ebook

All rights reserved, including the right to reproduce this book or portions thereof in any form whatsoever. For information, email info@colinryanspeaks.com.

Names and identifying characteristics of students, study participants, and others have been changed unless permission was granted.

First print edition January 1, 2026.

Cover Design by Colin Ryan, with inspiration from Steve Daugherty and Dale Baker. Layout by Carolyn Sheltraw. Edited by Jan Gleiter.

For information about special discounts for bulk purchases, contact the author at info@colinryanspeaks.com. Colin Ryan is a professional keynote speaker and entertainer. For more information or to book an event, visit www.colinryanspeaks.com.

. . .

Please note that I am not a licensed mental health professional, therapist, psychiatrist, or psychologist. The information, views, and opinions I express should not be considered professional advice or treatment recommendations.

Always consult with a licensed mental health professional before making any decisions related to your mental health. This book is not intended to diagnose, treat, or prevent any illness or to act as a substitute for advice from a doctor or psychiatrist.

Each individual's mental health needs are unique, and seeking personalized guidance from a qualified professional can be valuable. If you are experiencing a mental health crisis or have urgent concerns, please seek immediate assistance from a qualified healthcare provider, mental health hotline, or emergency services in your country.

This content is based on my personal experiences, research, and general knowledge up until the time of publication.

For Lindsey, Remy, and Enzo.

To my family, my friends, and the people who believe in me, challenge me, and stand beside me.

Thank you from the bottom of my heart.

Honestly, I should give you actual money out of my wallet, but how about this dedication instead?

TABLE OF CONTENTS

Prologue...ix

Part 1 1
  1. A Successful Depressive 3
  2. Unaccompanied.................................... 9
  3. Unreliable Narrators............................ 17
  4. The F-I-A-S-C-O................................. 23
  5. It Ain't Easy Being Wheezy...................... 29
  6. Saved by the Belle.............................. 37
  7. Holy(ish)....................................... 43
  8. Mayor of Campus................................. 53
  9. Once Upon a Huffy in Hollywood.................. 65
  10. Scotland Needs Subtitles....................... 75
  11. Pamplona Took My Breath Away................... 85
  12. Accidental Movie Star.......................... 93
  13. A Tourist in Other People's Passions.......... 101
  14. My Secret Sentence............................ 111
  15. Late to the Party............................. 119
  16. Ruptures...................................... 127
  17. An Audience of One............................ 137

Part 2 143
  18. From My Seat to the Stage..................... 145
  19. The Setup and the Punch....................... 153
  20. Somehow I Invent a Career..................... 159

21. Finding Life Funny 167
22. Story Therapy 177
23. The Heckler in My Head 187
24. The Big Picture 195
25. One Minute Less Afraid 203
26. The Complicated Art of Financial Compassion 211
27. We Were All 11 223
28. The Blurt, the Bat, and Being Seen 229
29. Social Anxiety on a Jumbotron 237
30. Breakthroughs at the Bottom 247
31. Diagnosed, at Last 259
32. A Photo of Us 269
33. Authorland 275
34. Reliable 285

Epilogue 293

Acknowledgements 297
About the Author 301
About the Editor 303
Easy Ways to Share This Book 305
Photo Gallery 313
Endnotes 315

PROLOGUE
BE STUBBORN AND BE KIND

I used to think, *There is something* wrong *with me*. I had this thought so many times that I lost count.

I wondered why I could feel crushingly depressed and constantly anxious both when things in my life were going badly *and* when things were great. I was convinced I would always feel this way.

For most of my life, I remained undiagnosed, so I couldn't figure out what to do to feel better. Later than I should have, I sought help, and things began to change.

Then one day, I started turning my struggles into stories. This didn't feel momentous; I simply needed material for open mics. But I liked how it felt to say my secrets out loud. I felt safer and more normal.

So I kept turning my struggles into stories. I had no idea that this was changing me, but it was. In fact, it was saving me. And it was leading me to who I am now.

I used to think, *There is something* wrong *with me.* I don't have this thought anymore.

• • •

In my adult life, I became a speaker, author, entrepreneur, and regular applause-getter, only to discover those things didn't help me the way I had hoped they would. In fact, the success I experienced didn't solve my deeper problems; it revealed them. It brought them to the surface in terribly stressful ways that I went to great lengths to hide.

In this way, my journey mirrors that of others'—maybe even yours. Because without the answers I needed, I just had to keep going. Surviving. Stumbling along in the dark. Doing my best, even on the days when it felt like my best was probably equal to other people's worst.

But I never gave up, and I'm so glad I didn't.

The effort to get a better grasp on exactly what my brain was up to was exhausting, and it sometimes seemed hopeless. But in my case, finally understanding what was happening inside my head was life-changing. Getting to that point required diligence, persistence, vulnerability, willingness to ask for help, true friends, and the counsel of people wiser than I am.

If dealing with your feelings about yourself and life in general has been painfully difficult at times, let me take this opportunity to state the capital-T truth, as I see it:

Struggling with your mental health does not mean something is wrong with you. You are not broken, and you are far from alone.

You are missing something you need, however. There is something that you must figure out, accept, overcome, or view differently so you can function better and live with more ease. Whatever this is must be clarified and then addressed, and that process requires time, effort, and determination.

I promise that if you stick with this long enough and find the determination—an on-and-off-and-on-again style of commitment is fine; it comes with the territory, after all—you will succeed. I know because I did.

Obviously, this is not easy. In fact, this is one of the hardest things that you can do. It also happens to be one of the most important and valuable. Understanding yourself better and managing your mental health will have enormous benefits. You'll be able to help yourself when challenges arise, share your story, summon the courage to show up for others who need you, and live with more peace—even joy at times.

You deserve to feel more joy. I'm going to repeat that. You absolutely deserve a joyful life.

Here are two things that should help in your quest for happiness:

Be Stubborn. Don't quit. Keep trying different things until you find the right mix of mental health tools. I managed to figure out mine *only* because I was stubborn enough not to give up. I wouldn't be here if I hadn't been.

Be Kind. Success in this mission will require you to be kind to yourself for as long as necessary. (It doesn't hurt to be kind to others, either!) As I see it, this is your foundation and protective armor. So, when you have a cruel thought about yourself, try to recognize that you are judging yourself unfairly. Then, instead of listening to that harsh judgment, try responding to yourself with kindness, until that thought floats away and is replaced by others.

Whenever you feel awful about things, refuse to stop believing in your inherent worth, and speak to yourself the way you would to a friend who needs your support. This can require a lot of effort, for sure. And that is why I recommend that you be stubborn and be kind.

• • •

While we may not know each other, I wrote this book in the hopes that you would read it. If you are a person navigating depression or anxiety, or you want to support someone who is, I think these stories should help.

Becoming the people we want to be *is* possible, and it's a worthy project. It's slow, though. My journey was confusing, awkward, humiliating, and, at times, really funny. Maybe yours has been, too. Like me, you're probably not "done" yet. There's always something else still to learn. But that's okay because we *are* getting better, braver, stronger, and smarter.

I have made two concerted efforts in writing this book: to be as honest as I can and to find as much humor in my experiences as I can. To be clear, the more important of these two goals is honesty. I'm confident we'll find some chances to laugh about all this, but at other points, we'll hang out together in the midst of our funk. I hope that's okay. But I'm also not aware of any rule that states that a book about depression needs to *be* depressing, too. If there is one, I'd break it anyway.

The first part of this book is essentially what a person's life looks like when they don't know what's happening in their head, and any progress feels almost invisible. Near constant confusion, paired with motivation that waxes and wanes, can make life seem to be happening *to* you rather than the result of choices made and actions taken *by* you. That was my experience throughout my childhood and into my twenties.

The second part is about my coming to see myself as a character in a story and wanting that story to be a good one—a story I could be proud of. My determination helped me muster the courage and motivation I needed to start making things happen instead of waiting for them to happen. It also helped that I sought support from friends and experts and found tools I could use to manage my mental health better than I ever had before.

This is why I'm convinced that it's possible to thrive (mostly!) with anxiety and depression. But let's face it, when it comes to dealing with mental health challenges, there aren't a lot of "and-the-crowd-goes-wild" types of victories. What there are a lot of, on the other hand, are *tiny* victories.

Forward motion can happen in such small increments that it's easy to miss. But those forward steps, however small, are a big deal. Once you learn to spot them, you'll discover that all these tiny victories matter, and they matter a lot. I believe that courage, transformation, and just plain great stories to reflect on and share can spring from those tiny victories just as much as they do from the epic ones.

Let me tell you about mine.

PART 1

CHAPTER 1
A SUCCESSFUL DEPRESSIVE

I managed to successfully avoid going to therapy until my mid-twenties. I wouldn't say I was smug about it or anything, but I suppose it did feel like some kind of an accomplishment.

Now, the streak was over. I was sitting in the lobby of a medical facility in a large, brick building with opaque windows, waiting for a complete stranger named Sam. The magazines on the coffee table were all out of date. The air smelled like industrial carpet cleaner and surrender.

I was meeting Sam because he was a psychotherapist, and I was in the worst depression of my life. Not only was it affecting my relationships and my sleep—it was now threatening my career. I'd started calling in sick to work, not because I was physically ill, but because I couldn't figure out how to get out of bed and pretend to be a functional human being. My boss had definitely noticed. I thought, *I'm not supposed to be here. I'm not supposed to be struggling so much with just being a person. How did my life get so far off-track?*

There were two clear reasons I'd never been to a therapist before: my mom and my dad. (Usually, they're why people *seek* therapy.) In my case, my mom was a born-again Christian, so I had grown up with a strong emphasis on *not* seeking secular therapy. It was considered "the wisdom of man" and something to be wary of. And my dad was Irish Catholic. Let me explain that group's mental health strategy in case it's not familiar to you. Basically, what you do is you hold your emotions in, well, until you die. And then you *win*. I had been trying both methods, and neither was even remotely helping. So there I was, waiting to meet Sam and hoping he had a third option.

He finally came up to me, shook my hand, and led me back to a small office. He had steely gray hair, kind eyes, and seemed to be a few years older than me. We sat down, and Sam asked, "So, what made you want to try therapy?"

I said, while staring at the floor, "I think something's wrong with me. The way I talk to myself . . . the way I think about myself . . . I don't know how much longer I can keep going like this." I ended, in defeat, "I think I'm really messed up."

Sam said, "Okay. And you thought, you know, now is as good a time as any?"

I thought, *No, man, this is not "as good a time as any." This is the end of the line for me. Why are you so chipper?*

I glanced at the diploma over his shoulder. It said Stanford, but probably anyone could print one of those out.

Then, I did something brilliant. Or more accurately, I didn't do something. I didn't leave.

Over the next hour, I said things to Sam I had never said out loud to anyone. No matter what I said, I couldn't faze him. Whatever awful thing I confessed about the carousel of

CHAPTER 1: A SUCCESSFUL DEPRESSIVE

criticism happening in my brain, he would just nod and say, "Okay" in a calm, even tone. And he'd encourage me to continue. I started to feel like I could breathe again.

By the end of the hour, I was drained, exhausted, and . . . hopeful.

Sam asked, "Should we schedule our next appointment?" (It turned out I wasn't all fixed in one session. Imagine my surprise.) We met again, and then again. Over the next several months, we did a lot of amazing work together.

It wasn't *all* good though. In the process, I developed a new phobia I'd not anticipated: the fear of seeing my therapist in public. If only I'd thought to explain, "Look Sam, you seem like a good guy, but the thing is, you simply know *too much*. I can't have you walking around out there, in life. I'm going to need you to stay in this little office. This is the deal I'm offering you. At least if you want my co-pay."

To make matters worse, he lived in my neighborhood. I saw him constantly. At least three mornings a week, he'd walk his daughter to school around the time I'd be heading to my car to go to work.

We never actually came close enough to engage with each other, but I imagined that if we did, his daughter would take one look at me and say, "Oh, that's *Colin*, isn't it?"

Sam would say, "Where?"

She'd respond, "Over there, hiding behind that Dodge Neon."

She'd be right. I would be hiding behind a Dodge Neon. My Dodge Neon. My forest-green, 1998 Dodge Neon with hideous white hubcaps and a crumpled roof, thanks to heavy snowfall from the previous winter. I had simply punched the ceiling up until it was somewhat close to its original shape because it wasn't worth having it properly repaired.

My imagined scenario would end with Sam saying, "Oh . . . *that's* his car. No wonder he's depressed."

Truthfully, despite this minor element of (potential) awkwardness, it was within only a few sessions that I realized the work Sam and I were doing was saving my life.

Like most people with mental health challenges, I thought therapy would lead to some profound realizations and a host of nuanced insights (that I could pepper into conversations to sound smart). And I did gain many of those. But, ultimately, the most profound thing I learned from Sam was embedded in the very first word he said to me. "Okay."

I had told him I believed something was deeply, perhaps fundamentally, wrong with me, and he had said, in a gentle voice, "Okay." I was often barraged by toxic, frightening thoughts like this. It was as though my brain had figured out how to create the perfect amount of poison. It wouldn't kill me but would paralyze me completely. And that "Okay" was the antivenom.

I experienced something with Sam I'd never experienced before: I was completely vulnerable, and I was completely accepted. It was transformative.

I knew if I were to have any hope of living a long life, instead of one that ended prematurely because of anxiety and depression, I would have to learn how to do this for myself.

I did. Quite easily, in fact. It only took thousands of dollars, 15 years, and roughly ten different medications. Gradually, I came to understand that, on my very darkest of days, *I* wasn't telling myself to give it all up; my disease was. This started me on a path of learning about my human brain, identifying techniques I could implement, and building a support system to lean on. I'd be lying if I didn't admit that many days felt impossible. But I kept going.

Now, I am not only alive, I am also what one might call a "successful depressive." I've learned how to thrive while having anxiety, depression, and a great many of the stresses and challenges a person can face.

All in all, I live a pretty good life. I'm a public speaker, an author, an entrepreneur, a husband, a dog dad, a son, a brother, and a friend. But I am also a person for whom depression has been a lifelong, unchosen companion and an undivorceable other half. Throughout my life, there have been many times I've been able to manage my depression, and many times my depression has managed me.

I might never *not* be a person who experiences depression. My brain might never *not* create overwhelming thoughts that tempt me to spiral. But when it does, I now know to say, "Okay." Now I have weapons I use against my mental illness instead of against myself.

There have been many times that I have looked back on those conversations with my very first therapist and felt certain that Sam had saved my life. That wasn't entirely accurate. *I* saved my life. I saved my life by being willing to sit in an unfamiliar room and share my worst thoughts aloud, so I could learn how to respond to them differently Wisely, I didn't attempt to take this on alone.

This taught me that we don't confront our mental health challenges and learn to live with them because something is wrong with us. Quite the opposite. We wrestle, grow, and face what needs to be faced because something is *right* with us.

Somewhere inside, the belief exists that doing this work makes a better life possible. And it does.

I started out my life feeling about as helpless as one can feel and afraid of pretty much everything. It took me a long time to realize that one way I could change my life was to see it as a story and myself as the author creating that story. To steer the story in the direction I wanted, I needed to learn how to recognize, celebrate, and leverage each small step I took.

So, where did all of this start, and what were the significant moments along the way that shaped my challenging, slow, and meaningful journey to become the person I always hoped I could be?

Let's go back and see.

CHAPTER 2
UNACCOMPANIED

By the time I reached my eighth birthday, I already had an impressive collection of those wings-pins that the airline gives children when they fly by themselves. An attendant would dramatically pin a little set of plastic wings on my shirt collar, and I'd say, "Oh, wow, a pin . . ." I wanted to ask, *Do you have any Red Vines you can give out instead?* That would have sparked real joy in me. I was twenty-plus flights in, and I was like a burned-out air marshal with a sweet tooth.

My mother and father had divorced when I was about three, and a few years after that, my mom and stepdad informed me that we would be moving across the country. We were leaving my birth state of California for some place called "New York," where there was something called "snow." Starting at age six, I took six cross-country trips (12 flying days) per year to be with each of my two families.

Traveling back and forth between two sets of parents was a familiar pattern for me. In fact, I couldn't remember anything else. Throughout my childhood, every year I had two Christmases, two birthdays, and two separate families. For me, they were two disconnected worlds that never intersected.

On those airplane days, I was an "Unaccompanied Minor." It was always exciting and a little scary. My parents would wake me while it was still dark, and we'd drive a long way to the airport. They'd walk me all the way up to the gate, where I'd be adorned with my latest pin. Then, I'd hug my parents and walk briskly down the long jet bridge, looking back a few times. They would stand there waving until I was out of sight.

I always got on the plane before the other passengers, and by the time the adults started filing in, I was already unwrapping the first (of several) watermelon Airheads. The passenger assigned the seat next to mine would usually give me a funny look. I took this to mean that they thought I was too little to be by myself, but I knew I could prove them wrong. Soon, I was regaling them with uproarious selections from my newest joke book and asking them what *their* favorite Roald Dahl novel was (mine was *The BFG*). I was sure I appeared to them to be positively brimming with confidence.

But I wasn't confident. Not at all. I was pretending. The whole time, I was trying not to wonder, *Is everything going to go okay? Will there be any big bumps in the air? Or a crash?* I was scared on those flying days, and truthfully, I was scared a lot of the time. I had these two completely separate families, and I was scared of not belonging to either one. Talking to the adult sitting next to me made me feel braver, even if it was just for that moment.

Once, a flight attendant asked me if I wanted to sit up in first class. *Heck, yes! I hope they have ice cream in first class!* I

CHAPTER 2: UNACCOMPANIED

hurried up there before she could change her mind, and soon, I was experiencing the lifestyle of the rich and famous! I could stretch out my legs as far as they would go. (Not that far.) I could order a steady stream of Cherry 7-Ups (in a whole can instead of a little glass stuffed full of ice). Best of all was the flight attendant's request that I read her a few of my favorite jokes.

Up in first class, I looked over at the woman sitting next to me. She was wearing business clothes and looked really busy and stressed. She had an open briefcase and folders and files spread everywhere. I babbled on at her anyway, until she eventually put down her work and paid attention to what I was saying. A few weeks later, my parents got a letter from this woman saying what a bright young man I was. She was the mayor of San Diego.

At age seven, with a full year of being a "frequent flyer" behind me, my parents sat me down and asked if I was okay with changing planes at some airport. Nonstop flights were quite expensive and getting harder to find. I could tell they felt bad asking, so I replied, "Of course!" But I was nervous about it. *How would I find my way around a strange airport without my parents?*

It was intimidating at first, but I quickly got used to it. I was always assigned an adult from the airline who walked with me to my next gate. Sometimes, this meant we'd walk together for about 30 feet. Other times, when there was a really long layover, they'd take me to a little room where I could wait. I was usually the only one there. Once, they tried to make the dull room more fun by adding Fisher-Price blocks, which I found a bit condescending. Another time, there was a tiny TV playing a movie about a heroic blonde man who fought aliens with a sword and a scantily clad woman who kept looking at him the whole time, which I found pretty intriguing.

I always felt that "Unaccompanied Minor" was kind of a bummer of a name. *Geez, American Airlines, are you trying to make me feel bad or something?* I tried to look on the bright side, but I didn't like having to fly 3,000 miles to see each half of my family. I didn't like being the only kid in my class whose parents lived that far away from each other. I didn't like how scared I felt at times.

I had no idea I would soon meet a person who had figured out how to be brave all the time, my Grandma Edmay. Because she lived in South Africa, the time and expense of air travel meant seeing her was a rare and incredibly special occasion.

My gran was four feet, nine inches tall. If she took her hat off, her hair would poof straight up, so technically she was more like five feet. (I don't want to deny her those inches.) Nonetheless, she seemed larger than life. She spoke both English and Afrikaans and a fair amount of Swahili, Xhosa, and Zulu, too. Her British accent made her sound like a posh, late-era Audrey Hepburn. She was not prim and proper, though. She often had a devilish twinkle in her eye, and she would teach me to play such British card games as Whist and Casino, where the object wasn't so much to win as to creatively and memorably heckle each other. My grandma was like my own personal Mary Poppins—I wasn't afraid of anything when she was around.

My gran and I had two very important bonds. The first was that, because my grandfather had passed away years earlier, when she came to America to visit us, she flew solo. We were

CHAPTER 2: UNACCOMPANIED

both unaccompanied. I was an unaccompanied minor, and she was, I liked to think, an unaccompanied senior.

The other thing we had in common was that my gran also loved to chat with people. But she took that confidence to a whole new level. She would talk to anyone and everyone around us. If no one came near enough, she'd chase after them. This was mortifying. Every time I looked away, she would march off towards the nearest group of people. Once, we were waiting in line to get into the Science Museum, and my mom and I realized we'd lost Gran. Mom sent me to go looking, and when I found her, she was further up the line, holding both the hands of a tall man we didn't know, staring up into his eyes, and asking him alarmingly personal questions.

Before I could step in, she asked, "How much money do you make?"

His expression told me he was thinking, *You didn't even ask my name yet.*

She went on, "Are you happy with your life?"

He looked at her like, *Holy crap, I just met you!*

Finally, she wondered aloud, sort of to him but also to anyone in earshot, "Do you know if this museum offers any discounts for an old woman?"

My gran asked for, and received, a lot of discounts.

Honestly, I needn't have been embarrassed. Although the man at the museum was (justifiably) taken aback, strangers almost universally responded positively. She didn't always ask such intrusive questions, and she brought kindness, humor, and genuine curiosity to every conversation she had. She would always find something about any person that she could connect with. She liked people, and people liked her. She was a really good listener—a second and third question person. As we watched her go through a group, having these conversations one by one, it was as though she was changing the energy of the entire room. Or line. (Or library.)

Eventually, I stopped worrying about whether she was going to talk to every single person she saw (she would), because I realized there was little to be embarrassed by and plenty to be inspired by. My gran taught me that one of the most interesting things about me was my interest in other people. I wanted to be like her.

As I got older, my mom shared more with me about her life growing up in South Africa and what both she and my gran had experienced living through decades of political upheaval. I understood them both in a more complex way. I could see that my gran had had many hard experiences in her life, that she and my grandfather had had a toxic and painful relationship, and that people in her life had made her feel insignificant. This meant that my gran *built* the confident version of herself that I knew. She had done it one conversation at a time. My gran gave me a path I could follow so I could be less scared and more confident.

She also made me consider the possibility that being "unaccompanied," and having the feeling that I didn't quite "fit" anywhere, wasn't all bad. In a way, it gave me a superpower: I could tell when other people felt alone, too.

I was at a friend's birthday party, and I saw a new kid standing off to the side, uncertain of who to talk to. So, I went over and talked to her. I asked her questions, and we chatted away, and I realized this was exactly what my gran would have done if she were there. It may even have been an improvement

CHAPTER 2: UNACCOMPANIED

on Gran, because I didn't ask this girl how much money she made.

Whenever my grandma was around, I felt better about everything. We were both Unaccompanied, after all. We played by our own rules. When she was around, I wasn't afraid. I wished she were around more, but she could never stay as long as I wanted her to. Just like ol' Mary Poppins, it seemed that she stayed only until the wind changed.

Whenever she flew back home to South Africa, I would try to keep her presence alive for a while by being more confident and trying to make everybody laugh. But eventually, the bad feelings always came back. Having two separate families on opposite ends of the country was difficult in a way I couldn't fully explain.

CHAPTER 3
UNRELIABLE NARRATORS

In addition to the good fortune of celebrating double Christmases and double birthdays, I also gained a unique kind of cachet among my bicoastal friend groups. They both seemed to think that being from a faraway place made me cool.

When I made new friends in California, I would tell them I lived in New York, and they would go, "Awesome! What part?" I'd say, "Schenectady." They would respond, "Wow!!!" (Clearly, they had never been to Schenectady.) When I made new friends in New York, I would tell them I was born in California. They would react almost identically. "Awesome! What part?" I'd reply, "Fresno." They would go, "Wow!!!" (Clearly, they had never been to Fresno.)

I went to school and spent most of the year on the East Coast with my mom and stepdad, and I spent Christmas break, February break, and summer break on the West Coast with my dad and stepmom. This uncommon arrangement was in no way abnormal for me, and in no way did it diminish the fact that I absolutely adored my mom and my dad.

My mom, Jackie, was an immigrant to this country. She was graceful and glamorous, and my whole life, she kept her refined South African accent. My mom was smart, hard-working, and a woman of remarkable faith. Growing up, I went to church with her, baked zucchini bread with her, and tried to make her laugh every chance I got. She would enthrall my sisters, Leigh and Claire, and me with stories about her life growing up in South Africa.

My dad, Tim, was also exotic. He was from Fresno. That may make him seem ordinary, but in reality, he was anything but. He had pitched in the minor leagues and then went on to have a successful career as an accountant. When I was growing up, my dad and I would go to San Diego Padres games, and we spent almost every summer night at the park playing baseball until it was too dark to see. And then we would go inside and watch movies. I have my dad to thank for my lifelong love of, and functional addiction to, film. As I got older, our passionate conversations about obscure baseball stats transferred to equally obscure movie trivia. At times, my dad could be a bit of a silent type. He reminded me of the stoic heroes in the movies we watched—a Steve McQueen or a Paul Newman. As I grew older, I came to appreciate that he also looked good holding a glass of scotch.

My parents met when they were in their mid-twenties, while my dad was traveling in South Africa. They quickly fell in love. She was a part-time model with an accent, and he was a handsome athlete who also had an accent. The next thing they knew, they were married, expecting a baby, and living in Fresno, California. My mom may have been geographically close to L.A., but in every other way, her new city was nothing like the Hollywood-esque place she had always imagined America to be.

Things got rocky quickly as they navigated the effects of a rapid romance, culture shock, personality differences, and more. Luckily, they had already done something splendid together. They had created one Colin Ryan.

They divorced when I was three, and throughout my childhood, I sensed there was some mystery and much pain connected to this brief marriage. I didn't know much more than that, though, because my parents were very classy. They almost never spoke ill of each other. Actually, they did one better: they almost never spoke of each other at all.

Instead, they addressed the reality of the divorce in their own ways. One of them took on more of the blame than seemed fair, while the other said as little about it as possible. One self-criticized and the other self-censored. The scant observations they did share about the other parent had no villains, few details, and ended as quickly as possible.

This meant that, despite their good intentions, my parents became unreliable narrators. An unreliable narrator isn't necessarily lying; they might just be editing. However, leaving things out, or overemphasizing the wrong things, can significantly impact what's understood as true. Each told me a version of their story they hoped would protect me.

This couldn't have been easy. It now seems impossible to me that two people could put a child through drama and confusion of the kind their tense custody battle over me must have created and *not* blame themselves for exposing me to it. I found myself speculating that perhaps this guilt and grief were part of the reason that each of my parents had a beloved pastime. A religion, if you will.

My dad's religion was movies. Maybe for him, movies were more than just a great escape (sidenote: also the name of his favorite movie). In movies, almost everything happens for a reason; every plot detail eventually makes sense and resolves poetically with a killer ending. Given the unchangeable, long-term fallout of that brief, doomed romance, this must have been cathartic.

My mom's religion was religion, which might have been less original, but she was every bit as devoted. She read her Bible daily, a book filled with examples of the consequences of wrong choices and the forgiveness that's offered anyway. Her religion was all about second chances. For a woman determined to be the best version of herself, this must have been good medicine.

My mom prayed, my dad watched movies, and they both practiced their religions, well, religiously. Sure, they were unreliable narrators, but for an understandable reason: They were trying to shield me. But when reality is rewritten to soften the edges, gaps are left—and gaps beg to be filled in.

This meant that their well-intentioned silence had an unintended consequence. I idolized my parents, and in the process, I set an impossibly high standard for myself—one to which I could never measure up. I failed to see that my parents were ordinary, messy, and imperfect humans. Missing that fact helped me miss another: I didn't know it was okay for me to be a screw-up sometimes, let alone often.

Overall, my life was happy and full, but it also contained a series of subtle absences. For one, there was never a family photo of my mom, my dad, and me on display in either household. If one existed, I didn't remember ever seeing it. I also didn't have a memory of the three of us ever being in the same physical space. That we were once a family had no concrete reality for me; it was just something I'd been told.

Yes, I still had my mom and my dad, but my parents had new spouses and new children with those spouses. I pretended that I was completely comfortable with these twin families, but in truth, I felt like a square peg that just didn't quite fit. Sometimes, when I saw my parents hugging and playing with my siblings, I would suddenly remember that they were more their actual children than I was because they were members of families that existed *now*—families my parents had chosen.

It was weird. I knew it wasn't my fault, exactly. But if I'd been a better kid . . . would the outcome have been different? Gradually, a stream of troubling thoughts emerged and began to play on a loop in my mind:

I'm a member of a family that no longer exists.

I'm a reminder of something everyone would rather forget.

My three siblings are half-siblings, so, in reality, I'm an only child.

All I want in life is to belong, but I am an outsider.

These thoughts felt as heavy as the world itself, because they represented the inarguable truth of my situation.

On one occasion, my mom told me that children of divorce often blame themselves for it in some way. She said she wanted to make sure I knew the divorce wasn't my fault, because it wasn't. I convincingly assured her I didn't think it was. But the truth was more complicated. Because my response to my parents' divorce, a response that permeated my childhood, was to hold them blameless and lean hard into blaming myself.

I never told either my mom or my dad this. I was worried that they were still hurting, and I didn't want to add to their pain. I put on a happy face for both of my parents to keep them from worrying about me. I emphasized what someone might see as advantages in having two families—double the number of parents, more siblings—to show everyone how content I was. "Imagine my luck!" I'd boast. "I have four parents, two half-sisters, and a half-brother. That's like 5.5 people!"

I believed it was my job to be brave, so I hid the fact that this hurt me at all. I had no idea that my success at this would take a toll and prove dangerous for me throughout the rest of my life. I learned to perform happiness in order to make other people's lives easier, even if it meant making mine harder.

My two fractured realities were confusing, scary, and overwhelming. With no way to change them, I started filling in the gaps on my own. Eventually, I landed on a conclusion I didn't realize would make things so much worse. I repeated it over and over: *My mom is on the East Coast with her family, and she is enough. My dad is on the West Coast with his family, and he is enough. I'm somewhere in the middle, and I'm just not enough.*

I had become an unreliable narrator myself.

CHAPTER 4
THE F-I-A-S-C-O

I was in fourth grade when I started wondering, *What am I good at? What's my "thing"?*

What am I bringing to the table here, talent-wise?

I took inventory. I was, at best, an average baseball player. I had a lot of heart—and a head full of baseball stats—but I was an unremarkable addition to my team. When it came to basketball, I was tragically below-average, especially considering that I practiced every night until it was too dark to see if I was making my shots or not. (Although I had a pretty good idea.) I was exceptionally talkative, which mostly meant I got sent to detention. Could *that* be a skill? Didn't seem like it.

When I compared myself to my peers, I wondered what my chances were of becoming "the smart one," "the funny one," or "the mysterious kid who talked only once a year, and everyone listened." I definitely wouldn't be that one.

Then our teacher, Mrs. Gottwald, announced we would be having a district-wide spelling bee. The winner would compete at regionals, then statewide, then nationals, and then that winner would . . . take over the world? I wasn't listening anymore, because I was thinking, *This is it. My moment. My legacy.* I raced home that day and began studying the booklet of words each student was given, from front to back. Winning this spelling bee would be my shortcut to universal acclaim, the chance to stand on the stage of the biggest theatre around, and guaranteed popularity, too.

When the big day arrived, I put on my luckiest sweater. It had the word "Princeton" across the front. No one in my family had ever gone to Princeton. My mom got it at Goodwill. I liked it mainly because it had a tiger on it.

I went up there, in my secondhand Princeton sweater, and I won that spelling bee.

(I'd weave this victory into conversations for years to come.)

The moment I correctly spelled my winning word, *I-S-T-H-M-U-S*, I became a champion. A living legend. A kid who knew how to spell a weird land formation.

A little while later, I was making an effort not to beam as I sat in class when our classroom door opened, and our principal, Mr. Shultz, appeared. He asked the teacher if he could speak to me in the hallway. Never a good sign, especially for a kid who had been to detention repeatedly. He said, "So, I just found out that one of the other students challenged her disqualification, and the judges ruled in her favor. So, we're going to have to redo the final round." I was still clutching my gleaming, plastic trophy as he said this to me.

I remembered the moment in question. Carissa, one of the students from another school in our district, had gotten the word "lynx." She had spelled it "L-I-N-K-S." I had spent

CHAPTER 4: THE F-I-A-S-C-O

hours reading and memorizing every word in the spelling bee booklet, so I knew immediately that she was wrong on a technicality. "Links," although a real word, was not in the booklet. "Lynx," however, was. I had looked the curious word up and been pleasantly intrigued to discover it was a wild, spotted cat found mainly in cold, northern climates. Even better, it was related to the tiger!

So, Carissa had been both correct and incorrect. Her spelling was correct, but she had waited too long to appeal the judges' decision. The rules stated that the contestant had to appeal before their turn in the next round. Once her parents found out what had happened, this rule (and the judge who timidly read it to them) crumbled in the face of their protective outrage.

As for me, I think I was still in shock when I walked into the room where they'd gathered the final five contestants again. When it was my turn, I stood to spell my new word. It was an easy one, but the adrenaline coursing through me during the competition had worn off, and I felt as if my brain was full of cotton. I stammered out my answer, forgetting to say a silent letter that I had actually known was there, sat back down, and watched as Carissa won the whole thing.

I felt awful. I was mad at Carissa and her parents, but only for a short while, because I knew she had spelled every word correctly that day. I was crushed that I wouldn't get to go to the regional spelling bee and stand on that grand, ornate theater's beautiful stage. My spelling adventure was over.

I walked up to Mr. Shultz and asked, "Should I give my trophy back?" He immediately broke eye contact and mumbled, "No, Colin, that's okay." All the other adults in the room who heard my question looked uncomfortable, too, as if they were all thinking, *Good for Carissa, but also, there's been some collateral damage here.*

They let me keep the trophy, but it now felt tarnished, well before the plastic coating started to peel off. In my angriest moment, I contemplated writing "Participation" on it with a Sharpie, but refrained.

I went through all the stages of grief: Denial ("I should wait by the phone, because maybe they'll call and say *actually* I did come in first.); Anger ("What kind of school lets you *un*-win something?"); Bargaining ("Maybe we'll be allowed to send *two* spellers to regionals?"); and Depression ("It turns out I can't spell 'kneadable' but I can definitely spell H-E-A-R-T-B-R-E-A-K.")

A week went by, and my fourth-grade heart still hurt. I just wanted to feel differently about this situation. Then I had an idea. I asked Mr. Shultz for Carissa's mailing address and wrote her a good-luck-at-Regionals letter. With perfect spelling.

When I dropped that letter in the mailbox, I felt . . . better. Even though the situation was beyond my control, I had taken a little bit of the power away from it. I still wasn't going to Regionals. But I had chosen to take a small action I could be proud of.

I surprised myself that day. In the face of something bigger than me—a challenge I couldn't understand or fix—I found a small way to respond that felt like *me*. Maybe *that* was my thing. It wasn't baseball or basketball or even, as things turned out, spelling. It was empathy. It was being kind. This small act of kindness helped me reframe the loss as a lesson: that I had the power to turn a disappointment into an opportunity to do something I could be proud of.

CHAPTER 4: THE F-I-A-S-C-O

I didn't know it then, but that was kind of the beginning of figuring out who I was. It taught me that, even when I couldn't control what was happening, I could still decide who I was going to be in the middle of it.

This was helpful to me in another way, too, because I was facing a health challenge in my life that was much bigger than losing a spelling bee. It was significant and likely to have a lasting impact, so learning to reframe it in some way would be crucial. Coincidentally, it wasn't very easy to spell.

CHAPTER 5
IT AIN'T EASY BEING WHEEZY

Like many people in the 1980s, I did a significant amount of drugs. But mine came with dosage instructions.

I had been less than a year old when I was diagnosed with asthma. From then on, my early life was peppered with rushed visits to the emergency room, rounds of allergy shots, numerous switches to the latest and greatest inhaler, and drugs. A whole lotta drugs.

For reasons that were hard to explain, I always had the feeling that, despite asthma being a life-threatening respiratory disease, it had a bit of an amusing side to it. Maybe that was because of all the wheezing, sniffing, and sneezing. Or maybe not, but it certainly wasn't the kind of disease that got "Donate Now" ads, backed by a plaintive Sarah McLachlan track. No one hosted 5K races to raise awareness for it. (Which would have been a little tone-deaf.)

Also, there was a noticeable lack of movie heroes with asthma. None who made it look cool, anyway. When I saw *The Boy in the Bubble* (we didn't have trigger warnings yet), I thought, *Oh, great . . . this is our Superman?* Then there was the movie *Goonies*. When the main character finally sees the mythical pirate ship and its infamous pirate captain, he calls out the captain's name excitedly, "Willy!" and then takes a puff on his inhaler. The main character finds himself unable to breathe, and that's . . . a punchline?

Movies may have done me no favors, but all in all, I lived a pretty normal life. Camping. Sports. Social events. So long as I had my inhaler with me. That three-inch plastic device helped me get air into my lungs when they, despite massive effort, could not perform the task. To add a little extra drama, I was the kid who constantly forgot where he put everything. *[Note from the future: and the adult who still does.]*

Asthma was a major challenge, so I concentrated on small actions I could take. I did my best to remember my medication, to avoid triggers (a seemingly endless list), and to stay calm even when I was gasping for breath. Panicking would tighten my airway even more.

My parents took on a lot of the burden. When they put me on those planes, they had to make sure the flight crew was aware of my asthma. When we went camping, they first had to find a park ranger and identify where an outlet was in case they needed to plug in my breathing device. It must have been great for them to really *relax* in nature.

Many nights, they sat up with me while I fought for air, listening to my chest, rubbing my back, and staying beside me until my breathing became steady again. They acted calm about it, but every now and then, I caught a private look of panic in their eyes.

CHAPTER 5: IT AIN'T EASY BEING WHEEZY

The 1980s were a bit of a pharmaceutical Wild West, so I was cycling through a series of new-and-improved (but not well-tested) medications. They would either help me breathe more easily or cause hallucinations and manic hyperactivity. I was once put on steroids that I was sure made me run and throw at an Olympic level. Several times, I had large plastic tubes fished down my throat, which caused vocal cord scarring and, I'm guessing, a fair amount of PTSD.

Somewhere in the midst of all this freakiness and abnormality, I noticed that making other people laugh always helped me feel better. I couldn't control my asthma, but humor could chase away the dark.

My mom was my first audience, and she had a great laugh, so I would try to get her going whenever I could. If I came up with something *really* hilarious, she'd snort and gasp and beg me to stop because she couldn't breathe. At that point, I would stop immediately, because, hey, been there.

One time, I was reading *Garfield's Thanksgiving*, and one of Garfield's sarcastic zingers aimed at his owner, Jon Arbuckle, jumped out at me. That night at dinner, I said the line to my mom. "You know what, Mom? I've always been a man . . ." Then I paused for a second, letting the suspense build, before I followed it up with, "A wimpy man, but still, a man." My mom just about *died* laughing. A number of times over the next few months, she urged me to say it again, and then she would crack up just like the first time. Her reaction made this silly little joke magical to me. It made me start to appreciate the economy of a good punchline—how it can tell a whole story in a single sentence.

Another reason I resonated with that "wimpy man" line and quoted it over dinner was that I didn't really see myself as being as tough as I was supposed to be. During that time, boys were inundated with such messages as: "Man up. Never show weakness. Stop crying. Don't be emotional." While I wanted to be seen as growing into the type of man that movies portrayed, I knew that I fell short. I had weak lungs and I was pretty much always blowing my nose, which I'd never seen Chuck Norris do. My emotions carried me even further off the mark. I cried when I watched *The Land Before Time*. I often felt afraid. I didn't even like getting outwardly angry, and all members of my gender were supposed to love that one. (I found it much easier, though, to direct anger inward.) I couldn't simply dismiss these norms and didn't know enough to openly mock them, but I found it easy to mock myself.

When trying to make others laugh, I would adopt personas inspired by things I didn't necessarily accept about myself but that I enjoyed exaggerating for humor. I would be hopelessly nerdy, ridiculously theatrical, timidly neurotic, or cartoonishly wheezy. Perhaps this is why I found asthma funny—it gave me a chance to make fun of myself, which I had no problem with. It made no difference to me if I told the joke or was the joke, so long as the joke could make someone laugh.

I needed to laugh, both at my asthma and at myself. I didn't know then that developing a sense of humor would eventually become a superpower and a secret weapon. I hadn't realized that by choosing to embrace "being" the joke, I had gained the power to control it rather than be its victim.

I didn't know those things yet. All I knew was that I needed to find some lighter side to living with this scary disease. One way or another, it *had* to be funny.

• • •

CHAPTER 5: IT AIN'T EASY BEING WHEEZY

My mom was a warrior against my asthma right alongside me. Having moved from California, with a strong interest in organic food and farmers' markets, she was what people in our small, rural town in New York state called "nutty-crunchy." She was determined to find some herbal remedies and healthier treatment options to offset all the medications I was constantly taking.

I was grateful for her efforts, but boy, oh, boy did we run the gamut. And the gauntlet.

First, she found an herbalist. His name was Herb. Of course it was. Herb proudly sold a concoction called "Kickaroo Juice." It looked like puddle water with sticks in it. It tasted even worse than I expected, and it did not fix my asthma.

Next, she read that cranberries could help with asthma, so she blended frozen cranberries until she had filled a pint glass with the bright pink liquid. I took one sip, and my cheeks were jolted with a shock of sourness like nothing I'd ever experienced. My eyes slammed shut, and I winced with my entire body, letting out a wail of anguish. My face felt like it was on fire. Unfortunately, my reaction was so over-the-top that my mom thought I was being dramatic in an effort to get out of drinking more.

She must've thought, *Is this my son or an Italian Nonna realizing the risotto is cold?* She made me keep drinking, and halfway through, I gave up and begged for mercy. "Give it to me," she said with an eye roll. She took one sip, turned her face away from me for a long moment, and then said without turning around, "You never have to drink that again." I noticed that her eyes were watering.

It later turned out that pureed cranberries, much like puddle water, lacked lung-healing properties. We continued our search.

Meanwhile, an unfortunate aspect of my disease was that ragweed pollen exposure, or even a common cold, could trigger my asthma and then escalate the problem to something much more serious. In my early teens, I got walking pneumonia, and instead of being able to take pills at home, I ended up in the hospital for several days. That is where I discovered I was a fan of all-you-can-eat Jello. My friends came and visited me, too, which was nice. It always felt good to know I wasn't alone.

Similarly, I kept my eyes peeled for other asthmatics. They were my people. Whenever I saw another person using an inhaler, I had this big, unspoken feeling: *I know you and I see you.* I hoped they didn't feel like an outsider the way I sometimes did. I'd chat with them, ask how they were doing, and encourage them in some way. I'd be tempted to high-five them, but I'd want them to conserve their energy.

As I got older, I realized that all the time I spent managing my asthma had some positive side effects. I had become powerful in ways I didn't expect. I'd developed a sense of gratitude for the gift of living despite this disease. I'd honed my ability to empathize with people who were having a hard time. I'd learned that, when confronted by a big challenge, I could aim for one small, smart action to take rather than do nothing. I eventually recognized that struggle can make a person stronger and wiser, sometimes in ways that only reveal themselves later on.

I had discovered early on that being funny felt better to me than being frightened. Since then, I'd been strengthening my humor skills. I liked making my parents laugh, but the true test of my abilities was whether I could make adults who didn't know me laugh. That was my holy grail. Once, a friend of my dad's heard that I was good at spelling, so she asked me if I could spell the absurdly easy word "potato." I remembered that vice-presidential candidate Dan Quayle had famously misspelled "potato" on TV by putting an "e" on the end, and I quipped, "In this scenario, am I Dan Quayle or not?"

What can I say? I was precocious. Their laughter had both volume and a note of respect in it. It was a pretty cool moment.

As a young person, I felt like an outsider, more often than I wanted to admit. But my repeated success with humor made me realize something. Any time I wanted to feel accepted by someone, all I had to do was figure out how to make them laugh. That sound was always pure joy.

CHAPTER 6
SAVED BY THE BELLE

Do you remember the moment when the approval of your peers suddenly mattered more than the approval of your parents?

For me, it was on the first day of middle school.

Up to that point, there had been some significant periods in my life when I needed no one's approval but my own. For example, as a toddler, I was *very* confident. I walked around shirtless, wearing only a diaper, with my belly pushed out, exuding an energy that communicated, "You're welcome."

I experienced another wave of unabashed confidence in fifth grade, when we suddenly became the oldest kids at our elementary school. We moved around the halls and at recess like royalty. My kinglike status must've gone to my head, because I was *unique*, and I would have changed for no one. Someone could have told me, "Just so you know, it's not cool to wear the same pair of sweatpants every single day of the school semester." And I would not have changed, because they were comfortable.

I could have been told, "It's also not cool to go to the school dance and do the Macarena for the entire duration of the Guns N' Roses song 'November Rain.'" (That's a *nine-minute* song!) Sure, my arms hurt, and everyone yelled at me to stop, but it was really my only move, and deep down, I was pretty sure they were just jealous of me.

Someone might even have told me, "It's *really* not cool to be an active member of your local church's clown troupe." Okay, I knew that one wasn't cool. But secretly, I thought it was super fun. And, even more secretly, I was still doing it when I entered middle school.

Now it was my first day of sixth grade, after all three elementary schools in the district had unceremoniously bid us farewell and dropped us into one large and terrifying new building. There were all these kids I didn't know, and down the hall from us, I saw an eighth grader who had a full beard, wore cologne, and possibly had kids of his own.

I had thought my sense of humor and open-hearted empathy could get me through anything. But, here, as I searched for acceptance from this horde of teenagers wearing sneakers much fancier than mine, listening to Walkmans playing bands I'd never heard of, and showing with their stone-faced expressions just how "over everything" they were, I sensed that I had met my match.

As far as I could tell, there were really only two options for fitting in in middle school:

Option 1: Be cool.

That wasn't happening.

Or, Option 2: Be invisible.

I went all-in on Option 2.

I managed to remain invisible for two whole class periods before I messed up and became extremely visible.

Our third-period teacher asked us to answer a series of get-to-know-you questions. I thought she was going to read them privately, so I answered with all of the honesty of the sweatpants-wearing, Macarena-dancing, Christian-clowning little gem that I was. I mean, I was *authentic*.

Then the teacher collected the questionnaires, shuffled them up, and redistributed them among the other students so we could go around, one by one, and read each student's answers out loud.

Mentally, I lamented, *I have got to start listening to instructions more carefully.*

The boy who got mine was this popular and really mean kid, and he read his three favorite answers from my sheet. They were also the three most mortifying things that I had written down.

Question number one: "What's your favorite movie?"

The other kids had listed horror movies and action movies. I thought to myself, *How are you guys even seeing R-rated movies? We're 11.*

He read my favorite movie: "*Beauty and the Beast.*"

The room burst out into laughter. Even though I was secretly confident that my favorite movie would hold up better than some of their favorites, like *Pet Sematary II* and *Universal Soldier*, I was in no way able to defend my answer. I also knew we were just getting started.

Question number two: "Where would you like to travel?"

So far, the other kids had said exotic places like France, Japan, and New Jersey. I took it in a different direction.

"Where would I like to travel?" I wrote, "Wherever a book takes me."

The thing about these particular sixth-graders is that they were not very supportive of my creativity. The laughter this time had an explosive quality to it. Kids were high-fiving in front of my face. One disapproving kid was just staring at me like, "I'm definitely gonna beat you up as soon as possible."

I felt about an inch tall. *Man, if only I really was an inch tall . . . then I could hide inside my brand-new Five Star First Gear Trapper Keeper.*

Suddenly I realized, in horror, what the third answer that he was going to read was. If only I could have pulled the fire alarm . . . but there was no time.

Question number three: "What do you usually like to do on the weekends?"

A lot of the other kids said "The mall," which, I assumed, is where they were sneaking into R-rated movies. My answer: "Performing and rehearsing with my clown troupe, Clowns for Christ."

That was a hard one to hear out loud. *[Note from the future: It still is.]* Thankfully, that's all I had written, because the painful details didn't stop at our group's name. My clown name was Scooter; I wore a plaid ladies' pantsuit that sported padded shoulders; and, not to brag, but we were in high demand on the local nursing home circuit. To me, the world needed more of two things I could offer: juggling and Jesus. So, clowning was a natural fit, and my church gave me a chance to do that.

School, on the other hand, was currently offering me a decidedly different reception. By this point, the kids were laughing

CHAPTER 6: SAVED BY THE BELLE

louder than ever. I was crushed. I felt my cheeks burn in humiliation. I had just been completely authentic, and I was universally rejected.

I wanted to jump up and yell out, "I get it! I'm gonna quit clowns. I'm gonna watch R-rated movies. I will do everything in my power to make sure you never hear from me until we graduate! And then maybe not after that, too, because I will change my name and get a new identity. Just tell me what you want me to be, and I'll be *that!*"

But I didn't say any of that. I didn't say anything at all. I just sat there.

Then, from the back of the room, a voice clear as a bell, said, "Guys, cut it out. Quit laughing at him."

The voice belonged to a student named Michelle Beaver. She had unshakable conviction, and her voice sounded like a warning.

The laughs were at least temporarily interrupted.

Michelle wasn't done. She turned to the teacher and said, "Why are you letting this happen? What is the point of this if we're just going to laugh at each other?"

To this day, I can't remember what subject this class was or even the name of the kid who read my answers, but I can still vividly picture Michelle.

I remember how it felt when she spoke up for me when I desperately needed someone on my side.

That day, Michelle showed me we actually have *three* options when it comes to fitting in.

We can be cool, and we'll be remembered for a little while.

We can be invisible, and we'll be forgotten immediately.

Or we can stand up for someone when they need us the most, and they will remember us as their hero for the rest of their life.

• • •

This three-options thing was clearly an amazing lesson . . . that I did not learn at all. Not while the sting of rejection was so powerful. The lesson I learned was that being my authentic self was just too risky.

That is why, the very next day, I leaned even harder into trying to blend in. I vowed to myself, "I will do whatever it takes to never be on the outside again. From now on, my only objective is to belong."

My mantra became, "Just tell me what you want me to be, and I'll be *that*."

I kept my head down at school and tried not to stand out. I couldn't seem to crack the code of fitting in there, so I set my sights on a different building, full of people who might accept me as I was. I hoped I would feel like I belonged there.

Even if I had to quit their clown troupe.

CHAPTER 7
HOLY(ISH)

Outside of school, I had a place where I felt I could be my full, unfiltered self: our church. The other people who went to this church every week became my "spiritual family." For my mom, my stepdad, my two sisters, and me, the whole world revolved around church.

There was Sunday School, followed by Sunday Service, and a worship service on Sunday night. Monday night was Bible study. On every other Tuesday night there was a potluck. On Wednesday night was Battalion, a Christian alternative to the Boy Scouts. Oh, and Friday night was rehearsal with Clowns for Christ. After my horrible experience in 6th grade, the following year I transferred to a Christian middle school and then went to a Christian high school, too. I couldn't get enough!

Church on Sunday morning was often a joyous place. There were smiles, memorable laughs, and passionate singing voices. There were many kind, caring, and intelligent people there, and it felt safe to be myself, be silly, and express my emotions. Listening to some of the stand-out sermons was when I first fell in love with speaking and storytelling. I felt safe and valued, and I appreciated being able to talk with thoughtful adults and other kids who were committed to being kind.

The pastor and the occasional guest pastors were so confident as they stood in front of our large church, sharing their knowledge about the Bible. They would crack jokes, tell stories, and put on their glasses to thoughtfully read and explain the original meanings of some of the words in that day's Bible passage.

They had the same assurance while teaching the doctrine of our Associate Reformed Presbyterian church. Our church was fundamentalist and adhered to the doctrine of Calvinism. We learned a handy acronym—TULIP[1]—to explain its key points. They were not as charming as that might sound. What stuck with me most were two ideas: that I was totally depraved and couldn't choose God on my own, and that if I ever turned away from my faith, it would only prove I'd never really been a Christian in the first place.

This last one was especially dark and scary to think about. *What if I'm not really saved? What if I lose my faith someday?* I started to worry that my occasional cookie-swiping, disobeying, and little-white-lying were, in God's eyes, the same as murdering and blaspheming. I had good reason to worry. Both in church and at my Christian high school, we studied Jonathan Edwards's "Sinners in the Hands of an Angry God" sermon. It painted a terrifying picture of God dangling us over the flames of hell, ready to let go at any moment. That image lodged itself in my brain. *What if that was me?*

CHAPTER 7: HOLY(ISH)

The thing we would excitedly tell visitors on Easter and Christmas was that all they had to do was accept Jesus into their hearts. One prayer and their lives would be different, and their eternal souls would be saved. It turned out that saying the prayer was just the beginning. To prove we were real Christians, we were expected to be what was referred to as "sold out for Jesus."

In our parlance, this meant loving Jesus more than anything else, waking up early for daily prayer and devotions, monitoring every thought for the presence of sin, attending church consistently, sharing the Bible with others, and treating every part of our lives as belonging to God.

We were told over and over that our fallen and wicked natures were the reason that Jesus was killed on the cross. To me, this indicated that when I read comic books I'd hidden inside my oversized Bible during the exceptionally long sermons, it wasn't just boredom—it was proof of my sinful nature. That thought made me feel ashamed, as if I was letting everyone down.

I read my Bible every day, did my daily devotionals, memorized Bible verses, wore a WWJD bracelet, prayed before every meal, and regularly quoted lines from *VeggieTales*, a Christian children's show, with my sisters. I liked to read and listen to music, but to live as a good Christian, it was essential that I monitor the content I absorbed. I read fiction and non-fiction books written exclusively by Christians and bought my music at a Christian bookstore that had a chart with dubious claims like "If you like Nirvana, you'll love DC Talk. If you like Pearl Jam, you'll love Audio Adrenaline." If you happened to like David Bowie, you were on your own.

I had soon developed a substantial music collection, consisting entirely of Christian artists. Still, I couldn't resist the radio. When Bush or Soundgarden would come on, I'd immediately fall off the Christian-music-only wagon. Backsliding never sounded so good. I'd feel guilty, and more than once, I cried while switching back to my Christian CDs (while also double-checking that I'd remembered to push the button for Bass Boost). Each time, I promised God this slip-up would be the last. But it never was.

...

I had already proven to myself I was dangerously weak around secular music, so when my interest expanded to movies, I was in trouble from the start. Whenever I watched a movie, I was completely enthralled. My heart would pound as I fed the VHS tape into the VCR and waited through the chunk-chunk and what seemed like forever before the screen flickered to life. I would immediately get lost in the world the movie created.

On weekends, I would sit close to the TV in the basement, watching rented movies with the volume low, my hand on the remote so I could turn the movie off the second my mom came down. I did my best to stay alert, but inevitably, she'd walk in on a gunfight scene, and there was no way for me to articulate that the violence on the TV wasn't something I wanted to participate in; it was just thrilling to watch. Whether the movie was funny, dramatic, or inventive, I enjoyed experiencing new places and different perspectives beyond those emphasized in my church. The TV room was in the basement of our house, as was my bedroom. I may have been below ground; still, through my TV, I could see entire worlds.

But my film appreciation was entirely self-guided until I met Abby and Paul.

Abby was one of my good friends from the youth group, and her dad, Paul, was the head media librarian at a nearby college. Abby and Paul were cinephiles on every level, and I quickly became a regular at their house for movie nights. Paul talked about movies the way John Cusack talked about vinyl albums in *High Fidelity*—I know because they showed me *High Fidelity*.

At Abby's house, I was tutored in both highbrow and lowbrow cinema, from Akira Kurosawa and Bernardo Bertolucci to Michael Bay and John Woo. On any given night, we might watch a foreign film, like *Cyrano de Bergerac*, a film noir classic like *The Maltese Falcon*, a movie with complicated adult themes like *American Beauty*, or a Hong Kong action bullet-fest like *Hard Boiled*.

Paul and Abby didn't cover their ears during swearing or avert their eyes at risqué parts. Instead, they concentrated on questions like whether a film was honest, if its story was well-told, and whether it had something to say. And they wanted to know my opinion as well. Paul and Abby encouraged me to fall in love with movies *because* they could be challenging art. Few in my church seemed to take this view. What mattered more to them was whether said art had a PG rating. When I left their house, Paul would hand me a scribbled list of movies to watch. Homework, if you will. All I needed to continue my education was a Blockbuster card and a bicycle, and I had both.

At one point, I picked up an old paperback copy of *The Last Temptation of Christ* at a garage sale, and I read it so many times that its cover fell off. I understood why it was controversial, but I also found it to be emotionally honest and beautifully written. My parents saw me reading it and got angry. But when I mentioned the book to Paul, he said, "Fantastic choice! Have you seen the movie version?" I felt trusted and respected by him, like I could think for myself and didn't have to just fall in line like everyone else did.

I often felt that my passion for movies complemented my faith rather than challenged it, but I couldn't discuss this with other Christians because they didn't seem to appreciate the ambiguity that I gravitated towards. Whether I was willing to admit it or not, I knew my film appreciation didn't align with the teachings of our religious elders. They reminded us often to "be not of this world." But movies didn't sort people so neatly. They showed sinners with sympathetic hearts and saints who stumbled. Maybe that's why I couldn't help but love them so much—they made space for contradiction.

It brought me relief when I met adults like Paul, adults who were complicated and curious. Square pegs. They didn't claim to have everything figured out already, and their company brought me relief. While adults like these were in short supply, over the years, I had the occasional teacher, youth group leader, or coach who didn't quite fit the mold. They were outsiders, too.

My social studies teacher, Mr. Hopkins, was another movie-lover. He had bright-red hair, wore quirky bow ties, and insisted we call him Matt. He was absolutely horrified the day he learned none of us in class had seen his favorite flick, the zany comedy-musical *Strictly Ballroom*. I rented it that weekend, and its central line hit me harder than most Bible verses:

"A life lived in fear is a life half-lived." I loved the idea, though I wondered how to apply it when I seemed afraid of everything—making mistakes, disappointing God, and constantly finding inspiration in secular sources.

I always gravitated to these kinds of grown-ups. They seemed to live in the gray, like me. Seeing them actively evolve in front of my eyes was inexplicably comforting. Most of the people in my church seemed fixed in their views and content to see everything as black-and-white, but I couldn't look at the world that way. I had a bad habit of wondering about everything. The adults who also wondered were, in one way or another, outsiders like me, but I started to notice that some of them paid a price for it—a price I found way too steep.

When I was around 12, I had a Sunday School teacher named Eunice. She was a tall, matter-of-fact woman who wore floral-print dresses and those half-glasses librarians always seemed to have. Eunice was a gifted teacher, but she only ever taught Sunday School. I asked my parents why she never gave the sermon, and they said, "She can't preach because the Bible says women can't teach men." *What?* I nodded as if that settled it, but inside, I bristled at this open example of sexism. I thought to myself, *That's wrong! I'm out of here! Oh wait, I can't drive.* I wanted to head for the exit then and there, but had no agency to act on my feelings. What stuck with me was that Eunice kept showing up anyway. Every Sunday, she stood there teaching us with warmth, brilliance, and insight, even though the church refused to see her as worthy of the pulpit. That made the unfairness sting even more.

I was challenged again when I was 16, and I finally got to know my stepmother's brother, Terry. While my mom and my stepdad remained devoted Protestant Christians, my dad and my stepmom's family had become lapsed, non-practicing Catholics over the years. When they flew to New York City to visit my stepmother's brother, Terry, I took a train to meet them. Uncle Terry lived in Manhattan, and he had a roommate named Stephen. It took me an improbably long time to realize that Stephen was not just his roommate. Even when Stephen read a book called *The Gay MANual* in the living room, I was still unsure. *Maybe he is just interested in the topic*, I thought.

Once I finally connected the dots on the relationship between Terry and Stephen, I knew I should be appalled by this "perversion" and stay spiritually strong in this "fallen and godless" studio apartment in Lower Manhattan (with really great views). But I surprised myself. I didn't react the way I'd been taught. What on earth would I judge *them* for? They were kind and thoughtful people. They made me feel completely welcome, even while knowing I was a Christian-teenager-time-bomb capable of erupting at any moment in a shower of Bible verses.

In light of their remarkable hospitality and warmth, the ugly talk in my church about "sodomites" and "The Gay Agenda" made me want to laugh to keep from crying. The only "agenda" I saw involved making nice dinners and being left alone to conduct their lives in peace. All I had to do was actually get to know two gay people, and the elaborately constructed world view my church had steeped me in started to disintegrate.

When I got on the train back home to my Christian family and community, I sensed it would be wiser to keep this entire experience to myself. Church was the only world I knew, and I didn't have the courage to risk losing it. Somehow, I knew that if I stopped believing like them and behaving like them, I would lose the community they offered me.

Unfortunately, I didn't see my change of heart as a mark of a strong and wise young man. Instead, I felt guilty for not recoiling, or quoting from the Bible, or being a good witness. The more I thought about it, the more I also felt guilty to realize that I wouldn't act any differently if I had another chance to.

Not long after that, I saw what happened when a respected pastor questioned the official line. My youth pastor was an incredibly kind and talented man named Tim. He was also the worship pastor and had an amazing singing voice. His wife and their three children also attended the church. He had a subtle lisp in his voice and a slightly effeminate affect. Although he served faithfully in the church, was an amazing dad, and tirelessly supported our youth group, it took only one Sunday School lesson to seal his fate. In a conversation with the students, Tim gently pointed out that, despite church leaders claiming that homosexuality is a choice, the Bible doesn't directly address this idea. A parent found out, and within the week, he was fired. He and his family were suddenly gone from the church, never to return. I can only imagine how awful an experience this must have been for him and his family. Even second-hand, it felt devastating to me.

But no matter the storm happening inside my head and heart, I took every action step I could in order to be—and be seen as—holy and righteous. I read my Bible every single morning. I prayed before every meal. I gave sermons in the youth group. I volunteered in the community. In church, I would hear about how my spiritual family loved me as I was, but I constantly felt the need to go to greater lengths to prove my loyalty.

Throughout high school, I was stuck between two groups: non-believing friends who were confused by but polite about my obvious faith, and my church community, which expected spiritual devotion but actively discouraged my questions and opinions.

The church side won simply because I believed those people knew better. Over and over, I would rededicate myself to God, only for the doubts to creep back in. The cycle never stopped. By my senior year of high school, I had decided that attending a Christian college would finally quiet my questions and provide me with clarity.

Spoiler: it did not do that.

CHAPTER 8
MAYOR OF CAMPUS

I attended a Christian liberal arts college in a single-stoplight town in rural New York state. Tucked away in the middle of nowhere, with the nearest city almost two hours away, this school was a little world of its own, full of farms, campus buildings, and nothing but Christians as far as the eye could see. And I was here for it.

I had finally put all my past struggles with doubt and questioning aside, and this time I was truly "sold out for Jesus." I knew it was for real. During our orientation session, we were given pledge statements to sign. I signed without hesitation, confirming that I would not smoke, drink, swear, have sex, or dance while a student there. It was a no-brainer.

The "no-drinking" rule would be easy to follow, because this town was dry and had been since Prohibition. But the "no-dancing" stipulation gave me pause. It struck me as a little odd that I was basically going to the school from the movie *Footloose* more than 20 years after that story took place. Was dancing the Unforgivable Sin[2] I'd heard so much about?

I would soon learn a familiar joke among students. "You know why we're not allowed to have sex? Because it could lead to dancing." I didn't really mind—I was an awkward and self-conscious dancer at best, and I'd be fine without it.

Given my lifestyle, values, relationship with God, and limited but negative experience of public school, it was so exciting to finally attend a school of all Christians. *[Note from the future: Wow.]* Suddenly, it was socially acceptable to pray before eating meals in the cafeteria and wear my WWJD bracelet without hiding it under my shirt sleeve.

We were required to attend campus-wide chapel services three days a week plus church services on Sundays. There were Bible studies all over campus and in every dorm. Ours was led by our resident advisor, and guys I saw as popular and confident would attend regularly and willingly.

I was surrounded by good-hearted, interesting people. Sure, some of them could be pretty intense, but most were funny, kind, friendly, adventurous, goofy, and intelligent. They came from many different places and had many different backgrounds. They were trying to figure themselves out, just like I was. It was pretty great to meet people and know immediately that their values and perspectives would line up with mine. I felt safe there.

We were constantly told "the world" would disagree with us. But here, everyone was in agreement. The only cracks in that harmony appeared when outside voices were invited in.

One time, controversial pastor Tony Campolo came to speak on campus. He had said publicly that homosexuality was just a sin like any other sin, not the utter horror I'd been taught. Given my experience, I appreciated this gentler attitude. His message was significantly more inclusive than anything I had heard before, and it reflected what he was known for—a belief that true Christianity should embody Jesus's teachings on social justice. I loved his message, but I kept that to myself.

In our classes later that day, we watched our professors debate and reshape Campolo's narrative. That was when I really noticed the powerful ideology shaping life on campus. We weren't lazy thinkers, but our beliefs were rarely challenged. We were inside what we occasionally called "the Bubble," shielded from the real world and its messy questions. It felt more like a Bible camp or a safe haven . . . with really hard classes. The worldview was consistent: sex belonged only in marriage, humanity was God's handiwork rather than the result of evolution, and positions on such issues as abortion, sexuality, and which political party to support were considered settled. Even when I wondered if I was falling into groupthink, the discomfort was fleeting. I could feel that something wasn't quite right, yet part of me wanted to believe the Bubble was the whole world. It became easy to simply think about something else. The social norms here were so intrinsic that they became almost invisible, much like water to a goldfish.

Overall, our behavior was quite similar as well. Almost no one smoked or drank or did drugs. (At least that I knew of). We had a lot of fun though, we just did it sober. I loved being there. I wanted to meet every student, and more than that, I wanted to make each person smile and see me as a likable guy. Everyone I met. All the time. It was fun at first, but I began to notice that the desire never let up.

Over time, I made more and more friends, which involved bouncing from one group to another. I'd feel terribly guilty for leaving the previous group, but the new group seemed to promise me an even greater sense of belonging, especially if I dressed like them and said I liked the same things they enjoyed. I would study each new group and think, "Tell me what you want me to be, and I'll be *that*."

I'd become a clique-jumper, which prevented lasting friendships, while the first group of friends I made, and ghosted, remained a tight-knit group for the entire time we were at college.

I eventually found a group I wanted to commit to for the long haul—a group of sophomores who lived on the same floor in my dorm and were a very tight crew. There were eight of them, and they formed a team for every intramural sport (they were all good athletes), they hung out at meals together, and they all had each other's backs.

When I finally met them, I played it cool enough to get the invite to hang out further, and gradually, a few of my freshman friends and I became add-on members. The guys were only a year older than I was, but they seemed to have had a more worldly upbringing than I'd had. Two of them, Ryan and Chris, were childhood friends from Long Island. They had strong accents, loved to shoot hoops, and constantly listened to gangsta rap on their stereo. With swearing and everything.

Ryan and Chris introduced me to many artists they were shocked I'd never heard of, like Nas, Lauryn Hill, and Tupac. (I was sheltered.) When Ryan learned I was really into a Christian rap group called GRITS, which he'd never heard of, he asked to borrow the CD. Sheepishly, I loaned it to him. He told me later, "Cols, I listened to those GRITS dudes, and they actually go pretty *hard*." He was being nice, but it still felt like a huge win.

CHAPTER 8: MAYOR OF CAMPUS

Another highlight of hanging out with the group was thanks to Motoi, who had the best gaming system and the biggest TV of the crew. One night we were in Mo's room, playing *GoldenEye 007* (and not drinking, which I'm still amazed by), when I started to get really tired. That's when I realized I couldn't leave. It wasn't that I was reluctant to leave. I couldn't.

A strange behavioral pattern had been developing for months, and I hadn't fully noticed it until now. I could exit a conversation, whether at a cafeteria table or an impromptu gathering between classes, only if I left with a final joke or clever phrase. I was convinced that failing to "leave 'em laughing" would expose my awkwardness.

I imagined that, were I to fail to do this, the group would exchange knowing looks, roll their eyes, and once I was gone, laugh at how odd I was. That would mean I had failed at my main goal: to be liked by everyone. If everyone didn't like me, then maybe no one really did—maybe I had just fooled them. I knew this was illogical, but my insecurity outweighed reason.

On the surface, I was funny and friendly, but it was a facade. I worked hard to hide what I thought was "the real me": unpredictable dips into depression, nervousness around girls, faith that waxed and waned, and worries about my hairline. So I smiled when I was sad, flirted but never dated, recommitted to God every few weeks, and wore hats.

My determination to be liked by every single person was becoming a full-time, unpaid campaign. I wanted to be seen as devout and likable, and I kept up the effort without knowing why. I was running for "mayor of campus"—a position that didn't exist—and the race never ended.

And now, there I was in Motoi's room, tired and trapped. I couldn't think of anything clever to say or find an organic moment to leave. Another half an hour went by, until my eyelids were so heavy I had no choice but to get up and head for the door. As I did, I tossed out a quip that didn't really make sense and definitely didn't quite land. As I walked down the hallway, I imagined them looking at each other like, "What a loser."

I still felt like an outsider, even though I was surrounded by nice people who never treated me like one. I should have felt like the ultimate insider, but I didn't at all.

Our school had more female students than male students, which unexpectedly increased my discomfort. Thanks to being raised in a house with three females, I was good at talking to women. In college, I basically always had a crush on one. Of course, I would want to be liked in return, and from time to time, my crush of the moment would reciprocate. And that's when my confidence disappeared. I had never dated. I had never kissed anyone. The moment she started flirting back, my hormone-filled body immediately betrayed me. It was humiliating. This made it challenging to listen effectively. Or to stand up.

• • •

My first summer break in college seemed to last forever. I was back in my small hometown, working a dull office job for the summer. All my coworkers went out every night and spent most of their paychecks partying, and due to all the not-drinking I was doing, I felt quite isolated socially. On the upside, I was saving a significant amount of money.

CHAPTER 8: MAYOR OF CAMPUS

Finally, my sophomore year of college began. I was psyched to be back because this time I wasn't a nobody just trying to prove myself. I was somebody now, and I was really well known! From the moment I arrived, I was reaping the rewards of my freshman-year campaign to meet and impress every person I could. As I walked around campus, I heard a constant stream of "Hey, Colin!" and "Let's hang out soon!" That first night back, there was a soccer game, and as I walked along the front of the bleachers to find a seat, it seemed that half the crowd yelled greetings to me. The Long Island guys started a chant of my name, which didn't last long, but still, I felt like a celebrity.

As classes became more challenging, and more and more homework was assigned, I started testing my ability to function without sleep. At night, alongside my classwork, I began using file-sharing apps like Napster (which easily broke through the "impenetrable" internet firewall our parents were promised) in order to catch up on all the music I'd missed during my mostly Christian-music-listening youth. I had soon built some truly eclectic playlists—British invasion, 80s hair metal, Miles Davis, and Christian bands, too. (Was I the first person to pair Jars of Clay with Rage Against the Machine? Quite possibly.) I could also download audio clips, GIFs, and short videos.

One night around three a.m., I was browsing Napster when I saw a video file with a woman's name and the words "on_a_boat_XXX." I sensed danger, but since all it took was one click, I added it to my queue. The small file downloaded quickly, and when I opened the file, it was *hardcore* pornography. I mean, it was grainy, the people seemed like they might be mad at each other, and as far as I could tell, no one was steering the boat.

I had somehow made it to this point in my life knowing almost nothing about sex. In sixth grade, I had been held out of a sex education class because my mom said the school had an agenda, so I hadn't even seen any awkward diagrams. My Christian high school didn't teach anything about sex in Biology. Apparently, statements along the lines of "Don't even think about it" or even "True love waits" included everything we needed to know. *[Note from the future: It didn't.]*[3] My youth group was a well-disguised and very effective abstinence program, where the whole point was to never be alone with members of the opposite sex and to remain virgins until marriage (or death, whichever came first). At this point, I had managed to see only a small number of naked breasts in carefully paused moments in VHS movies. Even then, there was a fuzzy line across the screen.

Now I was sitting at my dormitory desk, getting an education. It was not long before I had viewed this woman, not just on a boat, but in several other locations as well. I knew I shouldn't be watching, but it didn't matter. It was the best thing I'd ever seen. *This* was definitely the Unforgivable Sin, and I was spellbound by it.

Then the shame hit me. I felt like a monster. I quickly deleted all the files I had downloaded and headed straight to a small prayer chapel in the center of campus that was accessible 24/7.

It was a tiny room, with a dim, backlit cross. In the corner were journals, filled with other students' prayers and reflections. I didn't dare write anything in one of those journals for fear someone would find it and figure out what I was alluding to.

I sat there for hours, often in tears, and wrote every shameful thought about myself in my own journal. I wrote about myself in terms that were dark, vicious, and loathing. I questioned my worth, my right to attend this school, and even to call myself a Christian. This way of speaking to myself did not feel acceptable, yet I knew I deserved it, and I never came to my own defense.

Eventually, I saw dawn light in the hallway. I fervently rededicated my life to God and swore it would never happen again. Then I got off that floor and left the prayer chapel. I resumed my life as a student, but now I was one with a terrible secret. I didn't tell anyone about what had happened. Instead, I swept it under the rug—and directly into my nervous system.

That night marked the first time I felt the weight of shame so heavy it couldn't lift. I felt a rift between me and God and between me and my spiritual brothers and sisters. In the weeks and months that followed, I didn't like myself very much.

I began to feel sad at unexpected times—when I was in the middle of a party, at lunch, or in class. Some mornings, I didn't want to get out of bed. I started finding excuses to be alone more, but that didn't help much. I didn't know how to talk about this exhausting, deadening feeling that was always with me. I didn't know how much was spiritual shame and how much was brain chemistry—they tangled together until I couldn't tell them apart.

At the same time, I realized my efforts to be the unelected mayor of campus had created a form of popularity with an unenviable downside: I was liked by everyone but not known by anyone. I was well known without being known well. No one noticed that something was going on with me. Most of my friend groups thought that some other group must be my inner circle. No one asked me, "How are you doing, *really?*"

The fact that no one knew to ask me that only made me more depressed.

After all that time and effort to become popular, I had finally reached my goal, only to discover it had kept me from real relationships of the kind that I actually needed. If people like you for who they *think* you are, instead of who you actually are, are they your friends? They can't be. They can't have your back or help you with your problems because they don't know you need them to.

This was the first time I experienced depression as a noticeable condition, and it lasted for a long time despite my best efforts to shake it off. If I was going to be able to manage it going forward, I would need to get better at forming genuine friendships in which I could share both my proudest accomplishments *and* my humiliating experiences.

If I'd had a friendship like that, then I could have shared a bit about my "shameful downfall" with someone else. And if they were the kind of person who didn't take life quite as seriously as I did, they would have reminded me that no one can expect to run for mayor without a sex scandal.

. . .

By the time I reached my senior year, I had accomplished a lot of things to be proud of. I developed a few closer friendships than I'd had before, and I also got involved with the campus radio station. As a junior, I became the radio station president, running a team of seven managers and fifty hosts. I participated in student government, went on midnight adventures with my friends (often food-related), and made many great memories.

CHAPTER 8: MAYOR OF CAMPUS

For the spring semester of my senior year, I applied for a six-month film school program in L.A. I got accepted! And, yes, to stay on theme, it was a Christian film school.

As Christmas break and my departure for L.A. approached, I regretted not making enough of the kind of deep friendships that would last for years to come. But it was too late to fix it. So, I did what I knew best. I quietly disappeared from the many acquaintances I'd collected over the years—likely with a quick joke or a clever phrase as I walked away.

CHAPTER 9
ONCE UPON A HUFFY IN HOLLYWOOD

On my first day in Los Angeles, I got a ride to a nearby Kmart where I bought a Huffy bike. I also bought a bike lock, although I'm not sure I needed it. This bike cost $60 after sales tax, and the frame seemed to be made out of compressed tinfoil. But I didn't have a car, so this would be my sweet chariot for the next six months of living and studying in Hollywood.

I had been accepted into a film school program along with just 19 other students from across the country. I liked to think that meant it was more competitive than N.A.S.A., and we were chosen from thousands of applicants. (In fact, I still like to think that.)

For someone who loves movies as much as I do, it's hard to express how excited I was to be in Hollywood. Our school was located in Burbank, and we spent our days taking classes on movie producing, filmmaking, screenwriting, and the history of film. Our homework was writing screenplays, shooting short films, and watching as many movies as we could get our hands on. My fellow students loved movies like I did—maybe more. One guy, Kyle, had watched *Jaws* 50 times. Five zero. He watched it again with us, and it was like watching someone falling in love with movies all over again. *Man, I get it.* Kyle didn't just watch movies over and over, though. He had declared he wasn't going back to his college for graduation. He was determined to turn his internship into a job offer. I wished I had his fearlessness.

I had already begun my film studies in the basement of my house as a teenager, doing my best to watch every single movie in my tiny town's solitary Blockbuster Video. But now I was in Hollywood—the second biggest city in the U.S., in one of the most competitive industries in the world—and I felt seriously intimidated.

I quickly discovered that the City of Angels was also the City of Imminent Vehicular Homicide. Cycling there was not for the faint of heart. Every time I went for a ride, I half-jokingly said goodbye to my roommates as though it was for the last time. It wasn't so bad once I learned to forego blinking while looking in every direction at all times. Despite this, having the bike led to all manner of fun. When I wasn't using it to commute to school or to my job, I pedaled all over Los Angeles. I became fond of cemeteries because they were peaceful and traffic-free. I got to know a great deal of the city by bicycle. On weekends, I would ride around Griffith Park, up Mulholland Drive, up into the Hollywood Hills, up Laurel Canyon, or up to the Hollywood sign. A lot of riding up.

I had an unpaid internship three days a week on the Universal Pictures backlot, at a company called Larger Than Life

Productions. It was the production office for A-list screenwriter and director Gary Ross, whose credits included, among many others, *Dave* (starring Kevin Kline), *Big* (starring Tom Hanks), and the upcoming movie *Seabiscuit* (starring Popcorn Delights). OK, I had to look up the horse's name, but that's on me.

On the first day of my job, I rode my bike to the entrance of the Universal Pictures backlot. It was a secure area behind the famous Universal Studios amusement park. Many of the people who accessed this backlot were VIPs—movie industry bigwigs and their exclusive guests—so no one could enter without a pass that specified the exact number of hours of access allowed. Cars were backed up as security scrutinized entry passes and bomb-checked every car's backseat and trunk. They also checked underneath using mirrors.

When it was my turn, I was greeted sternly, but one guard broke into a good-natured smile as she followed protocol and awkwardly waved her bomb-detection mirror underneath my bike. Then I rode another mile, going through two more checkpoints before reaching the super-swanky production office. I went inside and looked for a discreet place to lean/hide my Kmart bike. That was when I saw two gleaming Bianchi road bicycles hanging on a rack. They looked like trophies. With a grimace, I leaned my bike against the wall near them. One of these things was not like the others.

I met the three producers' assistants, who introduced themselves and then promptly forgot about me. These assistants, who answered phones and scheduled meetings for their respective bosses, had graduated from Harvard, Yale, and MIT. They had all written multiple screenplays, and all aspired to direct movies someday. A lot of the film industry was staffed by people like this—incredibly creative, driven, and motivated. There were only so many opportunities to get the approval of the right people, so the cutthroat quality in the air was practically palpable. It felt like the first day of sixth grade all over again.

At my internship, I was virtually unknown to my production office co-workers—a nameless "gopher" (as in, "go-for-this, go-for-that") who copied tapes and ran errands. In my school program, I was writing screenplays, debating film theory with my peers and teachers, and directing numerous short films. I was putting myself out there, but not necessarily with the people who could create career opportunities in Hollywood for me.

I rarely saw the producers who worked there along with Gary Ross. When I did, they were always in a rush. Even when they nodded curtly in passing, I worried that trying to chat with them—and it not going well—could get me fired. It was also well known that even brief encounters with influential people like Gary Ross could make a huge difference—one small moment, one chance meeting, might launch a career.

My job was to sort screenplays from the mountain of them in the back room, organize VHS tapes, gopher across town for random items, and answer phones. Sometimes the voice on the other end of the line would say, "I have Kevin Smith for Robin" or "I have Jim Carrey for Alison." In these cases, I would connect the caller to the right assistant as fast as humanly possible. I was a writer and creative, and I knew *a lot* about film, but I felt like a Huffy in a world of Bianchis.

My friends and I had great fun, thanks to our frequent pastime of standing outside at film premieres hoping to see famous people. During my time in LA, I had several celebrity sightings, most notably Matthew McConaughey and Mr. T. (My younger sisters were more excited that I saw the dreamboat-of-the-moment Shane West.) But in the first three months I worked at Larger Than Life Productions, I still hadn't seen Gary Ross.

Ross was as A-list as it gets, and it turns out that success on that level means never having to go to work. He was adapting the screenplay for *Seabiscuit* at the time, so he was either working from home or on location. Occasionally, I was dispatched across town to buy a book he wanted "within the next thirty minutes," but I was too low in the pecking order to make the actual handoff. Every day, I sat three feet from his empty office, thinking that if I ever saw Gary Ross come to work, it would count as my next celebrity sighting.

Then one day, Gary Ross walked into the office. I knew who he was immediately because he had that *thing*. He just seemed famous. He was tan, handsome, had a great head of hair and an ageless quality. Later, I looked him up on the movie website IMDb and was surprised to learn he was 46. He looked a decade younger.

After chatting away with the producers and assistants, holding court, I heard Gary ask, "Whose bike is leaning against the wall?" With a hint of envy in her voice, one of the assistants said, "The intern's." I briefly wondered if she even remembered my name.

Then Gary came over to me and said, with a big smile, "Hi, I'm Gary Ross." I thought, *Yeah, I know.* I responded, "I'm Colin Ryan." *I'm sure you've heard of me as well.* Gary asked, "You want to go for a ride?" He said it with a laugh while walking in the direction of his office. *Is this a bit?* I wondered. *You're a famous guy with an elite racing bike, whereas I got mine from a store where it was hard to find one that didn't have handlebar tassels.*

Gary broke into a conspiratorial smile and said, "It's not like you have anything else to do, right?" I was starting to suspect he was being serious. He hadn't stopped walking and quickly disappeared into his beautiful office while my head swirled. In Hollywood, everybody hopes they'll be "discovered." Film industry lore is filled with stories about when a nobody met a director or a producer and their whole life changed in a moment. I'd secretly hoped for my own version of that story, though I never expected it to arrive in the form of a bike ride.

I had recently realized I wanted to be a writer and was hard at work on my first feature-length screenplay. What was the key to Gary Ross's success? He was a hell of a screenwriter. *Big* had one of the most relatable, wish-fulfillment story premises of all time. *Dave* was a near-perfect, feel-good, underdog story. *Pleasantville* somehow managed to blend the nostalgic longing for the old days portrayed in *Leave It to Beaver* with an incisive take on organized religion. And *Seabiscuit* was already a best-selling novel and, in his hands, would undoubtedly become a hit movie.

For a moment, I imagined myself riding next to Gary Ross and then getting drinks and chatting about our favorite movies, discussing where we found inspiration, and trading wry observations about life in Tinsel Town. I wouldn't be one of those weirdos around famous people, you know? I would be different. Confident. A promising, undiscovered talent with a laid-back demeanor. I would be *cool*—

My fantasy was suddenly cut short as Gary emerged from his office. He was now wearing a Spandex bike top and shorts, clip-in shoes, a slick helmet, and racing goggles. That's when I realized I had a few relevant problems: I was wearing jeans, it was 90 degrees outside, and I had a mountain bike with seven speeds, at least two of which had stopped working since I bought it.

Gary smiled at me again, and since I hadn't yet responded, he started clip-clopping toward the bike rack. He turned for a minute to grin one more time, throwing me a "You sure?" look. I smiled back . . . and broke eye contact. He shrugged, grabbed one of the Bianchis, and headed out the front door. Just like that, my moment was gone.

Ross returned a few hours later, walked back to the producers' offices, and exclaimed, "I just rode two mountains." So, it was probably for the best that I hadn't gone. But I still felt I'd blown it.

A week or two later, in my Screenwriting class, our professor taught us the concept of a "passive protagonist." This is a character who is more likely to say no than to say yes. These characters can drain the energy and excitement from a movie because they don't take action. They are constantly reacting to the plot and the other characters rather than driving the story forward. Some examples of frustratingly passive protagonists are Jimmy from *Yellowstone*, Jyn Erso in *Star Wars: Rogue One*, and Kevin Costner's character in *The Postman*. There are also some great passive protagonists, such as Forrest Gump and Jeffrey "The Dude" Lebowski, but they are rarer examples. Generally speaking, a movie's central characters, rightly or wrongly, wisely or foolishly, must take action. Otherwise, they don't grow or change, and the story becomes less compelling.

Uh oh, I thought. *Am I a passive protagonist?* The question hit harder because I already knew the answer. I had been hesitating in subtle ways since I'd arrived in Hollywood, and now I had been offered a key moment to step up, and I'd let it slip away. My story was happening to me, not because of me.

Many movies feature characters who switch from passive to active roles, and it's often to leave the world they know behind. Neo in *The Matrix*. Frodo in *The Lord of the Rings*. Shrek. I was doing the opposite. I could tell already that at the end of the semester, I was going back home. Hollywood was just too fast for me.

For our final school project, my pitch was selected, and I got the chance to direct the 10-minute short film I had written, *Split Second*, with a production team. The film turned out great, mainly thanks to the combined talents of our producer, editor, set designer, and actors. (And me.) The premiere screening of our film was a proud moment. Even then, I didn't mention it to anyone at the production company where I worked. I had already resigned myself to the belief that I hadn't made the most of my time there and settled for the unrealistic hope that somehow my work would speak for itself. When you're passive, missed opportunities tend to multiply. Each one makes the next one easier to miss.

• • •

One of my last weeks in Los Angeles, my supervisor at the production studio issued me a pass to come in on Sunday to do some extra work. There was no one there besides me. After I made all the requested photocopies and sorted the piles of screenplays, I hopped on my bike and rode, not toward the exit, but deeper into the backlot. Moments later, I was staring at the watchtower set from *Back to the Future*! "Great Scott!" I exclaimed, in full geeky reverence.

I continued and soon came upon the holy grail: the track for the Universal Pictures amusement park tram. There were no trams in sight, and after scanning the area for Security, I rode along the track and up a hill until I was facing the *Jurassic Park* gate! Sensors picked up my presence, and the doors slowly opened for me, revealing a jungle. Dinosaurs roared in the distance, and though danger was everywhere, I bravely pedaled on through.

Lastly, I rode down a street lined with old Hollywood sets: a Grecian palace next to a Mafia-owned Italian restaurant next to an Old Western saloon. At the bottom was the lake where "Bruce," Steven Spielberg's mechanized shark from the movie *Jaws*, lunges at the passing trams. I took a photo for my *Jaws*-loving friend.

The whole time, I boldly acted as if I belonged, and somehow, no one stopped me. I had just biked through one of the most memorable places I could imagine, and I couldn't have done it without my Huffy. We were quite a pair—we had teamed up to trespass on a magical movie experience, and every pedal forward had shown me I *did* have confidence. I just wasn't channeling it into the right places.

Yet.

I had been feeling small in Hollywood. Now, for the first time, I glimpsed what was possible when I didn't let fear dictate my path. Our six months ended soon after, with final screenings and tearful goodbyes. My friend who swore he wouldn't return for his graduation? He didn't. He turned his internship into a job and started building his Hollywood career. And me? I went home to New York State.

The day before I left LA and flew home to graduate with my class, I sold my bike. But I'd never forget it. Inspired by an upcoming movie by a director I'd met, I named my Huffy bike after a horse who was less impressive in stature than his peers but became legendary anyway. I would always remember it as Street Biscuit.

Courage doesn't always show up in the moment. Sometimes it arrives too late, after the opportunity has passed. But I could see that some, at least, had arrived. I had enjoyed exploring an unknown place like LA, and even more for having done it by bicycle. And it was this experience that led me to take a leap that landed me in Edinburgh, Scotland, where nothing felt familiar.

CHAPTER 10
SCOTLAND NEEDS SUBTITLES

I was definitely too young when I first watched the bloody story about the life of Scottish freedom fighter William Wallace. I must've watched *Braveheart* 50 times more since then, much like my friend had with *Jaws*. I said I loved the movie because I thought the battles were incredible, but it was something deeper than that and, in a way, ridiculous: I wanted to *be* William Wallace. As I understood his life—based on a movie, and filtered through the perspective of a teenage boy—I'd get to give inspiring speeches, run around the woods with a sword, and experience great interest from women, despite not having showered.

But as I entered adulthood, my tendency to retreat was becoming a noticeable pattern. What started with running home from Hollywood turned into not applying for certain jobs, not moving to interesting places, not speaking up for myself, and not asking out my crushes. I kept wanting to be a person who took risks, but when a meaningful chance presented itself, I took the easier path and did nothing. My anxiety and insecurity were clashing with my hunger for connection and courage, and the former were winning. So far, my actual track record was less "William Wallace" and more "Hiding Behind William Wallace."

And then one day, I surprised myself. Some of my friends had discovered a program that allowed recent graduates to get a six-month work visa in Scotland, and I decided to join them. This was not the easiest or most comfortable path, but it was an adventure that was too good to pass up. My friends and I got the visas and started planning our move to Edinburgh.

About a week before my flight, I was hit by an intense wave of second-guessing. *What was I thinking? How am I possibly going to get a job in a new country? How on earth am I going to remember to look right-left instead of left-right when crossing the street?* I shared my apprehension with James, a friend of my parents whom they had invited over for lunch. I told him I was excited but also worried about finding work there and adapting to a new country. James listened to what I had to say, thought about it, and then responded, "We don't know each other that well, but I can already tell you have a lot to offer. So remember: If they don't see it in you, it doesn't mean it's not there."

What was "it"? I had no clue (and I was fairly certain he didn't either). But his encouragement got me on the plane. It didn't, however, prepare me for the experience of taking the bus from the airport into the city of Edinburgh. Let me just say . . . if you are going to go live in Scotland, and everything you know came from watching the movie *Braveheart*, then you do not have enough information.

It turned out the Scots had made some updates since the 12th century. As I looked out the window, I saw more Pizza

CHAPTER 10: SCOTLAND NEEDS SUBTITLES

Huts than I'd expected. Then I saw Edinburgh Castle towering above us from the top of a hill. We wound our way through a city that seemed as though it was built for ghosts, with gothic, jagged spires and soot-stained brick, and dusk already descending even though it was still early afternoon. Despite its more modern flourishes, the city felt ancient and ominous. As I listened to people chatting on the bus, the accents were so thick and the turns of phrases so mysterious that I wondered if I had flown to Germany by mistake. *There is no way this is English.* (It was.)

As I arrived at the spot where I would transfer to my second bus, I would soon discover that, amid Edinburgh's industrial gloom, the city was full of people who were friendly, eager for a laugh, and, despite my best efforts to understand them, completely unintelligible.

Not being able to understand anyone was an immediate and decidedly inconvenient problem. I stood waiting at the transfer stop, feeling the effects of jet lag and the time difference, when a woman next to me turned and said, "Oy, pol, whyyanayenyerhoos?"

I stared at her for several beats. *C'mon brain, make it make sense . . . Nope, I can't.* I tried to be agreeable by responding politely, "Yes?" Now *she* looked puzzled, and the conversation ended there. In the silence that followed, I noted yet another difference from *Braveheart*: there was no option to turn on subtitles. When I checked into my hotel, the desk clerk finished his instructions, then added, "One more thing. Would you like me to knock you up in the morning?" Again, I responded politely, "No?" But I thought, *Wow, I definitely do* not *want you to do that.*

Later, I learned that he was offering to knock on the door the next morning at a scheduled time, like a friendly wake-up call. I wished I'd known that before I backed, horrified, out of the lobby.

The next day, I wandered the streets and eventually entered a small museum in the heart of the city. The Scots did not shy away from the darker details of their history. In fact, they were remarkably forthcoming. I read about all the bodies of impoverished citizens now buried under Edinburgh's modern buildings, the estimated murder count attributed to the legendary criminal Sawney Bean, and several other atrocities before I reached the exit.

By the door were two female volunteers, and one of them, who was petite, greeted me with a reedy voice. "I'm called Margaret, and this is Liz. Do you have any questions?"

"Yes, I'd like to go see Haymarket Plaza. Do you know why it's called that? Was it actually a hay market?"

"Nae. It was where they did the beheadings. The cobblestones in the plaza were designed that way to prevent the blood from pooling."

Good lord. I'm so glad I asked. I pivoted, "I'm also thinking about visiting a park called 'The Meadows.' Does it make more sense to walk or go by bus?"

The other woman, Liz, who had a gruff voice and the physique of a rugby player, grunted at me, "Neither. You shouldnae go there. You'll get murdered."

Margaret tut-tutted. "Och, Liz, don't be so dramatic. He wouldnae get murdered. He might get stabbed, though."

Fortunately, this time I understood them perfectly and skipped the park. I felt strongly that both outcomes were unacceptable.

CHAPTER 10: SCOTLAND NEEDS SUBTITLES

The following morning, I attended my scheduled orientation at the program's administrative office. It was time to go looking for a job. I printed out a stack of resumes on the office printer and hit the cobblestoned streets. For the next several days, I walked into every shop in Edinburgh and asked, "Would you hire me?"

I went into forty shops and asked this question and promptly got forty no's. I returned to the program office to print out more resumes. I saw the program manager and informed her, "I don't think anybody's hiring." She looked alarmed and asked, "You're not saying 'hiring,' are you?"

I nodded my head, and she stifled a laugh. "You should be saying, 'Will you *employ* me?' not 'Will you *hire* me?'"

I asked why, and she paused as she searched for the right words. "Well . . . 'hire me' has more of a connotation of 'I'm looking to offer you services of a sexual nature, in exchange for money.'"

I wish I had known that before I said it to forty strangers. Then I thought about how quickly they all said no. And what if someone had said yes?

I got back out there because I needed a wage. The British pound was worth twice the U.S. dollar, and the first and last month's rent on the flat I was sharing had consumed most of my meager savings. I had another reason, as well. In six months, some friends were embarking on a dream backpacking trip across Europe. If I earned enough, I could go with them.

The next afternoon, after my first round of asking, "Will you employ me?" (still getting no's, but less immediately), I happened across a little sandwich shop named The Globe Deli.

I walked in, asked for the manager, and said, "Would you employ me?" This got a much better reaction. Plus, the manager was Canadian, so I could understand him. I had an interview right then and there, and I got the job. It probably helped my case a lot that I managed not to laugh when he earnestly used the phrase "sandwich technician."

I started the next day and proceeded to mess up every single customer's order. This was because no two people spoke in the same dialect. Edinburgh is a very metropolitan city, and I took requests from people who were Irish, English, Australian, Scandinavian, Italian, and many other nationalities. I could barely understand anyone. Most of my misfortune, however, came from interacting with the Scottish-accented customers.

One of the locals stepped up and said to me, "Cheers, pol." (I'd figured out that "pol" was like "pal," which explained the first part of the question asked of me by that woman at the bus stop, but sadly not the rest.) And then this customer ordered . . . something. I didn't understand any part of what he said. Then, I had a great idea. I pointed to the speakers above us and said, "I couldn't hear you over the music. Would you mind repeating that?" He did, and I was right back where I started. Finally, a coworker rescued me and took over his order.

Soon after that, another Scottish customer stated her order. She requested a sandwich consisting of three ingredients. I understood the first and last items she requested, but the one in the middle? I was pretty sure she was saying, "Bdee." I asked her again, and again she said "bdee." I was truly stuck, and time seemed to slow down as even the music couldn't disguise the awkwardness of this exchange. Finally, my coworker jumped in again. "She wants a bacon, *brie*, and cranberry sandwich." I mean, obviously.

CHAPTER 10: SCOTLAND NEEDS SUBTITLES

I had many other interactions that were similar to that. I had no choice but to keep trying, no matter how embarrassing it got. In a way, it was like doing reps. *How many humiliations in a row can I take and still greet the next customer with a smile?*

My manager had noticed my frequent failures to translate, and I was quickly shuffled back to wash dishes, refill toppings, and mop floors. But how could someone who couldn't take sandwich orders be a sandwich technician? The second week, I got fewer shifts, and that Friday evening at the end of my shift, my manager handed me my paycheck and said, in his polite Canadian lilt, "Yeah, the thing is, I'm going to have to let you go."

As we stood there awkwardly, I thought, *I've never been fired before, and it's happening right now. This is so surreal. And I agree with this decision one-hundred percent. This has been a nightmare.*

Even though it was a good-riddance-to-all-involved situation, for some reason I asked him if there was anything I could have improved on. He looked thrown off for a second, then shrugged and said, "Honestly, Colin, you just don't have it in you."

Damn, that's a deep cut. I quickly left, with my pride in tatters. *Do I not have it in me? To make sandwiches?* But my brain immediately upped the stakes. *Do I not have it in me to be good at anything here?*

This moment of rejection stung. As I walked home to my flat, I remembered James's advice to me: "If they don't see it in you, it doesn't mean it's not there." That helped. I'd shown up and tried my best. The only real issue was that I'd applied for a job that required someone fluent in "Scottish," which isn't technically a language but might as well be. Still, I'd gone for it, and that was something.

A few weeks later, something clicked in my brain, and the thick Scottish brogue started to make sense to me. But it happened too late to save my sandwich career.

• • •

Soon after my deli dismissal, a temp agency connected me with a much better opportunity: a position at the Royal Bank of Scotland, located in an actual castle!

I soon learned that I would be working in the mailroom, which was in the basement of the castle. *Isn't that where the dungeon would have been?* I wondered, but didn't ask. The comparison felt appropriate because, all day, I sat and sorted huge bags of mail into slots, in a tiny room that was figuratively and literally far below the bank's higher-ups.

My mailroom duties in no way resembled the kind of work I dreamed of, but it was a good job nonetheless. That was in large part because I sat next to a highly entertaining co-worker. John was a fifty-two-year-old Scotsman who made me laugh every single day, including the first day, when I introduced myself. Upon hearing my accent, he immediately said, "Oh, right, you're American." He then mimed playing a banjo like a character in *Deliverance!* I was stunned, but I couldn't be mad, because it was such a funny way to casually sum up 320 million people. This was my first introduction to the Brits' predilection for good-natured teasing (or, as they refer to it, "taking the mickey.")

John was charismatic, well-liked, and brought a poetic flair to the act of complaining. Every day, when something or someone irritated him, he would stand up and loudly announce how many days he had left until he could retire: "Eight years, three months, and twenty-one days."

In his lilting Scottish accent, his retirement countdown (and its *eight* remaining years) managed to be amusing and depressing simultaneously. I thought, *We are a long way away from "They may take our lives, but they'll never take our freedom!"*

Thankfully, John's charmingly colorful (and off-color) stories took my mind off the monotonous work we did for hours on end. It certainly wasn't a dream job, but it helped me afford weekend excursions around England, Ireland, and Wales. Even better, I achieved my goal. I saved up enough money to join my friends on the backpacking trip.

On my last day at the bank, John gave me a meaningful handshake. Before letting go, he leaned in close and said, so only I could hear, "Seven years, nine months, and eight days." Despite his discomfort, I pulled him in for an actual hug. I would miss him. I would miss everything about this place.

I knew that "bonnie" Scotland would always hold a place in my heart. In my time there, I had grown more independent and confident, and I had definitely become more adept with the "language." All my little failures and rejections had shown me that I was resilient. I could show up, get knocked down, and (mostly) keep a grin on my face.

I was also leaving Scotland with something else I hadn't had before. A quiet, unlikely hope had emerged that someday I'd find work where what I had inside me—whatever "it" was—would matter. Scotland hadn't handed me the job of my dreams, but I was determined to find it, no matter how long it took.

The next day, I said goodbye to my flatmates, hoisted my newly-purchased backpack onto my shoulders, and boarded a train to Oxford to meet up with four American friends. Our six-week backpacking adventure across Europe lay ahead of us, and it promised to be an experience that would truly test my newfound courage.

Especially during a fateful trip to Spain, where I would come face-to-face with my greatest fear.

CHAPTER 11
PAMPLONA TOOK MY BREATH AWAY

As I stared out the window of the bullet train heading from Paris toward Biarritz, a coastal town in southwest France, I reflected on our whirlwind European adventure. Over the past few weeks, we took trains, planes, buses, and boats. We ate meals as if we would never get another, faced every fear we could think of, and we were having the time of our lives.

I'll put it this way: my friends were brave, and I was also there. I did my best to seem even a fraction as gung-ho as they were as we went skydiving in Switzerland, slept overnight on the decks of passenger ferries, and frequently faced navigating our way through unfamiliar cities where we didn't speak the language.

Little did I know that I was about to travel to Spain and come face-to-face with my greatest fear. It started when my friends excitedly suggested that we do something *really* scary. "Let's run with the bulls!" And I said, "Oh, no, thank you." Nope, that's not what I said. I was a 23-year-old male. I probably did a raucous whoop of agreement and hoped it was convincing. Now, I was on a very fast train headed for certain doom.

When we arrived in Biarritz, we hit up the French equivalent of a Kmart and found a rough approximation of the expected outfit for running with the bulls. We reluctantly purchased our findings: tight white T-shirts, shockingly-tighter white jeans, and red bandanas from the ladies' section.

All the hotels in Pamplona were sold out, so we decided we'd simply stay outside all night and do the run in the morning. We donned our new clothes and took only what we could fit in our pants pockets: a passport and a 20 euro note each. I also took my inhaler, because I don't leave home without it.

It quickly dawned on us that this plan meant walking across a French suburb, dressed head to toe in white, to reach the bus station where we'd catch a ride across the border to Pamplona. We were an outlandish sight: five tall foreigners in identical white outfits so bright they practically hurt the eyes. We looked like a cult. Or a boy band, but not one of the hot ones.

After our humiliating walk across town, we reached the bus stop, where I spotted a beautiful Australian backpacker. This was unfortunate because there was no way I could talk to her dressed like that. When the bus arrived, I slid into my seat and hunkered down for a bit. My inhaler was uncomfortable in the pocket of my white skinny jeans, so I put it in the magazine pouch on the seatback in front of me. Much better.

When we pulled into Pamplona a few hours later, it felt like we had parked in the middle of a *Where's Waldo?* convention. Everyone was dressed like us! These were our people! We got

CHAPTER 11: PAMPLONA TOOK MY BREATH AWAY

off the bus and merged with the crowd of revelers. It was a city-wide party.

As dusk approached, we felt the first sensation of chilliness. We looked around for a place to get inside, but every restaurant and bar was full. We ended up shuffling from pavilion to pavilion, trying to stay warm, while time seemed to slow down. None of us even had long sleeves.

That was when I felt my lungs tighten. Cold air is one of my asthma triggers. I hastily searched my pockets for my inhaler, that three-inch piece of plastic that I relied on. On the off-chance I didn't have it with me, I could be in serious trouble.

I didn't have it with me. It was in that magazine pouch on the bus.

I alerted my friends to my situation and assured them (and perhaps myself) I would be fine, but I would need to step away from the festivities so I could focus. I walked to a quiet park away from the throngs of people having the most fun night of their lives and proceeded to have a full-scale asthma attack.

My breath started coming in ragged gasps. My asthma felt like a wall at the back of my throat, an impassable border between my mouth and my chest. I fought to stay calm. But every inhale seemed to stop short, the oxygen never reaching my lungs. I could draw in just enough air to keep going, but never enough to fully breathe.

I didn't speak the language, and I didn't know how to find a doctor. All I could do was to continue trying to stay calm and draw in one partial breath after another. Maintaining slow, intentional breathing required focus. Sleep was not a possibility. Time slowed. Dying in Spain *before* the bull run hadn't previously occurred to me.

My attack lasted about four hours. As night slowly started to brighten into dawn, my breathing leveled off. It felt like I had smoked an entire carton of cigarettes, but I was going to make it.

I rejoined my friends, who had respected my need to be alone but were clearly relieved to see me. We wondered aloud where the track for the bull run was. We hadn't noticed the huge post holes throughout the city's downtown streets. Crews arrived and started putting a large post in each one and connecting them with fencing, quickly assembling the track for the bull run. They were building it with us inside. Those who were planning to run made sure to gather inside the fences, while those who were smart found a place outside to sit and watch.

After years of wondering what made Spanish people crazy enough to run with the bulls, I looked around me and realized there wasn't a single Spanish person in sight! The runners consisted entirely of Australians, Canadians, and Americans.

This is because the Spaniards were above us, on balconies, sipping their coffee and watching leisurely as a bunch of foreigners prepared to run for their lives. It must have been immensely satisfying.

I tried to suppress images of my imminent death as I focused on the rest of the white-and-red-clad crowd. They were stretching, chatting with friends, and trying to mask their fear with bravado.

We had taken our place just past what was known as Dead Man's Corner. This was where the alley turned at a full 90 degrees, and the running 1,000+ pound bulls occasionally slipped and skidded into the large plywood sheets that

CHAPTER 11: PAMPLONA TOOK MY BREATH AWAY

reinforced the outside corner. If someone got caught between them and the wall . . . well, it had that nickname for a reason.

The race was too popular this year, and with too many people on the track, some had to be removed. We discovered this when Spanish police in riot gear arrived and began pushing us toward the far end of the track. After a few hundred yards of herding us along (like cattle), the crew removed a section of fence posts, and we were unceremoniously shoved off the track. The fence quickly closed behind us, and the run commenced.

We desperately rushed to find a place to at least watch the race, but every available seat had been claimed hours ago. After a few minutes of frantic searching, we heard the runners and the bulls going by us. Through the crowd, I glimpsed a bull's leg as its owner hurtled by.

Dejected, we returned to the bus station and filed onto the bus back to France. I spent the first few minutes writing in my travel journal, culminating in the line "This was one of the greatest disappointments of my life." *[Note from the future: You're 23. There's plenty more to come . . .]*

Then I realized I was sitting in what seemed like the same row of the bus I had been sitting in the previous night. Surely this wasn't the same bus? I checked the pouch, and there was my inhaler! *Where were you 10 hours ago when I needed you?*

As we returned to France, I took comfort in knowing I had merely been *emotionally* crushed by this experience, not actually crushed by a 1,300-pound bull. Of course, I was relieved to be safe, but as the days and weeks passed, I became more and more troubled.

• • •

The asthma attack had traumatized me and left me wondering about ways I was in danger that I wasn't even aware of. I found myself fearing things that hadn't previously fazed me. I began obsessing over worst-possible-case scenarios and playing them over and over in my mind. Being in a plane crash. Breaking my leg. Having my passport stolen in the night. Being bitten by an animal. Being attacked by a mugger. And, once again, dying from asthma, which was something I hadn't worried about in years. These ominous possibilities gradually became all I could think about, and I couldn't turn the thoughts off.

I felt like my safety was a form of luck that could run out at any minute. I didn't breathe a word about my constant dread to my tripmates, but at an internet cafe, I opened up to my friend Christine about it in an email.

She replied and asked me if I thought I might have an "anxiety disorder." I had no idea what that meant, but at least now I had a phrase to Google. What I found was both reassuring and unsettling.

According to the DSM—short for *The Diagnostic and Statistical Manual of Mental Disorders* that psychiatrists use—anxiety is merely uneasiness or dread in response to danger, real or imagined. In other words, it's normal. Everyone feels it sometimes.

Anxiety *disorders*, though, involve worry that's constant, overwhelming, or disproportionate—so much so that it interferes with daily life. Those with the disorder may find it dominating their days, triggering panic attacks, and making them severely afraid of things that are extremely unlikely to happen.

Reading this, I caught myself arguing with the screen. "*Extremely unlikely?*" *Tell that to someone who's been in a natural*

CHAPTER 11: PAMPLONA TOOK MY BREATH AWAY

disaster or laid off or struck by a sudden illness. Bad things do *happen.* But then I saw something else: a lot of people with anxiety attribute their experience with it to having a "nervous temperament," as if it were merely part of their personality.[4]

That felt uncomfortably familiar. I'd always assumed my own nerves were just "me." It's no wonder that so many people never seek help. Anxiety is the most common mental health condition, yet 80 percent of Americans who screen positive for generalized anxiety have never been formally diagnosed. And, as Sarah Wilson points out in *First, We Make the Beast Beautiful*, anxiety among men is even more common than depression.[5] I was not alone in attempting to manage it on my own.

A week or so after our (non)run with the bulls, we were staying in a beachside apartment in Italy when I found myself experiencing an episode of extreme anxiety. During the night, the barred security door shook for several seconds, and I became immediately convinced that a crew of kidnappers with blowtorches was breaking in. My brain unspooled a vivid 4K horror reel of our future—tied up, tortured, accounts drained—all rendered in under a second. We soon learned the shaking was caused by a brief offshore earthquake, and there was no need to worry. My friends went back to sleep while my mind pivoted—to a tsunami. I sat in the bathroom to conceal the terror radiating through me. For hours, I desperately conducted research and tried to establish a plan for surviving the oncoming wall of water. I couldn't help but marvel at my brain's talent for catastrophizing. I made an observation that many others who face anxiety could relate to. *What a horrible skill to be amazing at—picturing doom in such detail.*

In an interview, comedian Baron Vaughn shared a personal insight as someone who navigates his own mental health challenges: "Anxiety is your own creative imagination turned into a weapon to beat yourself up."[6] My imagination wasn't an escape; it was becoming a prison. Over the remaining weeks of our backpacking trip, another big emotion took up residence. I was profoundly sad. There were times when I had to excuse myself in order to be alone, and I stole away to a stunning overlook or a rock outcropping, where I looked out over the city lights or lapping ocean waves. I wrote for hours in my journals about feelings I couldn't quite name or explain. I felt like I was grieving something, but I didn't know what. Or why.

I masked my sadness and fear around my travel companions pretty effectively. I felt fear but acted anyway and felt sad but smiled anyway. However, no matter how well I pretended to be courageous or how often I made people laugh, I couldn't shake my newly emerging feelings. Maybe they had been hidden inside me all along, but they surfaced with a vengeance during that long, terrible night when I had the worst asthma attack I'd ever had.

I had no way of knowing that it was also the *last* asthma attack I'd have.

But I did take consolation, even begrudging pride, in the fact that during my adventure in Pamplona, I had faced my greatest fear and lived to tell the tale. And bulls were also there.

CHAPTER 12
ACCIDENTAL MOVIE STAR

After eight months overseas, coming back home was harder than expected. The sudden silence at night was a sharp contrast to late-night hostel laughter and shared cheap meals with my backpacking friends. I craved community again, and as always, I turned to church for it. I didn't quite find a sense of belonging there this time, but I did experience something I never could have predicted.

Up to that point, I had been sure the most fun example I could give about growing up religious was that I was a Christian clown. Well, buckle up. Because, in my twenties, I became the star of a series of movies produced by a megachurch for Vacation Bible School.

(See? You *knew* you recognized me from somewhere!)

During my time abroad, my mom, stepdad, and sisters had moved to Vermont. When I returned, I joined them there while I attempted to come up with a plan for my life—starting with figuring out how to move out of my parents' basement. My family was attending a large church in the area, and one day my mom mentioned that the church was looking for an actor to star in a series of Indiana-Jones-style movies for Vacation Bible School. I thought, *I have found my purpose. This is what I was put on Earth to do.*

I was excited for three reasons. First, I'd always wanted to be in a movie; second, I grew up loving Indiana Jones; and third, I somehow ignored everything else about this scenario.

I didn't have any acting training, so I knew if I was going to nail my audition for the lead role of Dakota Joe, I was going to have to pull out all the stops. In my case, that meant doing a gruff voice *and* affecting an accent.

"'Ello, boys and girls! Oym Dakota Joe." I said in my audition, in the worst accent you've ever heard. If you were to point on a globe to how many countries my accent came from, you would need both hands. It was California by way of Australia, Wales, and western New York.

The production team *loved* the accent. So, I had to keep it going for almost a week of filming. For a costume, I had a torn and disheveled button-down shirt, a messenger bag with nothing in it, and a fedora hat. I submitted a prop request for a whip. I was denied.

Filming was so fun. I paddled in a canoe and capsized it. I climbed around in a cave. I ran around in the uncharted wilderness . . . next to the church parking lot. I had a sidekick, a dog named Denver, that was played by a sock puppet and voiced by a nine-year-old. It's not cool for me to say it, but this child was a major diva, and not in a spectacular way. While I spent the week soaked, dirty, and doing all my own stunts, he spent it complaining about the effort of reaching his sock

CHAPTER 12: ACCIDENTAL MOVIE STAR

puppet hand into the frame. *I'm sorry, is lying on a soft bed of grass for two minutes too hard for you?*

Okay. Pause. I realize I'm ranting about a nine-year-old, which I also realize I shouldn't do. So what? I wanted to give him a talking to, which would've started with "Look, fella." (This is Christian for something much worse.)

My sock-puppet sidekick's chief role seemed to be to drive home the already heavy-handed dialogue. Arguably, this was not necessary. At one point, I had to say (into a camera that was recording), "All this time I thought I was looking for a jewel, but I was really looking for Jesus." It's no *Shawshank Redemption*, I agree with you. Even the six-year-olds who would see this later would probably think, *We get it. It's a little on the nose.*

I was pretty sure the film we were creating would be a train wreck. At one point, I was paddling in "the rapids" to get away from the "giant waterfall," when behind me, two girls swam into the shot wearing floaty wings. At another point, I was supposed to uncover a box of treasure. (Spoiler alert: It contained a Bible.) I suggested it should be covered in dust I could blow off, but we could only find small pebbles as we looked around. We balanced them on the box, and then I went "Woaahhhhh" and brushed off the rocks, launching tiny projectiles dangerously across the cave. I almost maimed the camera operator.

I shuddered to think how bad this footage was going to look, but it turned out someone was on our side. No, not that Someone. The someone I mean was the youth pastor, who was a ridiculously talented filmmaker and editor. He took the footage and, through the magic of color grading and careful cropping, created five tightly edited short films featuring epic music and cliffhanger endings. Each day of the week, the kids got to watch a new episode of *The Adventures of Dakota Joe*.

It was the unparalleled hit of Vacation Bible School. The youth pastor called me in the middle of that week and said, "It's amazing—these kids cannot get enough. All they talk about is the next episode of Dakota Joe. I have a favor to ask... will you show up on Friday in costume to surprise the kids?"

He neglected to mention that the kids believed I actually was Dakota Joe or, at the very least, a professional actor from Hollywood—instead of, you know, an unemployed 20-something currently living in his mother's basement.

I said, "Sure, I'm free that day." I was free *every* day. I needed a win so badly I was probably wearing the fedora when he called. I told him I'd be there and hung up the phone. Because once again, I ignored everything else about this scenario.

Two days later, I was hiding in the broom closet of a church gymnasium, in a costume, waiting to surprise a bunch of children. (Hoo boy, now there's a sentence.)

I could hear a lot of kids, but I couldn't really tell how many there were. The program started, and I was guided to stand behind a curtain. Eventually, I heard the youth pastor say, "Boys and girls, we have a special guest: Dakota Joe!"

The curtain pulled back, and I ran out onto the stage as someone rolled a papier-mâché boulder for me to dodge. I was halfway through leaping over it, and in mid-air, when my brain processed what I was seeing: an audience of at least 400 children completely losing their minds.

They started screaming and clutching their faces. I went, "'Ello, boys and girls!" They screamed even louder, looking like they were going to cry or pass out or both. I felt like The

CHAPTER 12: ACCIDENTAL MOVIE STAR

Beatles must have felt when they first appeared on The Ed Sullivan Show. For a second I wondered, *Is SpongeBob standing behind me?* But no, they were screaming for me. It felt pretty great. I yelled out a couple of the catchphrases from the show, and they cheered and lost their minds all over again. I didn't know how long I was supposed to stay on stage, so I did a little call-and-response:

Me: "All this time I thought I was looking for a…"
Them: "JEWEL!"
Me: "But I was really looking for…"
Them: "JESUS!"

Oh, now I see why they wrote it that way. Very catchy.

When I ran out of stuff to say, I yelled, "Thank you!" I didn't realize that *I* was the big finale. Once I stopped talking, the program ended, and I failed to clear the room in time. I was left standing there, stuck in the gymnasium with 400 people, needing to maintain my character and his accent.

A woman I'd never seen before walked up to me in a dog costume and said, "Hi, Dakota Joe, it's me, Denver!"

It made sense why. You can't have a hand puppet walking around in a crowd. The illusion would be ruined. Even though this stranger was *not* my nine-year-old nemesis, but rather a different person altogether, it still reminded me of our experience working together, and I felt myself getting irritated all over again. I offered an unconvincing smile as "Denver" and I posed for a picture.

Right then, a little girl approached me. "Dakota Joe? Can I have your autograph?"

She was so nervous that her voice was shaking. I thought, *The lies I am telling to be standing here right now . . .*

I hadn't written in cursive since fifth grade, but of course, I wanted to give someone my autograph. Denver handed me a Sharpie (ever the sidekick). I turned back to the little girl and found her holding up her Bible.

Hmmmmmmm. What's the rule here? In this totally common situation that people might find themselves in at any time? I didn't know then, and I don't know now.

I was sure that there was something very wrong about signing it, but I couldn't bring myself to crush the girl's dreams. So I signed it with that permanent marker. In a fake name. In the word of the Lord.

As she ran away clutching her Bible, I thought, *At least that will never happen again.* But a little boy had seen what transpired. He turned to the crowd and yelled out, "He's signing Bibles!"

That's when a tsunami of three-foot-tall people rushed toward me. They backed me up against a wall. I was signing as fast as I could. I signed programs, I signed t-shirts, I think I signed a face . . . and a whole lot of Bibles. I lost count of how many.

You can judge me all you want. I certainly have. But it'll never diminish the fact that, for one day, I was the most famous I will ever be in my life . . . in the lamest way imaginable.

And I still have the fedora to prove it.

• • •

Later that night, I was sitting on the edge of my bed (and by this I mean the futon in my parents' basement), and I could still feel the reverberation of that crowd cheering. I kept replaying it while wondering what had just happened.

CHAPTER 12: ACCIDENTAL MOVIE STAR

I grew up going to Vacation Bible School, and from a young age, I had wanted to be a performer. I had just experienced the culmination of that childhood dream. It was this strange cocktail of hilarious, memorable, and mortifying.

I definitely remember thinking to myself, *Never tell this story to anyone.* (This turned out to be advice I would frequently ignore, and with good reason!)

But in addition to embarrassment, I felt a strange sort of guilt. While those kids were seeing a carefully edited final movie, I knew everything that had happened just outside the frame—my doubts and my feelings of phoniness. In these moments, I had forced myself to give voice to common Christian sentiments that I was no longer sure I believed. This led to a melancholy thought. *You've been disagreeing with some pretty central aspects of your religion for a long time, and those disagreements aren't going away. In fact, they're growing. Maybe it's time to do something about that.*

Even saying that silently to myself made my chest tighten in panic. My entire world was, and always had been, my faith, my church, and my belief in God. I knew that if I followed these doubts to where I was probably already heading, I was going to lose my community, my identity, and my salvation all at the same time.

So I did nothing. Instead, I took the combination of all that loneliness, confusion, and fear and buried it in a deep, painful place somewhere inside myself. And I kept the door to that distressing place shut as best I could.

It was for the best. It's not like being a Bible school movie star was paying my bills. I set those confusing thoughts aside and focused on what might.

CHAPTER 13
A TOURIST IN OTHER PEOPLE'S PASSIONS

Up to this point in my adult life, I had failed to find a job that tapped into what I was good at—one that interested me and that I could see a future in. I had to pay my rent (since, as soon as I could, I'd moved out of my parents' basement), and had taken a string of random office jobs that felt uncomfortably reminiscent of that mailroom in Scotland. Mind-numbing data entry. Endless spreadsheets. Answering phones and taking minutes for meetings.

After film school, my screenwriter dreams had morphed into a big dream for my future: I wanted to become a novelist. Of course, that was an incredibly long road to an unknown paycheck, if there would even be one. Thus far, I had written several essays and even a novella, but I hadn't submitted anything—not exactly a great business model.

After visiting Jamaica to help a small community rebuild its facilities after a series of hurricanes, I wrote an article about my experience and submitted it to a local newspaper. They published it. Seeing my name in the byline for the first time was a cool experience. So, I submitted more ideas, which led to more opportunities and my starting to create a career as a journalist. I was a "stringer" for various newspapers in the area, writing one-off articles for which I was paid by the project or by the word. It never seemed to bring in much money, but it was a fun side hustle.

One day, I found an open full-time reporter position at a local newspaper. With my portfolio of published articles in hand, I made a convincing case and walked out with my first assignment!

I now had a job that let me write, meet interesting people, learn how a city runs, and build a network of contacts. The job felt important, and I did, too. For someone who had spent years feeling aimless and anxious, having work that gave me structure and made me feel valuable did wonders for my mental health. I had a role and a purpose.

There was a ton of variety in the work, and I wrote a lot of different kinds of stories. Most were interesting, while others were less so, such as those that revolved around zoning meetings and other municipal happenings. One of those articles ended up with the headline "Zoning Board Remains Undecided on Parking Lot Layout." The rest of the piece was pretty boring to write (let alone read), since it was a bunch of words describing something that hadn't actually happened.

This type of coverage was part of the job, but fortunately, not all of it. I also had opportunities to write heartwarming "fluff pieces" about local people. At first, I treated the work like any freelancer would—just assignments to complete. But slowly, article by article, something started shifting in how I saw people.

I interviewed a group of middle-school students and their families participating in a charity Hunger Walk. Walking with them, I asked one girl, "Why are you here?" She said, "I'm doing the Hunger Walk because of my dog."

"Why is that?" I asked.

"Because he's always hungry."

I thought, *Aw, you don't know what this event is actually about, and that is an adorable quote I will definitely include.*

I attended, and then wrote a stirring review of, a middle-school play called *Romeo and Juliet: Ninjas vs. Pirates*. I also wrote an article about Mathletes heading to DC for a competition. (I wished featuring them in an article could give them some rockstar status among their non-math-inclined peers, but I'm guessing it didn't.)

These early stories were sweet, even amusing, but I was still an observer collecting quotes. Then I started noticing the gap between how people appeared and who they actually were.

I was surprised when my editor requested that I write a profile on a member of the school board. She had always seemed cold and unfriendly when confronted by frustrated parents and residents during public meetings. Kind of intimidating. She offered to meet me at one of the city's elementary schools, and she quickly began geeking out about her work as a coach for a districtwide girls' robotics team. We couldn't find any good place to sit, so we ended up half-crouched on a low bench made for children. With our knees practically up to our faces, I sat and listened as she lit up while talking about opportunities in tech for the next generation. I saw her as a mother, a coach, and once a girl herself. She wasn't who I'd expected her to be.

A local magazine hired me to write an article about long-standing bands in the area. I went to watch one of them perform, and the band members were in full 80s glam rock mode, complete with bandannas and tight leather pants. Their groupies were mostly screaming moms full of alcohol and hormones. Afterward, I gathered with the band to ask some questions for the article. At one point, the lead singer stopped me and asked, "Wait, what publication do you write for again?"

Boy, did I want to say *Spin* or *Pitchfork*, but I had to answer "*Vermont Maturity*," which was a free, monthly print magazine for people over 50. The band looked disappointed. The lead singer rallied and asked, "Could you at least not put our ages in the article?"

I broke eye contact and sheepishly explained that including their ages was the main reason I had gotten this assignment in the first place. It got awkward. I didn't think it would help to tell them the magazine was rebranding as *The Boom Times* (in a play on the word "Boomer"). But they accepted the information with wry smiles and more grace than I had expected. They weren't worried about their image; they just wanted the article to be about their music. I did my best to make them look cool in the final version, even though it also specified that they were 51, 54, 59, and 61.

I was learning to look past my assumptions. These experiences made me think about how we tend to whip past people in a hurry and form quick judgments. When I slowed down to appreciate the glimpse I was given into a stranger's life, I would often discover a deep ocean of experience and thoughtfulness.

CHAPTER 13: A TOURIST IN OTHER PEOPLE'S PASSIONS

For one story, I interviewed a mother who had written a book years earlier about her son dying young due to addiction. I told her I wanted to focus on her and her son's story. After our conversation, she sent me a long email relaying that because her son died of a drug overdose, she had been approached by a series of journalists who wanted to write an "issue piece" about the decline of youth in the community. She said, "You're the first press person who came to me and cared about what I've been through."

That's when I realized what I'd stumbled into—not just a job writing about people, but a chance to actually see them.

The stories I was writing and the people I was meeting were seeping into my life. One of my personal highlights was when I interviewed Lisa Loeb. In the 90s, few songs were as much of a mega-hit as her song "Stay," which was featured in the 1994 movie *Reality Bites*, and within a matter of months, Lisa had become the first unsigned artist to top the Billboard Hot 100. It had been a while, though, since 1994. Lisa Loeb was performing at a local music venue, and I got the assignment to interview her. She was legit-famous, so I was nervous about talking to her. My editor had stipulated that the story be about her being the writer of a famous one-hit wonder from 15 years ago. *Yikes.* I tried to find a more polite way to ask her about this, and I came up with, "What's your relationship to that song now, since you wrote it early on in your career?"

Loeb said, "I'm so grateful for 'Stay.' Because of that one song, I have had a whole life of creativity, exploration, and art. It makes people happy, so why wouldn't I be honored to sing it for them?" It was such a great answer that it became the pull quote in the article. Unfortunately, my editor changed the title without my knowledge to something that made her sound like a has-been, which really bothered me. But then I realized Lisa Loeb would never read that tiny, weekly newspaper anyway.

Preparing for each new article allowed me to travel like a tourist through other people's passions. I didn't know what I wanted to do with the rest of my life yet, but I got to be in close proximity to people who were doing things they cared about, whether grand or seemingly mundane. While I was still hoping to adapt my first screenplay into my first novel, journalism felt like an acceptable version of that dream. It was like being an author but in a hurry. The work was often compelling—most days, I couldn't believe I was making a living by writing. Until I remembered I was making only *half* a living.

I got paid $30 per article and $15 more if the paper used a photo I'd taken. I worked for this newspaper consistently, yet I was paid as a contractor, not an employee. I wrote eight to ten articles every single week, but that added up to only around $300. It was an unsustainable schedule of attending city meetings, coming up with ideas for features, arranging meetings with people and traveling to interview them, transcribing the interviews, writing and revising and submitting my articles by the deadline, and then making requested edits on short notice. Then Monday arrived, and it started all over again.

At the end of my first year as a writer, I had made $12,000. So, yeah. Not great. I didn't think to question why I could see the poverty line from my position as head reporter for a newspaper, or why I was on staff yet classified as an independent contractor. This was the best job I'd ever had, so I did my best to manage the financial challenges that came with it. I came up with many frugal ways to cut costs so I could keep doing this thing I found fulfilling.

CHAPTER 13: A TOURIST IN OTHER PEOPLE'S PASSIONS

I made Pad Thai, but I called my version Poor Man's Pad Thai because it was just ramen, a dollop of peanut butter, and some hot sauce. I sense your judgment, and I don't necessarily disagree. My Dodge Neon cost $1,500, and my DIY repair job on the caved-in roof was free. Unlimited data phone plans weren't particularly affordable yet, so I signed up for a Google Voice number to make free calls from home on my laptop. (It is amazing how fast something that was cutting-edge can sound prehistoric.) Unfortunately, even during short phone calls, my computer would heat up like I was playing *Call of Duty*.

I tried a pay-by-the-minute phone plan when interviewing a local veteran who had just written a memoir about his Vietnam War experience. My first question was, "So why did you write the book?" His response was to speak rapidly, in detail, without pausing, for almost 20 minutes. At that point, I mustered the courage to interrupt. "I'm sorry to stop you there, sir, but I have only 300 words for this article." He was clearly bummed but continued to keep talking at length. I said goodbye without mentioning that our phone call had cost me most of what I'd make on the article.

In my second year, I made more than $12,000! I made $15,000. Fortunately, I could make the rest I needed by having a 20-hour-a-week job answering phones in an office. One time, a coworker at that job asked, "What do you do when you're not here? Do you relax?"

I said, "No, I'm the head writer for a newspaper in a city of 20,000 people. That is why I work *here*."

In my third year as a journalist and an office worker, I made $30,000. It was an emotional moment because, for the first time, I was making enough money doing something I loved. It felt like a huge victory. But more income as a contractor meant more taxes were due. I owed almost $5,000 in taxes. Ouch.

I looked for more ways to cut my expenses. I discovered I could do this by eating PB&J sandwiches, pasta, and oatmeal, living with roommates in small apartments, and not going to restaurants, traveling, or dating. Or having fun. Fun was too expensive. So far, none of this was adding up to a particularly enviable life.

But I loved this job. By really noticing, asking, and caring, I was constantly reminded that everyone has stories worth telling. I also got to set my schedule and work wherever I wanted, so I felt like my own boss. These things felt worth the financial stress.

Nonetheless, I couldn't ignore that my dream was on life support. I approached my editor with a plan to take on more work in exchange for a higher salary, which was cautiously approved. I knew I would need to dazzle the whole team now that I had this next level of responsibility. But right when I most needed to be on my game, I wasn't. For a reason I couldn't pinpoint, my depression had returned in a big way.

• • •

After two remarkable years of confidence, purpose, and happiness, the depression that had plagued me since childhood descended once again.

This time was like nothing I'd ever experienced. I stayed in my apartment all the time, unable to go out. I still had to interview people for articles, but my social anxiety drove me to come up with creative excuses for interviewing them on the

CHAPTER 13: A TOURIST IN OTHER PEOPLE'S PASSIONS

phone or by email. I was in a fog all the time, with little ability to verbalize my thoughts.

This was odd because I was usually comfortable when thrown into a conversation. I was good with words and good at making an awkward situation somewhat less awkward. (Paradoxically, another of my talents was the ability to make an awkward situation much *more* awkward. Being a human is complicated sometimes.)

Have you ever tried to summon the courage to call your crush or someone you looked up to but found that you kept hanging up because you didn't know what you would say? I was that way with every single phone call. Every time my eyes landed on the number I needed to dial, my heart would pound, and my hands would shake.

I was so paralyzed by self-doubt that, even when I powered through and picked up the phone, I first imagined the conversation in my head from start to finish. No matter how I played it out, it always ended with whoever I had called thinking, "*Whoa, this guy is weird.*" Once I finally called and they answered, my skin crawled during the entire conversation, and I would interpret even the slightest pause from them as judgment.

I was in deep trouble. I figured I'd be fired at any moment. But worse than that, I kept thinking how much easier it would be not to be around anymore.

I wasn't sleeping, and I was up at strange hours. I was watching too many movies and struggling to do my work. For the first time, I missed deadlines.

Depression has no sense of scale. Any failure or misstep can feel inordinately shameful. Whether I couldn't make a phone call, think of the right thing to say, or stubbed my toe on something I should've seen, I reacted with self-loathing.

I didn't tell anyone this, but I was harming myself. Nothing dangerous or permanent, but it really hurt, which, for some reason, helped. I knew I was on the wrong road, but I couldn't change directions and didn't know who to talk to. One day, my editor called me and, despite my protestations, required that I come to the office. When I arrived, he said, "Colin, what's going on with you?"

I couldn't make eye contact. My voice was completely flat. I just shrugged, and then my eyes began to fill with tears.

"Are you depressed?" he asked. I froze, feeling caught. Then, I did the only thing left to do. I nodded.

He opened his desk, searched for something, and then reached over and handed me a business card. Below the person's name was the word "Therapist."

CHAPTER 14
MY SECRET SENTENCE

I had never talked to a therapist before, so even though I now had the business card and phone number for one, there were suddenly lots of reasons not to call. I was afraid this man would be like one of the kooky therapists that Matt Damon in *Good Will Hunting* chews through in a matter of minutes. I was scared to share my authentic self and my secrets, even if that was the whole point of therapy. I was worried he would look at me in disgust and say, "You're being kind of a baby. Be a man." I was afraid at some point, he'd become uncomfortable and stop me by saying, "You're freaking me out." I was also concerned he'd be clinical and impersonal, more focused on writing a prescription than actually engaging in conversation.

My conflict was internal and intense and significantly more common than I had any idea at the time. Podcaster and author John Moe describes it this way:

The longest road a person with depression travels can often be the one between where they are at present and where they can get help to improve. Seeking that out, making that appointment, and keeping that appointment can be a Herculean task ... What keeps people away is a fear, one that depression itself is delighted to stoke, that as long as you don't find out you have mental health problems, then somehow you don't have mental health problems. If you never get a good look at the monster, then there's no need to fight the monster. The problem there is that yeah, that monster is real, and if you opt out of fighting it, the monster simply beats the crap out of you all the time.[7]

The next day, I picked up the card and dialed the therapist's number, and I didn't hang up when he answered. He was friendly, upbeat, and conversational. While I questioned his cheerful nature, in light of my reasons for calling him, I didn't exactly have any other therapists' business cards lying around. So, despite my misgivings, I made an appointment.

A small win, I thought at the time. It was considerably more than that.

As I said earlier, his name was Sam. After I'd answered his first question about why I wanted to try therapy, he encouraged me to elaborate. What came next was a vulnerability avalanche.

My words came out slowly at first, but I soon picked up speed. "Well, there are a couple of things that are pretty big problems. I've never really been in a relationship. I can't relax around someone I like that way. I need to keep my distance, or I'll get hurt. Even with friends, I can be standoffish. I'm not interesting enough or cool enough, and I don't want anyone to

CHAPTER 14: MY SECRET SENTENCE

know that. And my thoughts . . . My head is full of thoughts that I don't know how to deal with."

Once I ran out of words, I wondered briefly if it was possible to actually pass out from embarrassment. But Sam simply took it in. He nodded and steered me back to more casual waters. He asked me about myself—my background, my job, my family and social circle, my hobbies. It turned out we had writing in common. He'd written for a magazine in New York, which immediately sounded cooler than my writing career thus far. But I felt more at ease.

We veered back into the tougher things I needed to discuss. As I talked, I felt as if I was outside of my body. Just as I had feared, I was now saying those things that I'd never said to anyone. Sam didn't recoil at all. Whatever I told him, he just went, "Okay." Every time he said that word, I felt the tiniest flicker of hope.

Sam seemed excited about the possibilities ahead for me, unfazed by my self-doubts. He was showing me I could acknowledge my most difficult thoughts without adding further judgment to them. They were just thoughts. Some were true and some were not. Discussing them with Sam helped me distinguish one from the other.

My head was a busy place during this first conversation. I had really opened up, but I was also monitoring and managing myself the whole time. Sure, I was stating my most frightening thoughts in the hope that I could get help processing them, but then I would quickly add things like, "It's not that big a deal, though." Because, apparently, everything was going great? *All I need is a quick tune-up, and I'll be on my way.*

For some reason, I really wanted to make sure I wasn't coming off *too* crazy. This attempt proved disastrous. At the end of the hour, Sam asked when I wanted to meet again (because, clearly, there was plenty left to be done). I threw out a date, and he said, "Shoot, I can't do it that week. I'm taking my family on vacation."

I replied, "Oh, that's okay! Where are you going?" He hesitated for just a second. I would never find out why, because I immediately assumed I'd made him uncomfortable, or that as a patient I wasn't allowed to ask him that. To fix things, I quickly added, "Don't worry, I'm not going to go all *Cape Fear* on you."

Panic hit me immediately. *Why did I say that?* In trying to put him at ease, I'd just compared myself to a psychopath. I wondered if "I'm not going to go all *What About Bob?* on you" would've at least been slightly less disconcerting.

Instead of calling for Security, Sam just laughed along with me at my unfortunate phrasing. We found a different time, and we kept meeting. He was proving to be a cool therapist. Sam revealed himself to be a skilled listener to whom I could talk about my life, my fears, my hopes, my weaknesses, my frustrations, and my doubts about my own potential. I was an eager and focused client, and I put in a lot of effort.

Sam helped me approach my mental health in a variety of ways. He described antidepressants as simply one "tool" in our toolbox, and I overcame my hesitancy and began taking an SSRI. I did not, in contrast to my fears, become addicted to it. Taking it became part of my daily regimen, while most of our work was focused on changing my lifestyle in specific ways. Sam helped me identify simple, positive steps I could take to help each area of my life feel more hopeful, and I took a number of them. I was beginning to take an active role in my own life. I wanted it to be a better one—a good story, even.

CHAPTER 14: MY SECRET SENTENCE

Sam accepted me, no matter what I told him. He patiently guided me into conversations about the areas of my life I needed to explore. He helped me lift the rocks I was afraid to lift so that all the hideous secrets wriggled out in every direction, which revealed to me that they weren't actually all that horrible or shameful. He was empowering me to develop a sense of agency in my life and shedding light on the ways I had become accustomed to speaking to myself.

Being conscious of my self-talk was quickly proving to be one of the most eye-opening aspects of therapy for me. Author and psychotherapist Lori Gottlieb explains its significance this way:

> We talk to ourselves more than we'll talk to any other person over the course of our lives, but our words aren't always kind or true or helpful—or even respectful. Most of what we say to ourselves we'd never say to people we love or care about, like our friends or children. In therapy, we learn to pay close attention to those voices in our heads so that we can learn a better way to communicate with ourselves.[8]

Sam taught me not to give my self-doubt more power than it deserved, to respond to it calmly and rationally, rather than by adding fuel to the fire. He taught me that when I had a terrible thought about myself, I could respond to the thought as though it were a voice coming from outside of me instead of inside. When I told him I would often tell myself I'm worthless, he asked, "How would you like to respond to that thought?" I considered this and replied that I'd say that statement was inaccurate and unfair, considering all the good things I have to offer.

I had missed this opportunity many times in the past, but once I learned to "hear" my thoughts this way, I realized that I could choose how to interpret the ones that were critical of me. I could learn to defend myself from, well, myself.

This mattered most when it came to something I had repeatedly thought but never expressed to anyone. I thought of it as my secret sentence.

It was this: "If you really knew me, you would reject me."

Explaining this to Sam and hearing it aloud in the presence of another person, it sounded vindictive, undeserved, and unsustainable. Sam responded, "When did you first start thinking this about yourself?" I found myself talking about the times as a child when I felt like an outsider even among friends or family. I relayed the relief I felt when I got someone to laugh, and the panic I sometimes felt when a joke fell flat or I couldn't think of anything to say. I retraced the way I had opened up only in spaces where I thought I could be myself, and in places where I thought I couldn't, I had tended to hide as much as possible. Among religious peers, I subverted my tendency to swear and my love of poking too much at accepted wisdom, and around non-religious people, I was reserved and evasive when I was invited to parties. I always felt like an outsider until I couldn't stop being one. I had been rejected at one point, yes, but then I'd fallen into a pattern of rejecting myself.

I was finally beginning to recognize that putting on a mask in order to show only the *right* version of myself was causing me more pain, not less. Since I had never let anyone see the real me, never revealed the parts of me that were scared and filled

CHAPTER 14: MY SECRET SENTENCE

with self-doubt, no one had ever really "seen" me. I couldn't possibly know what the reaction would be. It might not be what I feared.

Sam was my first evidence of this. No matter how authentic I was with him, he didn't recoil. Through this pattern, Sam earned my trust and my respect, which is why I felt emboldened to make another big confession. One that I really, really, really didn't want to say out loud. Finally, I worked up the courage. "Sam, there's another reason I'm here," I admitted. "It might even be *the* reason I'm here . . . I'm a virgin. And, man, I need help."

CHAPTER 15
LATE TO THE PARTY

Before I tell you how old I was when I lost my virginity, I'll give you a fun fact: I was a virgin when the movie *The 40-Year-Old Virgin* came out. This fact was much less fun for me than it might have been for others. I'm told the movie was a comedy. I just sat in the theater thinking, "Yup, this all checks out." It was like a documentary about my life.

I'll put it to you this way: I was late to the party. More than late, actually; I had lost my invitation. And kind of like the hapless main character in the movie, I wasn't sure why this time-honored rite of passage had never happened for me.

When I had confessed my (unwanted) sexual purity to Sam and asked for his help, he'd slowly gotten me to talk more about it. I'd already told him about my fear of rejection, so it was time to delve deeper into the other major factor: religion. Might this situation have had something to do with my being raised fundamentalist? Why, yes, it did. It had *everything* to do with that.

I attempted to unpack how exactly I ended up at this juncture. I had grown up being told, and believing, that if I ever wanted to find real love, I had to wait for marriage to have sex. I prayed for the soulmate I would someday meet, who would make all this waiting worth it. She would be all the virtuous things I was hoping for, and our first time together would be amazing.

Between the ages of 14 and 21, my social life had been limited to friends I made in church, at my Christian high school, and at my Christian college. Almost every friend I had was taught, like I was, that sex was only acceptable in a marriage. My own path to believing in this idea, and committing to it, was less than ideal.

When I was about 15, our youth group read the book *I Kissed Dating Goodbye* by Joshua Harris. In the book, Harris (who was just 22 when he wrote it), outlined a different approach to romance that encouraged young Christians to "court" instead of date. This meant we should only have a relationship with someone we intended to marry, and we would carry on that relationship under the supervision of adults to avoid temptation. This was because, as the book warned, premarital sex would taint us. We would be like used gum. We would have given parts of our hearts away—parts we would no longer have when we met our eventual spouses.[9]

As a result, we all kissed dating goodbye. I'd never even come close to dating, so I wasn't sure what I was kissing goodbye, but I was doing it anyway. Anything I could do to become purer and ensure I would find that godly soulmate someday was something I believed I needed to do.

In the hands of the Evangelical church, the book would quickly become the unofficial adolescent rulebook for "Purity

CHAPTER 15: LATE TO THE PARTY

Culture"—a church mentality that elevated sexual purity above everything else. This meant abstinence became not only the expectation for one's body but also the standard for one's mind. We were encouraged to scrutinize every impure thought we had and repent. We were quite sure that anyone who admitted that they were "struggling with pornography" would be regarded as a full-blown sex addict. I know this because I did admit to it, and that's exactly how I was treated.

Then, as I got older and relaxed my views a bit, I still found dating to be oddly stressful. I had crushes on women constantly, but as soon as the crush became mutual, I freaked out. This continued through college and into the present. Each time I was intrigued by someone new, it wouldn't be long until I felt waves of discomfort and panic, which would result in ghosting my new crush or just feigning disinterest and totally confusing her. Instead of being excited about where we were heading next, I treated it like the end of the line. Because the more she got to know me, the more things she'd find that she didn't like. Once she really knew me, she'd reject me.

From a young age, I had been taught to war against my own body, to conquer my natural admiration for the female form, and to ignore my desires and every biological instinct I had when it came to seeking physical intimacy. I'd been fighting this battle for so many years now I wasn't sure I could stop, even though I was experiencing both pain in my loneliness and shame at my longing.

Sam listened as I shared this backstory, thought for a moment, and then said with a curious expression, "I'm noticing something that I want to check in with you about. Earlier when you talked about your parents' divorce, you sort of made it sound like you don't believe in marriage."

I said, "Yeah, that's true. I don't."

Then he said, "But it also sounds like you believe you can't have sex until you are married."

Now it was my turn to make a curious face. I said, "I've never actually put that together until now."

"How's that been for you, Colin?"

"Well, it's gotten hard."

And then we high-fived. (I told you he was a cool therapist.)

Sam went on, "I'm just going to give you my perspective, and you may disagree with it, and that's fine. I believe sex is a gift to be shared with someone you really care about. And maybe that's enough rules to put on something so special."

Despite Sam not being a Christian, this was the first time he'd challenged a belief of mine. He did it respectfully, and it was clear his goal wasn't so much to dispute my point of view as to have me consider whether it was helping me or hurting me. I thought about his words and knew immediately that I agreed with him.

At this point, though, I also knew that there was nowhere in my entire paradigm to apply his advice. So, I filed it away.

About a month later, I saw a pretty girl in a coffee shop. I knew I wanted to talk to her. I thought, *Don't drag this out. Don't try to figure out what days she's here so you can bump into her again. You're 27 years old. Let's move this thing along.*

So I got up. And I walked over to her. And I was like, *Yeah . . . no*, and I just kept walking until I reached the water fountain. Obviously, that's all I really wanted.

When I got there, I told myself, *You are not allowed to sit back down until you talk to her.* So I had about nine cups of water.

CHAPTER 15: LATE TO THE PARTY

Then I sloshed myself back toward her table and, this time, managed to start talking to her. I tried to make her laugh and succeeded. It was going pretty well.

I said, "What's your name?"

She said, "Robin."

And I said, "My name is Colin. Our names are so similar." (I have a lot of game.)

Somehow, she looked past this and gave me her number. A few days later, we went on an actual date.

The whole thing had been going great when suddenly—probably because of the honesty I had been experiencing with Sam—I just said *the thing*.

"Robin, I don't want to ruin this night or anything, but I feel like I should tell you . . . I'm a virgin."

I was so ashamed that I actually looked down. I caught myself and looked back up at her. She had this funny expression on her face.

She said, "I can help you with that."

And she did.

. . .

The next morning, I expected to feel the regret and shame that I had been taught my whole life I had just earned.

But what I felt instead was gratitude, affection for Robin, and pride in myself. I had made a decision on my terms. I had trusted myself, and I liked what happened when I trusted myself.

Robin was still sleeping next to me, so I had to stifle a laugh when I realized I had just gotten the answer to a prayer of mine since my teen years. I was taught to pray for my future, godly soulmate—the person I would share myself with for the first time in this special way.

Now I knew that the "soulmate" I'd been praying for all those years was 31, divorced, bisexual, and an atheist. It was a real classic answer to prayer.

Robin and I ended up seeing each other for a little while. But with the differences we had, it wasn't a huge surprise when we went our separate ways.

I was very sad, of course, because I did feel attached to her, but I also totally understood her reasons for moving on. As my post-breakup sadness eventually faded, I was keenly aware that my heart remained intact. There were no missing pieces. I was grateful to have known her and for how she'd helped me come out of my shell. And I really liked this (slightly) more confident version of myself.

When I looked back on this whole experience, I realized how critical it was that I could be vulnerable with Robin. It couldn't have happened if I hadn't first been vulnerable with Sam. This journey hinged on all those times I sat in a small office, sharing my truth with Sam, saying things I had never told anyone, and *not* being rejected. On the contrary, while I was being totally authentic, I was also being totally accepted.

The acceptance I'd received from Sam as well as from Robin helped me enormously in feeling, for the first time, that I might be able to accept myself.

I had an interesting thought. *What if the best version of myself isn't the one I'm performing in order to hide the real me from the world? What if the best version of myself is the real one?*

Now there's a thought. Easier said than done, but still.

CHAPTER 15: LATE TO THE PARTY

I felt that I had moved the needle a little bit on my depression. It was taking on a different shape. The problem was that it was just beginning to morph into something else. While I felt myself becoming more of the man I had always wanted to be, I also felt myself becoming less of the man my mother had always wanted me to be.

It was a thought that truly scared me. Because, for many reasons other than this recent experience—reasons that went back a long, long way—I was pretty sure I was losing my faith.

CHAPTER 16
RUPTURES

Whenever I found myself questioning my spiritual convictions, I would be flooded with fear. I had wrestled with it almost my whole life, but I knew that if I rejected my faith entirely, I'd lose everything—my salvation, my identity, my community. The cost felt unbearable.

The thought of abandoning my beliefs terrified me, so I'd block it out by quoting a verse from the New Testament, "For God has not given us a spirit of fear, but of power and of love and of a sound mind."[10] It never helped, though. Then there was the knowledge that my own church family would view me as "lost," "fallen," or "damned." Podcaster Shelby Bennett Hanson described her experience of losing her fundamentalist faith this way:

> I felt flattened when Christians portrayed people like me as wanting the "easy path," as if grief and alienation and upending your own life was an easy path [. . .] I felt sick

when deconstruction was painted as a personal problem for people who prefer their truth to God's truth. All I have ever sought is truth.[11]

There was nothing easy about this path, or the price I'd eventually have to pay if I kept walking it. And yet, somehow, I couldn't seem to stop questioning everything. I was starting to feel a bit like the main character in one of my favorite movies, *The Truman Show*. In it, Jim Carrey plays Truman Burbank, a man who slowly realizes his entire life has been staged. This results from a series of incidents—a falling stage light, a rainstorm that soaks only him, his high-school crush trying to warn him of something before being mysteriously pulled away—that don't fit Truman's beliefs of what is normal and possible. They function, in effect, as ruptures in the confines of his reality and slowly add up until he can't ignore them. Truman realizes he's trapped and that, if he is to break free, he'll need to confront his biggest fears and exchange the familiar for the unknown.[12]

I had been experiencing ruptures for years. Ruptures of a religious kind. Like cracks in a wall, they were small at first but had gradually widened. Just as Truman's doubts finally rose up to confront him, mine had accumulated until I could no longer ignore them or the unsettling questions they carried with them.

• • •

The shift began when, a few months into therapy with Sam, I noticed that I wasn't just surviving; I was happy. I was breathing a little easier, for the first time in a long time. *I am still here,*

CHAPTER 16: RUPTURES

I realized. *I just went through a very dark and dangerous period in my life, and without therapy, I wouldn't have made it.*

The things I had been told—that being in therapy meant I was damaged, that believing it was needed made me faithless—sounded less like warnings and more like willful narrow-mindedness. This left me staring down a new puzzle: If this work was healing me, why had I been told to stay away from it?

Even though I'd shown clear signs of depression as a young person, the message I heard in my churches was that therapy was something to avoid. Depression and anxiety were sometimes described as spiritual shortcomings. They represented challenges to be addressed through prayer, not professional help.

At the same time, a heavy sense of shame and a laundry list of fears were woven into my church experience.[13] A few of the things I feared: eternal damnation, being "Left Behind" should the Rapture suddenly occur, the Devil and demonic spirits, spending too much time with non-Christians who might sway my beliefs, and even trusting my own mind over the authority of church leaders (which I was taught was prideful and rebellious).

One of my main stresses was managing intrusive thoughts, like lust or anger. Nobody can control every thought, so I routinely felt guilty—whether because I felt attraction for someone or I indulged in a satisfying string of expletives.

My earliest religious ruptures occurred when people I found admirable were limited, excluded, and even vilified by my church for reasons I couldn't agree with. Like Eunice, my Sunday School teacher who wasn't allowed to teach men. Or Tim, my youth pastor who lost the job he was amazing at because he voiced a controversial opinion. And then there was my step-uncle, Terry, a kind and generous man who accepted me even though I had been taught not to accept him. (Years later, his partner, Stephen, told me he had expected me to be a "Creepy Christian Teen" when we first met. All three of us expressed our relief that I hadn't lived up to that stereotype, and we had a good laugh about the label.)

Even though I had been told otherwise, I cared more about building a relationship with Terry and Stephen than accepting what I'd been taught about them.

• • •

The mistreatment of queer and non-conforming people would trouble me further when it appeared again in one of my closest friendships. A year after college, my best friend, Matt, sent me a momentous email. It consisted of just one line: "Just so you know, I like guys."

I knew why he didn't tell me in person. We were both Christians, and he was afraid of how I might respond. As I read his message, I didn't blame or disapprove of him. My eyes suddenly filled with tears, and I cried for my friend. It broke me to realize that, throughout our years of friendship, my best friend hadn't felt safe to be himself with me or with many of the people around him. I immediately called Matt and told him nothing had changed. He was, and always would be, my best friend.

• • •

CHAPTER 16: RUPTURES

There were other discomfiting experiences that would stay with me. You may remember my mentioning that in my mid-twenties, I traveled to an impoverished part of southern Jamaica on a hurricane relief trip. Among the people in our group were some missionaries, and I started to become uncomfortable when I heard one of them pointedly ask our hapless Jamaican driver, Terrence, "How do you know if you'll go to heaven?"

Terrence gave a friendly wave to a car that sped by, missing us by inches, then removed his faded ball cap and wiped his brow in the heat. He answered haltingly, as he thought through how best to respond. "I'm a good man, miss. I keep my word . . . I share what I have . . . I stand up for what matters . . . If someone needs help, I'm there. I figure that should count for something."

The missionary shook her head and said none of that mattered unless he accepted Jesus into his heart. Her words made my stomach drop. To me, what Terrence had said was as good an answer as I'd ever heard, maybe better than any I'd been taught.

His words reminded me of how many different ways there are to see the world. I'd been taught to sort people into "us" and "them," but in light of my realization that Terrence would fall into the "them" group, that way of thinking seemed simplistic and small.

• • •

These ruptures made me question the idea that my perspective was the only, or even the best, way to understand the world. I wasn't sure how to examine this further, but it remained unresolved in my mind.

I really enjoyed the comedian Pete Holmes, but I became fascinated when I found out he was a former Evangelical, or "Exvangelical." Like me, Holmes had grown up as an evangelical Christian in the heights of purity culture, and he had found a natural well of humor in his religious upbringing. Some had described Holmes as almost suspiciously friendly, and since I had also been characterized that way, I related to Pete's funny description of his wholesome vibe in his comedy special "Faces and Sounds."

> If you've ever considered the idea of a multiverse, of millions of separate realities happening at the same time, in which there are millions of different versions of every single one of us, I'm pretty sure this is the only universe where I look like I do and I'm *not* a youth pastor.[14]

In many ways, Holmes's story was similar to mine, but with one major difference: He had left his Christian faith and found a way of living that seemed to fit him better. On his podcast, *You Made It Weird*, Pete often asked his guests where they found, or didn't find, meaning in life and then exhibited genuine interest in their answers. He didn't argue or try to convince them of anything. Instead, he looked for common ground and new ideas worth considering.

In these conversations, Pete was the person I'd always wanted to be—someone more interested in learning from people than changing them. In fact, I had always *been* that person. I'd always admired the people I knew who felt things deeply, asked big questions, and didn't always need to be right. I, too, had never cared much about being "right." Who learns anything that way? To me, what good was winning a point in an argument if it meant losing the person?

I realized that if Pete could leave his religious views behind to give freedom to the curious, interested part of himself, so could I. Like Truman looking toward the horizon, I was starting to sense that my freedom lived on the other side of my fear.

I began to feel cautiously hopeful but also, for some reason, very alone. From my conversations with others who had gone through a faith deconstruction, I knew that nearing the point of ultimate decision brought with it a profound sense of isolation—of disconnection. I could see why. Luckily, in my case, the loneliness was tempered by the happy accident of where I lived.

* * *

When I had first moved to Burlington, Vermont, several years earlier, I'd encountered "non-believers" everywhere. I quickly saw that the people I met didn't match the warnings I'd been issued. An adult in my church in New York had cautioned me to "stay on my guard" there, because Vermont was "one of the most godless, unchurched places there is." He made it sound like an open-air Balkan prison or something. I mean, it was also the home of Ben and Jerry's! A thought struck me: *Will I meet the devil there, only to discover his name is Cherry Garcia?*

Even though I had arrived in the state shaped by the worldview I was raised with, and was still carrying some hurtful beliefs about others I wasn't even aware of yet, it felt as if Vermont itself took a long, concerned look at me and said in a kind voice, "Let me love you." Over the next several years, I went on yoga retreats, discovered Grade A maple syrup, and soon found that most of my closest friends were lesbians. It was a success story.

At one point, I opened up to a new friend about my religious childhood. (Okay, yes, we were at a yoga retreat.) I told him that, from a young age, I was raised to believe I was fundamentally bad and sinful. He replied quickly and with so much compassion that it caught me off guard, "I'm really sorry that happened to you." I felt completely understood.

As I continued opening up to people who looked at life differently than I did, I felt less anger at the Church, because I didn't need it to be my everything anymore. I wasn't becoming the "angry atheist" I'd once feared I might turn into. I still wondered about life's mysteries; I just didn't give myself a label. And I loved people—freely and without needing to convert or convince.

This included Christians. I wished the good-hearted ones the best. I had experienced firsthand how organized religion could provide feelings of security, certainty, hope, belonging, and purpose. But when continuing to enjoy those feelings required excluding people I cared about, I could no longer make that trade.

On reflection, there was one thing that still grieved me, and always would. In church, I was told again and again not to be ashamed of the gospel, but not once was I told not to be ashamed of myself.

• • •

Slowly, I began to believe that I could build a life rooted in love and integrity, independent of the beliefs I had inherited.

CHAPTER 16: RUPTURES

As I saw it, this journey toward becoming who I really was had been longer and tougher than any other I'd traveled. It was also the most important.

The process of "falling" from my faith was bringing me closer to myself. I was becoming the kind of adult I had needed for most of my life, and I was teaching myself about shame and how to heal from it. I started to like and trust myself more.

Letting go of my rigid grip on faith gave me the freedom to become who I wanted to be—someone who placed people above ideology. Finally, I had priorities that mattered to me every bit as much as the old ones had. They weren't tied to a formal belief system, but they felt solid and true. The result was a quiet, grounded moral code I'd learned years earlier from a matter-of-fact Jamaican man: Keep your word. Share what you have. Stand up for what matters. If someone needs help, be there.

At long last, after more than two decades of calling myself a Christian, I let go of that label. It happened like a whisper, not a shout. Like Truman, I simply walked out the door.

Of course, as I'd long anticipated, leaving came with a cost. The reactions from others varied—some friends were supportive, while others drifted away. There were no interventions or desperate attempts to save my soul. But I felt a growing dread from knowing that this decision would test my relationship with my mother more than ever before. It might even break her heart. She never asked me why I left, only made it clear she disapproved. That unspoken gulf between us hurt more than I'd expected, but I knew that staying would have broken something in me that I'd worked too hard to repair. Ultimately, I had no choice but to listen to myself.

To mark this recognition, I imagined myself repeating Truman's gentle goodbye: "In case I don't see ya, good afternoon, good evening, and good night." But unlike Truman, there was no audience—just me, both tentative and triumphant, stepping into whatever came next.

CHAPTER 17
AN AUDIENCE OF ONE

Therapy had given me the self-assurance to face the things in my life I had been trying to ignore. One of those things was the question of whether a $15,000 annual salary as a journalist was worth so much effort. Or was financially sustainable. But there was something else that felt equally important. This wasn't the goal I had originally set out to achieve.

Journalism had been an interesting—and meaningful—detour, but it was a detour, nonetheless. What I'd really wanted, since before I'd ever written my first article, was to see my name on a published book. Now that I was feeling better about myself, I could finally acknowledge that without guilt.

My frugal lifestyle had amounted to some savings, and so I decided to take the leap and turn a screenplay I'd written in film school, *The Myth of Oceans*, into a full-length novel.

I was drawn to the imaginative adventure of crafting characters, guiding them through conflict, and leading them to fateful decisions that would affect the direction of their lives. As my writing transitioned into a full-time pursuit, it also became my first tool for thinking about what makes for an interesting life.

I ached to create something to share with the world, but I was also afraid of rejection. I tried to understand why it scared me so much. I realized I had always worked hard to be an interesting and articulate person. So, if someone read my work and thought it was dull or poorly phrased, that would feel like rejection on an existential level—not just of my work, but of me. I wrote and wrote and wrote, but I dreaded the moment when friends would ask if they could read what I was writing.

I became that type of writer who is always working on something but always has an excuse for why no one can see it. Someone might say something like, "You seem like you're writing a lot lately. Can I read something you've written?" I would reply immediately and with unnecessary intensity, "No! I mean, no. It's not ready." Any follow-up question about when it might be ready would be met with, "Never! Let's change the subject."

The Myth of Oceans was a story about a young widower, emotionally closed off after losing his bride on their wedding day, and the unusual cast of characters who take an interest in his recovery. Let me sum it up in one word: sad. Now, I can see that the character's tragic loss might have been an excellent setup for some John-Wick-style revenge, but this wasn't that. This was a slow, contemplative, character drama. Just a man and his melancholy. When I wrote, I would listen to sad songs and describe the slow journey of a grief-stricken young man with the weight of the world on his shoulders. My teacher had said, "Write what you know," after all.

It wasn't long until my life started imitating my art. Just like my protagonist, I couldn't move forward. Every day, I'd write

CHAPTER 17: AN AUDIENCE OF ONE

a few pages, read them, hate them, and delete them. I wasn't writing a novel—I was being an asshole to myself, with no one to intervene. All I wanted was to share my work, but I was sure that sharing it would guarantee rejection. So instead, I ate Doritos. And watched movies.

I had shown real talent for being a movie junkie even back in the pre-streaming times. Sure, I would sometimes rent Federico Fellini movies, but I also watched the Chris Tucker action-comedy *Money Talks* multiple times in the same day. (I'm not some Italian-cinema *elitist*—I have range.) I binge-watched movies before Netflix made it cool, and now I was putting that habit to good use. Movies worked like white noise, drowning out my inner critic's stress-inducing commentary.

It was fun for a while, but it wasn't a great formula for writing a book. On the other hand, was it any worse than typing all day and then keeping the work hidden away from curious eyes? Either way, my approach to authorship was turning out to be miserable, unproductive, and the opposite of lucrative.

• • •

Like a lot of creatives (and depressives), I thought that being an artist meant one had to struggle. Feeling heavy things without dulling their edges was required. You know, for the art. One of my favorite quotes at the time came from the Danish philosopher Soren Kierkegaard, which essentially said that a poet is an unhappy being whose cries of pain sound like beautiful music to others.[15] *Um . . . Yikes.* It's telling that my favorite quote reinforced the idea that suffering is essential to making good art.

Objectively, I could see that when I wasn't depressed, I created more work. I also liked doing it more. But what started as hopeful and exciting was gradually being choked by struggles with discouragement, relentless perfectionism, and deteriorating mental health.

In addition to experiencing depression, I had a mysterious three-week period when I could sleep no more than one or two hours each night. With an overactive mind and a lot of extra time to kill, I would go on bike rides in the middle of the night, pedaling along dark, empty streets, passing closed gas stations and vending machines that glowed like beacons.

After about a week and a half of insomnia, I wandered into a 24/7 grocery store around 3 a.m. and experienced what felt like a comedy sketch, as written by David Lynch. The lights were impossibly bright. Polka music blared, seeming to speed up and then slow down, as if it were being played on a system with a dying battery. An old woman asked me if the fruit was fresh, then laughed for no reason and walked away. A shopping cart with a kid in it rolled by—no driver in sight—and came to a stop after tapping into a Little Debbie display. This was starting to feel like an unplanned supermarket vision quest. Once I saw the uninjured child being reunited with a relieved parent, I decided it was probably a good time to head back to my house.

By the end of week three, I decided to visit a nutrition store, where I bought various herbal supplements that finally ended my streak of sleepless nights. Still, between my depression and my insomnia, it seemed like the improvements I'd experienced around my mental health had evaporated. Even worse, my therapist, Sam, had closed his practice to take a full-time staff position at an organization, so I was on my own. I was pouring my whole heart into my book, giving it all my creative energy and effort. But unchecked, unevaluated sadness was crushing my spirit. The tortured artist thing was getting old.

With no deadlines, no audience, and no feedback, I might have sat in an echo chamber of self-doubt forever. Luckily, I ran out of money first. This meant there was only one thing to do. I saved my book document for the final time and closed the file. I knew I would never open it again. I metaphorically handed over my pen and moleskin notebook (I couldn't resist imagining it as though I was a cop handing in his gun and badge—a writer till the end).

Giving up on my "life's work" carried its own strange grief. It was like losing a friend or a job without anyone noticing. I didn't talk about it to many people. I was sure I would never be a writer again and that it was probably for the best.

I had been writing for an audience of one, and the audience was impossible to please. In all that time, I never experienced the benefits of sharing my work with others. I let only one close friend read my novel, and I never read his comments when he sent it back. I just knew my book wasn't good enough. How could it be when *I* wasn't good enough?

There it was: the mental trap I'd created. Recognizing this belief as self-defeating led me to another valuable realization: *Someone needs to get out of the house a bit more. Ideally, for exercise and walks in nature, rather than exploring 24-hour grocery stores.* So I started doing that, and it helped make the demise of my dream a little less sad than it might have been otherwise.

I even developed a sense of humor about my situation. It finally dawned on me that my chosen genre of writing had been basically "the sad young man chronicles," and that a shorter, more memorable name for that genre was "Unsellable." I smiled despite myself, maybe for the first time in weeks.

While I didn't know precisely what this thought meant, I found myself wondering whether the best art might be to create a good life. Writing had been my big dream for nearly a decade, and I ended up with little to show for it but stacks of unshared manuscript pages. But the thing I regretted the most was that, in all that time, I had never dealt with my fear of rejection. I had named it, but I still had no idea how I could get past it.

I felt like saying to the universe, "Help me out here. What would you do with a creative person who wants to share his work with the world but is too insecure and afraid of rejection to do it?"

I had no idea the universe was about to answer me with a plot twist I couldn't have seen coming. I was about to leave my comfort zone in a big way, and the audience to witness it would be larger than I could ever have expected.

PART 2

CHAPTER 18
FROM MY SEAT TO THE STAGE

As my 30th birthday approached, I looked at my life and thought, *Hmm. I was* sure *I would be further along by now.*

I felt directionless and stuck. My dream of becoming a novelist had ground to a halt, my journalism position had been downsized, and I was "between jobs" in a pretty big way. I didn't have a girlfriend or even a goldfish.

I had noticed that, right before I entered each new decade of my life, I would experience a brief existential crisis. At nine-and-a-half years old, I sent a fan-mail marriage proposal to Elizabeth Shue (no response) (*yet*) and secretly hid comic books inside my Bible to read during church. At 19 and a half, I attended an off-campus, unsanctioned school dance that featured bumping *and* grinding. I also started telling people my new favorite book of the Bible was Philemon. Those were wild times.

Now, at 29 and a half, I didn't feel like I had much to show for my first decade of adulthood. I'd graduated from college, lived overseas, and lost my virginity. Those were pretty cool things, to be sure, but I felt that I should have accomplished more.

The tagline from *Strictly Ballroom*, a movie I'd loved in my youth, now seemed uncomfortably prophetic: "A life lived in fear is a life half-lived." Well, I was clearly half-living. I wasn't taking any risks because my fears had paralyzed me. I was afraid of rejection, failure, embarrassment, and wasting my time. I was scared of making the wrong decisions, so I wasn't making any decisions at all.

Somewhere I'd heard the expression "When you need a change, any change will do." I think it may have been referring to getting a haircut. But I was about to make a much bigger change than that. It happened when the universe answered my rhetorical question about how I might overcome my intense fear of rejection by saying, "Let's have you try stand-up comedy. Maybe you'll be good, maybe you won't, but either way, it should toughen you up fast."

It started when a friend told me he'd signed up for a stand-up comedy class at Burlington's Flynn Center. The class consisted of seven workshop sessions and then a public performance at their 150-seat showcase venue.

This idea was terrifying. I had always loved watching and listening to stand-up comedy, but *doing* stand-up comedy seemed way too risky. I loved joking around with my friends, but I wasn't on stage when I did it. Nobody had paid money to get into the conversation.

There was another reason this scared me. I was deathly afraid of public speaking. As Jerry Seinfeld explained, "According to many studies, people's number one fear is public speaking. Number two is death. This means to the average person, if you

CHAPTER 18: FROM MY SEAT TO THE STAGE

go to a funeral, you'd rather be in the casket than doing the eulogy."

Well, stand-up comedy seemed like public speaking on steroids. Not only would I need to talk in front of people, I would also need to get an audible reaction out of them, preferably a positive one. I played this scenario out in my head . . . If they didn't laugh, I'd have failed right out in the open. And I doubted there was a trapdoor I could use to disappear under the floorboards (and then leave the country and change my identity). So, I'd have to just stand up there and absorb the rejection in real time.

I noticed my heart was doing a drumroll. This idea scared the daylights out of me, but there was something else there, too. I *wanted* to do it. And I realized, with total clarity, *If I don't do this now, I never will.*

The next day, I registered for the class. And then did my best to put it out of my mind. Way too quickly, the day of the first session arrived. As I walked from my car to that class, I felt like I was heading to my death.

I had plenty of time to feel that way because I was walking a lot slower than usual. The day before, I had sprained my ankle and been told to use crutches for a week. During my long hobble, I attempted to calm my pounding heart by telling myself we probably wouldn't perform the first night. We'd just talk about comedy theory or something. What on earth did that mean? This was a class for casual amateurs—we weren't going to sit around deconstructing the comedic timing of Lenny Bruce.

I walked into the classroom, which was clearly also a dance studio, given its floor-to-ceiling mirrors and ballet barres. I found a seat among the half-circle of chairs. There were 14 of us, from young adults to retirees. The teacher, a comedian named Josie Leavitt, stood and welcomed us to the class.

After a preamble that was way too brief for my liking, she said, "Everybody, take the next five minutes and write some jokes down. Because each of you will perform today." All I could think was, *Where's a brown paper bag to hyperventilate into?*

As the clock ticked, I tried to think of jokes. Then my eyes fell on my crutches and, realizing I would be using them to get on stage, I started scribbling. Soon names were being called, and then Josie said, "Colin, you're up."

That's when I discovered that the walk from my car to the class was *nothing* compared to the walk from my seat to the stage. Despite being only 15 feet, it was the most difficult walk of my life. I turned, faced the class, and tried to ignore my life-sized, panicked reflection in the wall of mirrors behind the group. Then I pretended to be a comedian.

"You're probably wondering about these," I said, nodding to the crutches. "Turns out I injure myself with some frequency. And each time I do, two thoughts pop into my head. First: 'Ow!' Second: 'Now I have to explain this humiliating story to everyone.'"

It didn't quite get a laugh, but it did get what I might have described as a "group smile." A few people nodded. I could at least be glad I hadn't blacked out. I tried to make eye contact, sensing that if I let my gaze drift over my classmates' shoulders to the mirror, I would forget my place and start fixating on why I was standing so awkwardly.

I continued, "A few years ago, I tore a ligament while I was rock-climbing. And a small part of me was thrilled. Because

CHAPTER 18: FROM MY SEAT TO THE STAGE

when people asked about my injury, I could lower my voice an octave and say, 'Oh, this? I was leaping for a hold. It happens.' That's a cool way to get hurt."

They laughed. *(They laughed!)*

"It's definitely cooler than a guy my doctor told me about who tore the same ligament that I did—by turning to sit down in an airplane seat. Imagine telling *that* story: 'I got as far as seat 12F . . . and then it was all over.'"

More laughs—actual audible laughs. My nerves started to settle.

"Well, this time I didn't injure myself rock-climbing. I did it while chatting with someone. I was mid-sentence when I stepped backward onto an angled chair leg. And that was it. Now I know I'm the kind of person who can sprain their ankle in the middle of a casual conversation."

I got a solid laugh! Before I knew it, my time was up, and the class applauded as I returned to my seat.

What a rush! I couldn't believe what had just happened. I had done it! Sure, my material wasn't very polished or well-delivered, but that wasn't really the point. The point was that I had just done something I was certain I would never have the skill or the guts to do. Even better, I had made people laugh.

I knew immediately that the sound of those people laughing was the sound of my life changing. I had just discovered a path forward I couldn't have seen before, and I'd uncovered a new truth: I was capable of doing this exciting, scary thing. Following on the heels of that new truth was a new desire: to do it again as soon as, and as much as, possible.

Joseph Campbell is often quoted as saying, "The cave you fear to enter holds the treasure you seek."[16] I had just done the thing that scared me most—and discovered I might actually be good at it. It upended what I thought I knew about myself. I had walked into a room that scared me, stood in a spot that scared me even more, and liked the result.

It felt momentous. I knew that I had been quietly taking risks in small, stubborn ways for a few years now, but that first comedy class was when I *noticed* I was doing it. In real time.

Over the years, I'd heard many inspiring stories about soldiers, mountain climbers, cancer survivors, and people who became rich or got famous. The stories were great, but they were also kind of intimidating. I'd hear them and feel ordinary. Why hadn't I heard more stories on the level of what I had just done? Stories about the quiet victories of everyday people facing things that scared them? Couldn't those stories be inspiring, too?

I suddenly saw myself, not as the author of the first draft of a failed book but as the author of my own autobiography. As the author, I could decide which bold risk might make the story more interesting. Since I was also the central character, I'd then have to get up the courage to actually do it.

• • •

Over the next few months, I continued walking those "15 feet" between my seat and a stage as much as possible. I kept going to the class every week, but I also jumped on opportunities to go to open mics. Right after our third class, I drove with a few other students to a comedy contest audition, where I signed up and told a few jokes to an audience of more than a hundred. I didn't get into the actual contest, but I also didn't throw up.

CHAPTER 18: FROM MY SEAT TO THE STAGE

This felt like an accomplishment, because each time I got on stage, the butterflies in my stomach threw a full-scale riot.

I never got more than a few minutes of stage time, but slowly, three minutes on stage became four, then five, and then six. This was one minute beyond my comfort zone, followed by another, and then another. I was building confidence, but the progress was so incremental I could barely register it. Not to mention that, once I got myself onto the stage, I had a new challenge: My body would betray me.

At one of my first featured shows, I stepped on stage in front of 75 people and immediately blinded myself by looking directly into the stage lights. My hands were already sweating profusely, and I clutched the microphone stand like it was the only thing keeping me upright. I said my first line, and it came out as a shaky-voiced string of gibberish. I thought in a panic, *Uh oh, I'm so nervous I can't form English words.* My mouth felt dry, and my heart pounded as an awkward silence filled the room. I glanced at the door to the bar, which, tantalizingly, was right by the stage.

I thought about leaving and didn't only because I was stopped by how bizarre that would be for the audience. I imagined their description to others later on. "Yeah, it was wild! He just muttered something and walked out into the night." Or I could buy time with a drink of water. I tried the water-drinking idea, and when I spoke again, I had more control over my words. Within a minute, I was past it and actually doing just fine. My performance went really well, and I sure was glad I hadn't walked out the door three seconds into it.

Getting on stage was about one percent easier the next time and the time after that. There was no shortcut to overcoming my fear of standing in front of an audience and trying to be funny on command, but I'd discovered that there was a shortest route: Head right toward the thing that scared me. It was a path of almost imperceptible progress, but my hands and voice shook less each time I stood on stage. I proved to myself, in one way at least, that I was stronger than my fears.

As a result, I also became less nervous when called upon to do public speaking, whether at a Toastmasters meeting or a friend's wedding. At times, I felt almost comfortable doing a thing I used to avoid at all costs. I was looking at fear differently—not as a reason to retreat, but as an invitation to advance. Feel the fear, and then act anyway. All I had to do was walk that metaphorical "15 feet." And that's what I kept doing.

For the first time in a long while, I wasn't just being carried along by life; I was steering.

CHAPTER 19
THE SETUP AND THE PUNCH

Over the next few months, I sought out as many comedy opportunities as I could. I discovered I had solid instincts for connecting with the crowd and recreating funny moments from my life well enough to make the audience laugh.

Despite the nerves that still came and went, nearly every performance so far had resulted in laughter. I was proud of that streak, especially when I saw how rejection onstage had rattled my peers.

My very first real show came at the end of our seven-week comedy class. I was extremely nervous, but when I stepped onstage in front of 150 people, I crushed it. The energy, the laughter, the applause—it was electric. All I could think was, *I can't believe it! I'm a real comedian!*

I felt transformed. I'd gone from a shy wallflower, terrified of rejection, to a comedian and regular performer. I was sure I was ready for anything. Hungry for more, I found two opportunities for comedians in ads on Craigslist. The first was vague to the point of seeming ominous, like I might have ended up the unwitting star of a series on the dark web called iHostage. So, iPassed. But the second was more legitimate: a comedy show in a town about two hours away. I emailed them and was promptly offered 20 minutes, which would be the longest set I'd ever done. I eagerly prepared.

The show had drawn a rowdy, drunk crowd that loudly ignored the comedians. When my name was called, I went on stage, and my worst fear became a reality. Comedians call what happened next "bombing." No matter what I tried, I could not get a laugh. It was humiliating.

It felt like the crowd was rejecting me on a molecular level. The people in the audience hated me. I couldn't get them to stop their conversations and listen for even a moment. My sense of humor is a big part of who I am and how I connect, so this felt like a highly personal rejection, one that could be extremely difficult to recover from.

I had written my setlist on my hand as a guide. "CANDY. AIRPORT. YOGA. DONUTS." Each word prompted a five-minute story, so once I started one of the stories and no one laughed, I had to keep going for a long time until I could start the next one. I kept re-checking the words on my hand, wishing they were prompts for better jokes.

Boxer Joe Louis once said, "Everyone has a plan until they get hit." Well, I was hit. There is no one to save a comedian who's bombing. And leaving early means not getting paid.

After 20 agonizing minutes of trying for laughs I didn't get, I crawled off the stage, stung and startled. I returned to my seat—right in the middle of the room filled with disapproving strangers. Also, the woman I was seeing at the time *and* her parents were

CHAPTER 19: THE SETUP AND THE PUNCH

there. I plastered a fake smile onto my face to hide my embarrassment. Inside, though, I was thinking, *Clearly, I'm quitting. There's no reason for any human being to subject themselves to something this humiliating. Surely not for $15 and one free drink.*

I had heard several comedians at open mics say they had bombed once, a long time earlier, and it had taken them years to get the courage to try again. Now I knew why. I was already contemplating my own immediate resignation from comedy, until I thought about my life, only a few months earlier, before I tried this new pursuit. It wasn't great. It wasn't that safe either. I had come too far to go back to being that scared, self-conscious writer, mercilessly torn apart by an audience of one.

After years of keeping my creative ideas hidden away, I was now regularly sharing them with others. I had just discovered that this process could hurt deeply, in a way that felt traumatizing. I couldn't go back, but how could I keep going forward?

The next day, all I could picture was that failure. I kept replaying it in my mind. But on the day after that, I noticed I was reworking my material in my head. I looked down at my hand and saw that the setlist I'd written on it had gotten fainter. The ink was fading, just as the feeling of failure was fading.

That's when I realized that I didn't want to quit—I wanted to keep going. I wanted a do-over. I understood it now. *This is what it means to be a real comedian. It means getting up after a setback, walking the next 15 feet, and standing on the next stage. Real comedians keep getting back up.*

And I was going to do just that.

Sometimes we surprise ourselves with what we can get through. When we discover we have more grit than we thought. When we have every reason to give up but don't.

I had learned more from my first epic misfire than I had from all my successful shows combined. It taught me that failure is *valuable*. Failing gave me data on what worked and what could be improved. Failing gave me the opportunity to come back smarter, stronger, and more resolute. Most importantly, failing made me want, with every ounce of my being, to succeed on my next attempt. I was starting to see that there's no better classroom than failure.

My onstage disaster was also how I learned that context mattered when evaluating a performance. I could now see that my comedy class's final show, in which I had done so well, was in front of an audience packed with friends and family, who were all primed to cheer for every performer. We were also in a gorgeous venue. Oh yeah, and the tickets were free. But this time, I performed in a venue with so much background noise and alcohol that having a good show wasn't even possible. So, had I experienced a rejection at all? Maybe not. If I had never had the audience's attention, how could I lose it?

My friend and fellow comic, Pat Lynch, has had his share of rough shows, too. I once asked him to share his philosophy on comedic failure, and he emailed me his thoughts with the subject line "Nobody really cares about you." Here's my favorite part of Pat's message:

> When you put yourself out there, you're often sharing something personal in a very public way. Which means there's the potential to get hurt. Badly. When it doesn't land, it feels like a direct indictment of you—your creativity, your ideas. That silence and rejection can feel like public shaming. But most of that punishment is your

own creation. It takes maturity to realize you're not as important as you think and that your failures haven't captured anyone's long-term attention. After your horrible, soul-crushing experience, nobody else is thinking about it. Join them.[17]

Great, right? For me, the deeper fear, the one underneath the fear of public speaking and stand-up comedy, was the fear that the audience might not like me. I don't mean that they might not like my speaking or my performance. I mean that they might not like *me*.

After all, I had dedicated half of my collegiate experience to making sure everyone on campus liked me. It was an impossible task, but one I attempted anyway, because I couldn't abide the idea of being disliked. But now I'd acquired some confidence—not a lot, but some—and I could see that no one was thinking about me enough to hate me at all or even think about me for very long. They'd already moved on to something else they'd rather think about, like themselves.

As I failed my way forward, my confidence grew. Every bit of it was earned because I was building it one act of courage at a time. I kept doing those brave minutes. I'd had enough of waiting for confidence to arrive magically on its own. A series of performances was like a journey involving incremental boosts in self-assurance. Eventually, I didn't have to pretend anymore.

I had finally pinpointed the simple practice behind a lot of highly accomplished people, which is to fail forward. They ask themselves, "What would I pursue if failure didn't scare me? What would I be willing to fail at if I knew it could be a step toward success?"

So far, my experiences in comedy had made me braver and tougher in ways that were also helping me outside of comedy. It was thanks to my newfound confidence that I said yes to something possibly even more daunting than doing comedy for strangers: going back to high school. Not as a student, thankfully, but potentially worse—as a guest speaker, faced with the challenge of teaching finances to teenagers.

CHAPTER 20
SOMEHOW I INVENT A CAREER

As I stood in front of a room of more than 60 high school sophomores, I knew I was in way over my head. For the next 80 minutes, I was going to talk about retirement and investing. To tenth graders. On their second-to-last day before summer break.

Six months earlier, a friend had sent me a job posting from a local credit union looking for a "financial literacy champion"—someone who could teach youth about personal finance. According to the ad, the ideal candidate should be able to connect with people but didn't need to be a financial expert.

Well, that was good, because all I knew about money was how to scrape by on as little of it as possible. Before attending the job interview, I had to look up the definition of "financial literacy." (It meant having the basic skills needed to manage money.) *Why not call it that?* I wondered.

Between being underemployed and doing stand-up comedy, I had the right mix of desperation and emerging confidence to at least apply for a job I was unqualified for. Finance wasn't a subject I was particularly interested in, but a year earlier, there had been a major collapse in the American housing market, and I realized I should probably learn how money works—especially if I wanted to have some of it someday.

The American Dream, as it had been taught to me, was the idea that those who worked hard and earned enough money could own their own homes and be financially better off. There was clearly a huge need for financial literacy; otherwise, why would so many people have signed up for loans they couldn't afford to pay back? Without a stronger foundation of financial knowledge, the American dream was becoming less achievable. The solution to the whole mess seemed simple: teach people about money, and they'd make better choices. It was a tidy explanation.

In preparing for the interview, my quick research revealed that consumer credit card debt was on the rise, less than half of adults in the U.S. used a monthly budget, and retirement savings participation was declining in the wake of the financial crisis. At that time, only 10 states required any personal finance education for high school graduation. This job would be an opportunity to help more people develop a stronger understanding of their personal finances. If everyone understood the basics, the problem would solve itself. Right?

Unfortunately for me, reading these stats made it clear that, financially, I was a lot more like the public I hoped to be addressing than the employer I hoped to be working for. I had never earned more than $30,000 a year because random cubicle jobs and freelance journalism never paid well. I had no retirement savings or the faintest idea what a 401(k) is (or why it has "k" in it). I had rarely negotiated for a higher salary or a better price on a car, because the very thought of negotiating made me want to barf. I had certainly never made a budget.

Nonetheless, I had the people skills and approachable personality the credit union was looking for, and I was offered the job. Suddenly, the responsibility of this opportunity felt real. Over the next several months, I read every personal finance book I could find. I attended credit workshops, started budgeting, and started building my credit score. I wanted to be sure I was practicing what I would soon be preaching. I even began contributing to my first 401(k). In the process, I managed to learn the reason it has a "k" in it. The name comes from the part of the U.S. Internal Revenue tax code that allows for such a plan: section 401, subsection k. Now that I knew that, I suddenly felt like I'd aged about 15 years.

It was sinking in that my job would be to teach teenagers a complicated subject their own parents probably struggled to get across to them—a subject full of depressing data, endless statistics, and abstract advice. In other words, I'd be teaching the driest topic imaginable to the toughest audience possible.

My first experience of doing that was about to begin. The sophomores had just arrived for an hour-plus guest presentation on personal finance, and as they had filed in, they looked like they were walking to their doom.

My instincts warned me that it wouldn't matter how good my advice was if no one paid attention to it. Whatever I told these students had to be both understandable and relevant to them. I knew I needed to do more than just dump data and recommendations on them. I needed to engage them and make the information and ideas matter. So, I played clips from popular movies and shows to prompt conversations about financial ideas. I asked questions to learn what they thought about money, and then I celebrated their answers rather than lecturing them. I did my best to be as authentic and interested as possible. It worked, and they started opening up.

At one point, I asked them, "If you could get a credit card with a maximum limit of $5,000, what would you buy with it?"

I got a range of answers from the students in the room.

"I'd buy a used car."

"I'd buy something that costs exactly $5,000."

"I'd buy sneakers made out of real gold with soles made of pure silver."

"I probably owe my parents that much by now."

After each of these responses, I'd laugh good-naturedly and listen non-judgmentally. Perhaps because of this, they opened up more than I had expected. They admitted that when it came to this question about finances, they didn't actually know the right answer. Then Sneakers spoke up, "You know what? I'm really nervous about credit cards. I don't want to get into debt and then not have enough money to live a normal life when I'm older."

There were a few students whose parents had already discussed finances with them. One of these students said, "Personally, I wouldn't spend the money on my credit card until I had saved enough money to pay it off." Since this was a great way to earn free air miles, build credit, and avoid late fees and interest charges, I was delighted by her answer. She beamed, and her proud reaction made me realize that the word "champion" in my job title worked better as a verb than a noun.

By the end of my time with the group, I felt that it had gone well. As they filed out, the teacher approached me and said,

CHAPTER 20: SOMEHOW I INVENT A CAREER

"You know that boy with the sneaker obsession? The one who asked you a lot of questions? Well, he hasn't talked in this class all semester. Whatever you're doing, keep doing it."

So I did, and I went on quite a public-speaking journey for a person still working through stage fright. I spoke in schools all over the state, pretty much weekly, and my audience size kept increasing. I noticed I was becoming remarkably comfortable with public speaking, and when I was calm in front of the crowd, I could even go off-script and bring students' questions and shared stories into the mix.

What I was doing started to feel less like a job and more like a career. I was creating my own style and methodology around communicating the information I'd been hired to cover. And I was finally earning a living doing work I could be proud of and that I was good at—achieving the vision I had for myself back in that Scottish dungeon/mailroom.

I was on a meaningful path now, and it was one I could possibly pursue for a long time. By combining two unlikely things, comedy and financial speaking, I'd landed on something new. It was a creative leap, but also a practical response to the recognition of a pattern. Success in both comedy and speaking depended on connecting with the audience. In comedy, if I wasn't entertaining my audience, I wasn't succeeding. In classrooms, if I wasn't engaging my listeners, I wasn't educating.

Talking to students about how expensive adulthood would be could easily be dry or depressing, so adding jokes, video clips, or unexpected examples from pop culture helped both to lighten the mood and make the information stick in their minds. The combination of these things may have seemed unique to others, but to me, it was the best way I could think of to answer my own unspoken question. *When I was a student, what would have made me care about this subject if some random adult had come in and talked about it?*

Even though I was a self-professed non-numbers person—charts and long columns of data had always made me sleepy—I found that I was genuinely becoming more interested in finances. I was practicing what I preached. While my grant-funded salary was modest, my personal budgeting and improved spending habits enabled me to move into a slightly better apartment, buy a more reliable car, and begin saving for retirement. I came up with a simple tagline to convey the transformation I was experiencing: "Your ability to manage your money directly affects your ability to have the life you want."

My humorous approach even attracted the attention of the media. Back in my journalism days, as I wrote articles about other people, I wondered if I would someday be part of a news story—the subject, rather than the byline. Oh, I'd been shown in a televised news clip and in the newspaper, but neither instance had anything to do with my being newsworthy.

The first was from a few years prior, at a minor league baseball game. I was standing near the home run line, eating an ice cream sandwich when someone hit one out of the park. That night's news clip showed the ball flying overhead—and me, mid-bite, frozen on screen with a mouthful of ice cream.

The second involved the grand opening of a yoga room at the airport. (This is what constituted breaking news in Vermont at the time.) I thought it'd be a press conference, but it turned out to be a full-on yoga class. I wasn't dressed for public stretching, so I stood in the back, by the snacks, and still managed to end up in the photo accompanying the article. The picture they published was accurate, and unfortunate: 30 people in downward dog, and me behind them, happily snacking on vegan banana bread.

Luckily, I would soon get a third chance, when a newspaper covered a series of presentations I gave for several large groups of prospective college students. The journalist who interviewed me was intrigued that I was both a comedian and a financial speaker. I explained that these pursuits were different aspects of my life, and I didn't want the story to combine them into one thing, because my job was hard enough without having to take on the burden of trying to perform "financial comedy," whatever that might be. The following week, the article was released under the title "Funny with Money." It described me, in no uncertain terms, as a comedian who taught personal finances. I facepalmed a bit, but mostly I felt elated about being the subject of a feature in the newspaper. I had become a story worth writing about. And I wasn't eating anything!

Ultimately, this news coverage helped me recognize the broader appeal of using humor to teach an important subject, and I was able to modify it into a brand I felt good about. Later that year, I applied and was accepted to speak at a national conference about ways to make financial education more engaging. When the conference organizers asked for my job title, I said, "Comedic Financial Speaker." It sounded made up, but that was because I had made it up. And it stuck.

CHAPTER 21
FINDING LIFE FUNNY

Between speaking in schools and doing stand-up comedy, I was now traveling all over the state, and every gig felt like a fresh, new adventure. As a speaker, I'd usually end up in a classroom or an auditorium. As a comedian, though, it was much harder to predict where I'd end up performing.

So far, I'd done stand-up in a truly odd mix of places: bars and restaurants, sure, but also between rounds at a local MMA fight, in the library of an elementary school, and even at a retreat center in the woods. Tougher than any of those, though, were the times I had to follow a raffle. (No performer can ever bring people as much joy as a raffle can.)

But when my friend Tony booked me and a few others to perform at a family reunion at a campground, I had a hunch this would be my strangest show yet. My hunch was confirmed when I saw Tony's driving directions. "Once you're south of Middlebury, go until you see the pig farm, turn left, and after a few miles, you'll see a giant squirrel."

Sure enough, I pulled into the parking lot of the campground's main office, and then stared upwards in awe at a 15-foot-tall squirrel statue. *I think this is the place.* I glanced over, and next to the squirrel, a sign read, "Welcome to Kampersville!" That quirky "K" was fair warning—this gig would be anything but ordinary.

As I drove along an endless line of RVs, I passed a man in a sleeveless t-shirt that allowed an unobscured view of his barbed-wire tattoo. Both of his hands were full. With one arm, he clutched a stack of crushed beer cans against his side so they wouldn't fall. With the other arm, he tenderly held his baby daughter.

This place was like a fun combination of *Dirty Dancing* and *Deliverance*. I found myself wondering, *Did he crush those beer cans with his boot or with his forehead? Did his daughter help?*

I arrived at the dining hall where the performance would take place. A crowd awaited—one that could sit comfortably at a single picnic table. The hall had a huge window through which a bunch of children could be seen playing in the pool, and this window was directly behind the stage.

I took it all in and thought, *This is about right.*

From the beginning, the show was a disaster. No one was listening, kids were screaming in the pool, and the microphone didn't work. But as I waited for my turn to perform, I was struck by the realization that this would be a pretty good scene in a story. Every odd detail and strange character from this day could be part of an anecdote I would tell later.

I suddenly had a warm, almost giddy feeling, as I found amusement in every absurd detail of this experience. The gig might have been a joke, but I was *in* on the joke. I started making a mental list of the things worth remembering so I could

CHAPTER 21: FINDING LIFE FUNNY

get them into my notebook as soon as I returned to my car. They included:
  —The dad who was loaded down with beer cans and a baby.
  —The zany misspelling of the name of the campground.
  —The directions that included a pig farm and a giant squirrel.
  —The matching yellow jerseys worn by every member of the audience, all proudly displaying the name "Swanson." (Before I remembered it was their family reunion, I took them for an all-ages softball team, with a very lazy t-shirt printer.)
  —The fact that this show was happening in a dining hall, in full daylight, while shrieking kids played in a pool behind us.
  —The considerable distance I had driven in order to be paid $9.

This whole experience delighted me. Sure, the jokes I would tell about this ridiculous comedy show in a campground might be more than a little at my own expense, but they would also be a way of removing any feelings of humiliation or foolishness. The other performers appeared to be three different versions of miserable, but I had a blast. To top things off, I told a story about my 30-something awkwardness in social situations. A young teenage girl in the audience connected so visibly and profoundly to every line in my story that I briefly considered taking my act to middle schools. *They get me.*

As I drove home and the giant squirrel grew smaller in my rearview mirror, I reflected on the awkward show in Kampersville and something bigger as well: the power of finding life funny. That night could be a launching point for beginning to take difficult, even humiliating, moments—both those from the distant past and those that were uncomfortably recent—and turning them into jokes.

If I was willing to laugh at my own embarrassing experiences, then there were *a lot* more stories I could tell on stage. A lifetime's worth. In fact, I'd had so many awkward social experiences that I often found myself wishing I could be a ninja.

As a boy, I thought ninjas looked cool. As an adult, I was more jealous of their smoke bombs. My grown-up life had been an endless series of awkward situations (usually because of something I said or did). How great would it be to just throw down a smoke bomb and vanish? Like an infinite, restore-your-game option for real life.

One time, I was in a public pool and saw a little boy wearing a comically oversized life preserver. He looked like a turtle—arms and legs barely sticking out. He jumped into the water, bobbed directly over to me, pointed at his life preserver, and said, "You can't spank me in this." Like most adult males, I find the idea of being mistaken for a creep terrifying, so this child's out-of-the-blue remark was the stuff of my nightmares. Before I could react, the boy's father called out, "What are you saying to that man?" The boy replied in a voice that seemed to echo across the pool. "I'm telling him he can't spank me."

All heads turned toward me. What could I do? There is no training for a moment like that. Besides, I was trapped in the pool. I couldn't just go under the surface and stay there. I panicked and responded in a defensive voice. "No! That's not . . . er, he . . . I wasn't . . . I'm just . . . uh, *standing* here!" I could not have sounded more guilty.

Oh thank god! Smoke bomb.

I had an awkward moment when I was a kid myself. I was going through the airport baggage scanning area and forgot I had a couple of pens hooked onto the front pocket of my jeans.

CHAPTER 21: FINDING LIFE FUNNY

Before I could go through the X-ray machine, an intimidating security guard stopped me and said, "Son, you'll need to go ahead and take those pens off." The man had said *pens*, but that's not what I heard. I looked at him in confusion, and he gestured for me to hurry up. So I took my pants off.

Now, I know as well as anybody that the airport is not a great place for a smoke bomb, but, man, I would've loved to vanish in a cloud of smoke right then! In my defense, I did it only that one time. Because that is how I learn things: in the most public and embarrassing way possible.

Mining my history of embarrassment did more than add enormously to my available material. It affected how the audience related to me. When I talked about an embarrassing moment, they felt better! They felt better knowing they weren't alone. And they felt better knowing they weren't me.

Being embarrassed is a universal experience, and when I shared one of my awkward moments, most people could identify with it. I was learning that almost nobody has it all together; they just seem like they do.

Laughing at myself reminded me that it's alright to be imperfect. The more I did it, the more I realized I could change how an experience felt –for the better.

Now that I had momentum, I decided to confront another part of myself that had always been framed as culturally uncool: asthma. As a child, I'd noticed the curious lack of movie heroes with asthma. While my lungs had improved in the years since then, the portrayal of asthma in movies definitely had not.

Asthma continued to be a condition reserved for movie characters who were either hopeless dorks or super-villains. No heroes—which we asthmatics would appreciate seeing now and then. Just once, it'd be great to have Wolverine strap on a nebulizer. Or have James Bond halt during a foot chase, take a puff of his inhaler, then pause for a long time to let the medicine in . . . before finally exhaling and safely resuming pursuit.

This is not to say asthma is never featured in the James Bond movies. In *Casino Royale*, there's a villain who sells illegal weapons to terrorists and plots world domination, then pauses to use his inhaler. When I saw this, I thought, *That's the character who has asthma? Some of us are nice.*

I've also wondered about the greatest movie villain of all time. Darth Vader. Asthma is never specified, but it's pretty clear there's a respiratory problem.

The movie *Hitch* features a main character with asthma, and he isn't a villain. He is, however, hopelessly incapable of looking cool around women. So, not much better. He's on a date with the woman of his dreams when he has an asthma attack. (Thanks, Hollywood.) So he pulls out his inhaler, thinks for a second, then hurls it down the street and goes and kisses his date. Big romantic moment. It took me right out of the movie. All I could think was, *What is your co-pay, man? You're gonna need that.*

So yes, when seen in that light, asthma remained one of the funnier varieties of respiratory diseases.

• • •

As I continued to make the challenging aspects of life humorous, I began to feel untouchable. But not for long. In the midst of all my comedy high points, something unexpected happened. My depression came back. How could this be? It seemed that having people clap for me multiple nights every week should be a foolproof cure against feeling low. Yet, by the time I got four blocks away from the club after a show, the happiness I had just felt had already vanished.

I kept getting on stages, but I was in the grip of a terrible, painful wave of numbness. My brain seemed smothered by a heavy fog. I felt happy only during the precious few minutes I was performing.

I truly didn't know what to do. So one night at an open mic, with 30 seconds left on my time, I tried telling a joke about my depression. I said, "It's hard to engage in small talk when I'm depressed. People ask, 'How are you?' and all I want to say is, 'Me? Oh, I'm slipping into the void. How are you?'"

When I got off the stage, a couple of comedian buddies of mine gave me a thumbs up. One of them said, "That was dark! We like Dark Colin." And I thought, *Can you help me? I'm not doing great right now. I don't want to talk about my comedy persona at the moment.* But their reaction was exactly what I would have expected. Comedians are a hit-or-miss support group. A bunch of comedians together is still a bunch of outsiders together. Go to any open mic, and you'll witness a buffet of individuals with diagnosable mental health conditions, which they are currently treating via the attention of strangers. This perfectly describes me too, so I fit right in. But once I got a laugh at that joke, I wondered if I could joke-write my way through this bout of misery.

It would be no easy task. Talking about depression had an emotional weight to it, and if I dug in too much or lost the thread, I'd just make the room uncomfortable. I'd also be taking more of a risk. Awkwardness was automatically relatable, but would anyone connect with my jokes about being depressed? I felt like I had to try. At the next open mic, I got up and tried out some more depression jokes I had come up with.

"If you live in New England, or anywhere there's a long winter, you're familiar with this thing called Seasonal Affective Disorder (or S.A.D. for short). All winter I tell myself it's just my Seasonal Affective Disorder, and then the weather turns nice in spring and I realize, Oh, I have the all-season kind.

"I also have something called Doritos Affective Disorder. It's when you eat an entire bag of Doritos and then just hate yourself. Do you know people who use Chip Clips? Who are these monsters who eat a few chips, then close the bag and say, 'I'll save these for next month'? You're supposed to eat them as fast as possible, in the dark, fingers covered in cheesy dust, thinking *No one will ever love me*—while reaching for a second bag. That's Doritos Affective Disorder. Or 'D.A.D.' for short. If a therapist were to realize its initials are D.A.D., their eyes would just light up. Because that's, like, 12 more sessions.

"Some people lose their appetite when they get depressed. Do they think they're better than me? Not to brag, but they'll never achieve the kind of snacking-related records I'm setting. I once ate a Costco-sized jar of Raisinets for two days. And only that. I told myself there were raisins in there. That did not make me feel better."

The crowd was laughing, which was always a good sign. But there was something else—a few people were nudging each other in recognition. These total strangers also had their versions of my "I'm a monster, and I'll die alone" moments.

They weren't judging me; they were relating to me. They weren't pulling back; they were leaning in. I'd just shown the real me, the one I actively hid from everybody, and they were okay with it.

This was a tectonic-plate-shifting epiphany. It meant I could look at anything in my life—a painful or embarrassing experience or a notable failure—decide it was funny, then figure out how to prove that by turning it into a joke. This didn't change the past, but it changed the way I looked at it. Writing a joke about something distressing was simply making a choice. It was choosing to use a different lens to re-imagine a moment in order to feel differently about it.

With a recent or ongoing difficult experience, I would have to wait a little while. I could notice it and write it down, but then I'd need to give it some time. Struggling is often too painful in the present. It only becomes funny *later*. After enough time has passed and the wound has become a scar, the experience might be worth revisiting from a more playful perspective.

To find life funny, I simply had to decide it was funny *already* and view the experience from that perspective until I could find the proof. This realization gave me a way to process some tough experiences, and it also strengthened my belief in what was becoming my new truth with a capital-T: We are the authors of the stories of our lives.

Now, I was authoring mine. Over time, I created jokes about trying to be somewhat holy, finding the lighter side of having asthma, spending years working on a novel that was unsellable, and the very strange experience of becoming a Bible School movie star. I found that every laugh I got was like the audience telling me, "We've got your back!" I was starting to believe they did.

This lifted my depression, at least for the moment. I would still feel down at times, but I had a tool I hadn't had before.

Being sad didn't go anywhere interesting. But finding life and all its torments funny? That was a game-changer. That opened all the doors. My jokes were no longer at my expense but in my arsenal.

I was learning to find the awesomeness in awkwardness. I was starting to transform pain into punchlines. I was finding comedy in unlikely places, just by remembering to look for it.

Humor had given me a way to take difficult memories and change their *feeling*. But I was about to learn a skill that would allow me to change their *meaning*.

CHAPTER 22
STORY THERAPY

Soon after I started doing stand-up, I got hooked on stage time. I was obsessed with making people laugh and, to be honest, having people pay attention to me, which meant I was always looking for that next rush.

One night, I saw a poster that said, "Storytelling Open Mic." I wasn't entirely sure what that meant, but it had the words "open mic," so I was in.

At that point, my only frame of reference for a "storyteller" was from some brief volunteer work at a local shelter a few years earlier. One night, the staff brought in a storyteller to entertain the guests. I kid you not, he showed up in old-timey clothes—a frilly blouse shirt tucked into brown deerskin pants, suspenders, a porkpie hat with a feather, the whole thing. He told well-known fairy tales, such as "Jack and the Beanstalk" and "The Princess and the Pea." At first, it seemed a little silly, but a few minutes into each story, all of us adults were listening with rapt attention—transported.

Still, I hoped this was not what was meant by "storytelling," because I didn't have the confidence for deerskin pants. (I once wore lederhosen to a school parade, but I was very young, and it was my parents' idea, and I cried most of the way there and even a little bit during.) Fortunately, the bottom of the poster included a short list of rules: no notes, six minutes or less, true stories only. There was no rule requiring a hat, porkpie or otherwise. I was relieved.

I arrived at the venue, a bar called The Half Lounge. It was aptly named because it was half the width of a regular bar. It had a place to order drinks at one end and a small, elevated nook of a stage at the other. I signed my name on the list and was surprised when I was called up first.

Before I began, the host got up, welcomed us, and repeated the rules, then added one: "Don't do comedy, please." *No comedy?* I wondered, *I don't have to try to make people laugh and should just talk about something genuine? Is this a trick?* My love of performing had landed me in a place where the goal wasn't to perform but just to be myself. *Ugh, who wants to hear that?*

I had decided to tell the story from sixth grade about accidentally revealing to my sociopathic classmates that I liked to moonlight as a Christian clown. (I'm sure you remember this story from earlier in the book, but the version I had sketched out for this open mic was shorter and not yet fully developed.)

The memory of that entire class laughing still made me shudder with embarrassment, a few decades later. But I was an adult now, and I could certainly see the humor in it, too. This was the first time I would tell it, and it consisted only of the three cringeworthy things I had admitted and ended with the kids laughing in my face.

CHAPTER 22: STORY THERAPY

In other words, it was much more of a comedy bit than a story, but it was all I had. I went onstage and, admittedly, ignored the host's "no comedy routine" rule completely. The audience ate it up, and I returned the mic to the host while avoiding her chiding glance for breaking one of only four rules.

As I listened to the other tellers, I noticed that their stories often had humor, but they also had an arc. They revealed how the experience they were sharing had changed them in some way. The tellers gave more weight to emotion and left in quiet spaces, too. During such spaces, the audience wasn't bored and restless, like a comedy audience might be. They were engaged and supportive. They seemed perfectly happy to go on a journey with the storyteller. I was kind of in awe. This was shared humanity among people in a bar—authenticity and acceptance on a large scale. We were huddled in our modern-day version of the cave, regaling each other with tales of faraway places as firelight danced on the walls.

I could see now that my story wasn't really a *story*. Not yet, anyway. It was a funny example of the "My Most Embarrassing Moment" sub-genre, but the problem it detailed wasn't resolved, and I hadn't changed. Unlike the other storytellers, I had learned no useful lesson from the experience. In fact, the way I told it, the only lesson was "Be careful what you reveal about yourself, because people will bully the bejesus out of you." *Grim.*

But was that all I had learned from it? As I revisited my memories of that day and pictured the room where it happened, I remembered a girl named Michelle and that she had defended me. I could remember what she said and even where her seat was in the room.

It was so vivid that it gave me an idea. *What if I made my embarrassing moment simply the set-up for a star appearance by Michelle?*

As I rewrote the story this way, the feeling around the memory changed, just as it had with the memories I'd rewritten through humor. But this was more than that; this was changing the memory's meaning. By spotlighting Michelle, the story was no longer about someone *conforming* to a peer group; it was about someone *transforming* that group. I liked this subtle evolution a lot.

But would an audience find this as cool as I did? I knew from my experience with stand-up comedy that the only way to know for sure was to tell it and see. At the next storytelling open mic, in the same small, lamplit venue—two qualities that suddenly reminded me of Sam's office from years earlier—I told this new version and the audience laughed in the right places and leaned in in the right places, too. They sympathized with me, but they cheered for Michelle.

With their reaction as reinforcement, I thought to myself, *This is the real story.* And, thanks to a curious collaboration involving me, an open mic, and an audience of strangers, it was.

• • •

I continued doing comedy, but I also spent more time writing and performing stories. I noticed a benefit that went way beyond getting the extra stage time. I was reconsidering past experiences in a way that made them feel more meaningful.

Soon after, I jumped at the chance to attend a lecture on storytelling, taught by an unforgettable member of the local storytelling scene. Recille was a 77-year-old storyteller who was at every storytelling event, no matter how late in the evening it was held. She was always impeccably dressed, and once someone had assisted her onto the stage, she would come alive and captivate us with her gusto. She reminded me of my lively Grandma Edmay.

In her lecture, Recille Hamrell explained the concept of neuroplasticity, the brain's ability to reorganize itself by forming new neural connections. Neuroplasticity can have tremendously beneficial effects, valuable both for brain health and life expectancy. And—this intrigued me—it can be activated through writing and telling stories about our experiences. As we revisit memories, narrate them, and assign meaning, we engage in a form of reflective processing that strengthens connections between our prefrontal cortex (thinking and decision-making) and our limbic system (emotions and memory).[18]

This leads to another equally interesting idea: our brains are already storytellers, by default. They both gather data and interpret it as well. Since this happens quickly and mostly without our awareness, the brain's interpretation of something could be highly emotional, subjective, and misguided. It could prop up a particular meaning or message that, upon thoughtful reconsideration, doesn't hold up at all.

I applied what I'd learned to my Christian clown story, which I had automatically interpreted as a shameful, regrettable moment. I realized that, with some effort, I could write a better version of that memory and do it on purpose. Learning about the science behind storytelling made me even more motivated to continue. By turning some of my struggles into stories, I could rewire my brain. And that's exactly what happened.

The process of that rewiring was both simple and profound. I would externalize a memory as a story, view it from arm's length with some objectivity, and then rewrite it. Finally, I would use my own and others' reactions to the story to rewrite it again, remaking it into something new. Over time, I would start to internalize the new message it offered. I was rewriting old, unexamined stories into better ones. I was having a conversation between who I had been in the past and who I was in the present.

After doing this for a while and becoming increasingly practiced at it, something dawned on me. *Wait a minute!* I thought. *Am I writing again?* Years earlier, I had been so terrified of rejection that I refused to show my personal writing to anyone. But now, I was writing my own stories and delivering them out loud—to total strangers. And I was doing it without fear. Instead of avoiding people's reactions to shield myself from negative feedback, I was seeking out their reactions for guidance on what was working and what wasn't. Laughter and nods told me I was on the right track. Confused looks and closed body language told me I wasn't there yet. But these moments weren't rejection; they were research.

Storytelling tricked me into being a writer again, and I was glad it had. I discovered that I had gained the confidence around writing I had previously lacked. I could do something I really loved with less of the isolation and insecurity. I still experienced a lot of obsessing and perfectionism, but now I had a deadline—the next show. Over time, I wrote more and more stories, and it became a creative form of self-therapy. I called it "Story Therapy."

• • •

CHAPTER 22: STORY THERAPY

The most significant benefit I received from storytelling would become clear only over time. For me, each performance was a small but important act of vulnerability. I said things aloud I'd always kept to myself, and this normalized those things. The first time this happened was when a few of us storytellers got together to brainstorm ideas for a Moth event the next night. (The Moth is an organization dedicated to the art and craft of storytelling, centered around true, personal stories. It hosts a popular podcast, *The Moth Radio Hour* and live storytelling competitions in which people are given five minutes each to tell a true, personal story on a given theme.)

The theme for the stories at the next night's event was "Pride," and since I was a person who mostly regretted everything, I was drawing a serious blank. As we went around the circle and shared our ideas, something occurred to me that sparked an unplanned confession.

I told the group, "This isn't really something I would say I'm *proud* of, but I lost my virginity way later than most people did. But you know, I did eventually lose it. Come to think of it, I'm proud of that, at least."

Suddenly, I noticed I had the group's attention, and so I told them the story. When I was done, I said, "I just realized I've never told that to anyone."

They replied, without hesitation, "*Please* tell it tomorrow night."

So I did. I took a story I'd told only once before, to three close friends, and told it to an audience of two hundred strangers. Because the theme was Pride, I didn't tell it sheepishly. I owned it. Sure, I had been "late to the party," but I had also made a big decision on my terms instead of those imposed by others. I had trusted myself, despite countless hours of being taught that I couldn't trust myself in this area and that having sex before marriage would be a shameful, permanent mistake I'd always regret. But it wasn't and I didn't.

Now, I had the chance to tell my story and acknowledge the pride I felt, and the crowd ate it up. It received the highest score of the night and qualified me for the upcoming Moth GrandSLAM, which was great, to be sure. But way more importantly, in under 24 hours, I had transformed a source of shame into a point of pride. The audience had responded with overwhelming support. From now on, I would choose to feel about the story the way *they* did.

Each storytelling event offered an opportunity to take a risk like this, and as I told more stories, I built confidence in being open with my emotions. Within me, a war raged between my desire to acknowledge my emotions and the rigid confines of what I had been taught about what heterosexual masculinity was supposed to look like. But storytelling wasn't like that at all. The way the audiences at storytelling events offered comfort and support during raw retellings of messy moments presented an intriguing alternative. They offered an unspoken and unshakeable social contract: "We will go where you take us—we are here *for* the vulnerability, and we're not freaked out by it."

At this time, Dr. Brené Brown's work was impacting the cultural conversation about vulnerability. As she put it in her book *Atlas of the Heart*, "Vulnerability is not weakness; it's our greatest measure of courage."[19] It took courage for me to say things into a microphone, especially when they were things I'd never admitted to anyone.

CHAPTER 22: STORY THERAPY

Learning how to be more vulnerable brought me external and internal benefits. I began thinking about it this way: The things we find hard to say are often the things we need to say. In fact, the toughest parts of an experience in the past are the *best* parts of the story we tell about it later.

This even served as an emotional survival skill in the present. Whenever I could, I would think, *Pay attention to the painful details, because when I tell this later, it'll make the story more relatable, more real, and more complete.* That usually wasn't enough to overpower the heaviness of the low moment I'd be in, but it definitely helped me keep my eyes on the horizon a little more.

Whenever I felt like I was going through hell, I reminded myself I was in the middle of a story.

CHAPTER 23
THE HECKLER IN MY HEAD

As far as I can tell, heckling is almost exclusively reserved for comedy. I highly doubt anyone has stood up during a concerto and yelled out, "This sucks! But I've brought a clarinet, and I'll take it from here." Did Mozart have to deal with this type of thing?

Yet, anyone can, at any point, yell at a stand-up comedian. And routinely will. Every so often, a comedy audience member has a few drinks and thinks, *You know what? I don't have any material. I didn't practice. But I've got something to say, and I'm the show now.*

As a rule, comedians despise hecklers. They are the bane of any performance. Generally, I agree, but I'll also admit that I've had a few yell out some truly amusing things at me.

The first came from a woman at a bar show who yelled in the middle of my act, "Must be hard for you not to get punched in the face." I responded, "Actually, it's not hard at all. I'm great at not getting punched in the face. I've designed my whole life around it."

The second happened when I did a comedy show at a college during finals week. It was the main event that night, and we performed for an audience of about 900 students. They were a rowdy and intoxicated bunch. At some point, a female student in the front row, clad head-to-toe in pink spandex, yelled loudly to me, "I wanna have your babies!" *What do I say to that?* I knew that, as a man, I was supposed to be psyched at this invitation. But what I said was, "No, thank you. That seems like a very neighborly offer . . . with long-term consequences."

The third is still my favorite heckle of all time. After Hurricane Irene swept through Vermont, a bunch of us donated our time and hosted a charity relief show for the small, hard-hit town of Brandon. It was held in the town's main theater and completely sold out. As the crowd entered, I saw this little old lady come in using a walker. She appeared to be nearing 90, and I thought, *How adorable.* I was incorrect.

Soon after we started, this woman, who I later learned was named Priscilla, said two of the most memorable things that would be said during that night's comedy show. The first came when the second comic, who was Canadian, got a little too crass for her tastes. Suddenly, she called out in a firm voice, "Watch your language!" This was an amazing thing to yell out during a memorized performance. But even more amazing was watching this comic on stage, as his comedian-ness and his Canadian-ness collided, and he started trying to censor himself mid-act. At one point, he said, "All in all, it was a pretty shi—um, poopy turn of events."

The next comedian was even dirtier, so after a few infractions, Priscilla was done. She yelled out, "Bring on Gene Childers!" He turned out to be a local jazz musician who

Priscilla would rather watch than the show she was currently part of the audience for.

As far as heckles went, that was one for which the only response was to think, *Well, I don't know what to do with that.* Because she wasn't telling us to clean it up. Rather, she was communicating, "Let's have something else. We're finished with all of this, only 15 minutes into the show. Bring on the soothing sounds of Gene Childers."

I knew I was supposed to be on Team Comedian, but all I could think was, *I want to hear Gene Childers. This guy is so good that people demand him in the middle of other shows. Think how adept he must be at—I'm hoping—the jazz flute.*

Priscilla was a great example of what a heckler is: a harsh but vocal minority. When hecklers yelled out during one of my performances, it was easy to assume they spoke on behalf of the entire room, and everyone hated me. But more likely, everyone hated the heckler for ruining the good time and rooted for me to respond by putting them in their place.

Priscilla had already exited in a huff by the time I got on stage. But we had an extra big laugh at her expense anyway. It had to be done. That's the price of being the only person outraged at a fundraiser.

. . .

Priscilla was my favorite heckler. But my toughest heckler? She was in my audience at a teachers' conference, not a comedy show.

I had been asked to speak at a teacher's conference about how I used humor, told stories, and got students involved in dialogue. I assumed a group of teachers on a Tuesday afternoon would be an easy audience. I was incorrect. I was about to get leveled by a force at least as formidable as Priscilla.

For the conference, I created a brand-new presentation called "Money in the Movies," in which I played movie clips and talked about the money messages in them. It was meant to be a template teachers could use that would be fun for students—lots of videos and relevant examples. I have always wanted to grow as a speaker, so I passed out evaluation forms afterward.

A little while later, I was sitting in my car, glowing from how well my first big speech went, and I decided to read the evaluations. I got mostly good reviews, and a few that were not so good. Two of those not-so-good ones were particularly memorable.

The first of the not-so-good ones said, "Given the name of the presentation, I assumed we would be watching a movie. Perhaps choose a different title next time?" *Fair enough,* I thought. *Imagine how irritated I would be if I was expecting a movie, and all I got was someone talking for 45 minutes.*

The other negative evaluation made all the positive ones disappear from my mind. My cheeks burned with embarrassment.

This teacher started with, "This suffered in comparison to the keynote speaker."

The keynote speaker had been a professional speaker for 30 years, so I wasn't sure how to apply that. *I guess I should do this for 30 years before I dare to darken her doorstep again?*

Then she wrote, "This was dry and very talky."

Um, I'm a speaker! I don't have a lot of options besides talking! Did she want to see me build a diorama? (Also, I

CHAPTER 23: THE HECKLER IN MY HEAD

played about ten movie clips, so I wasn't sure I could have been *less* talky.)

The third and final thing she wrote was, "Much of this was stuff that I already." *Already what?* She didn't say, and I'll never know.

Her typo wasn't enough to lighten my mood. Sitting there in my car, feeling defeated, I told myself, "Don't you dare let this one negative criticism eclipse all the positive reviews you got, all the laughter, all the sense of accomplishment you feel." This was great advice.

It's strange how often I ignore great advice. Instead, I let the criticism in. This person's words dug into my brain, ruining the sense of accomplishment I had been feeling just a moment earlier. For a few minutes at least, it made me question my job and my worth as an educator. I had recently started saving up the money and building up the courage to become a professional speaker, and it felt like this person was saying that would never happen.

I went home and went to bed, drained and seriously rattled. At 7:30 p.m., I got a notification on my phone for an open mic that started that night in about 30 minutes. I dragged myself out of bed and downtown to the open mic. When it was my turn, I simply read that nasty evaluation to the audience verbatim—and it killed.

I thought, *Oh yeah, a good story needs a good villain.* I mentally thanked the disgruntled teacher for volunteering her services.

I decided to agree with the audience, who howled in response to the vicious critique. This didn't have to be painful; this could be funny. I liked to imagine that teacher heckling me at a comedy show. In front of a whole room of people, she'd yell out, "This suffers in comparison to (insert name of world-famous comedian here)."

I'd respond, "I have to agree with you. I would also rather see that comedian. Too bad we can only afford to see me."

Then she'd unleash her show-stopper: "Much of this is stuff I already!"

I wouldn't even need to win the point back on this one. It's hard for someone to be smug when yelling a typo.

Internalizing shame helps it grow, while externalizing it tends to help it shrink. Thanks to an open mic that happened directly after this presentation, I never had time to internalize her feedback. At least, not for long. This was the fastest I'd ever gotten over harsh criticism, and the swiftness of recovery was due to my choice to vocalize it instead of keeping it to myself.

It might seem counterintuitive, but voicing embarrassments, regrets, and mistakes is a great way to diminish their power. It took being blindsided by a negative review for me to realize that I could always choose how I responded to rejections. I didn't need to suppress them; I could learn from them and even find humor in them.

When someone heckles you, you can always respond.

• • •

Comedy had become a way to build my confidence, but it wasn't a cure-all. My big, bold dream was to pursue speaking on a larger scale. When I thought about this dream—not to mention my current lack of a romantic partner—I felt less self-assured. I had some feelings of unworthiness that jokes couldn't fix.

CHAPTER 23: THE HECKLER IN MY HEAD

When it came to considering my own potential, doubts started to creep in. I began to realize that something, or someone, had arrived to hold me back. That someone was a heckler, too. A heckler in my head. A bully in my brain.

This was not good news, because my inner heckler was a much tougher adversary than some random audience member who was intoxicated, inconsiderate, or both. It was someone with the deepest possible expertise about where my vulnerable spots were. He fought dirtier than a stranger would because he knew how to criticize me more precisely than any stranger ever could.

He'd say, "Much of your early writing is derivative."

Damn. That is something I'm very insecure about, actually. I'd love it if you didn't bring that up.

Or he'd say, "The thing about you, Colin, is that you're nice and you're funny, which is why people can't tell right away how weird you are."

Wait a minute, that one's like a trick. It started out as a compliment and turned into an insult through emotional ninjitsu.

But the thing the heckler said most often was something I didn't have a quippy response for. He'd say, "Whatever you do, whatever you achieve, you're never going to be enough."

I'd been hearing this one my whole life, and with this heckle, my growing resilience through humor failed me. I didn't defend myself. I ceded the stage and the microphone to the heckler. I simply didn't have an adequate response, and I was filled with fear that I never would.

I knew that being a comedian was not going to be my end goal in life. While I loved hanging out with comedians, I knew I would need a community around me that could offer better support for my mental health and would push me toward the bigger goals I felt drawn to.

Comedy had already given me so much. It showed me how to reframe tough memories, develop tools to deal with rejection, and take meaningful risks in life that boosted my belief in myself. But before I was through with it, comedy would give me something of far greater value.

CHAPTER 24
THE BIG PICTURE

As I took stock of my life in this moment, I saw a lot of progress to be proud of. Thanks to my work for the credit union, I had developed the ability to present helpful financial and life advice in an engaging way and had graduated to speaking mainly at assemblies for hundreds of students at a time. My comedy career didn't pay much, but it was progressing, too. I had just been offered my first headliner gig.

This was definitely a milestone for a comedian. I was the final act, with my photo on the poster and the most time on stage. But what weighed on me more than stage nerves was a recent, quieter ache. I had spent the last year living like a comedy monk—on stage numerous times per month making strangers laugh, but avoiding intimacy ever since the painful wreckage of my last relationship.

After Robin, I had dated a few women briefly before I had my first long, serious relationship. It was wonderful, until it wasn't. It ended painfully—the kind of experience that left me vowing never to date again and convinced me that doing stand-up comedy was less risky than being in love.

Now, I had some distance from that past heartbreak and had put a lot of those memories behind me. I recognized that, while I had been putting all my energy into getting laughs, I'd been preventing anyone from getting too close. What I really wanted wasn't just applause. I wanted someone who would still be there when the audience went home.

Unexpectedly, on the way to the headlining gig, I found myself in the middle of a blizzard. My drive took me up and down a dangerous mountain road, but the other route to the venue was twice as long and would have made me an hour late. The road had a sign saying it was closed for the winter, but it wasn't actually gated, so I white-knuckled the steering wheel and drove straight up the mountain road. I would soon realize my mistake.

As I left the sign behind and steadily climbed, I was struck by the quietness of my surroundings, which were now blanketed in snow. There were no street lights, and the night was so dark that the falling snowflakes made light trails when they reached my headlights. I felt as if I were traveling at warp speed in the Millennium Falcon. In reality, I was doing 15 mph in a Ford Focus. I made it to the top, and on the way down, I miraculously avoided ditches on both sides and only tapped into two snowbanks. A respectable number.

At last, through the swirling snow, the venue's sign appeared—The Big Picture. A tucked-away movie theater and restaurant glowing like a lighthouse in the storm. Inside, the crowd buzzed with that particular mix of relief and anticipation people carry after surviving a harrowing drive. I had

CHAPTER 24: THE BIG PICTURE

survived the trip, too, but my nerves weren't just from the weather. Something about the night felt charged.

And then she walked in.

She was gorgeous, with long brown hair and high cheekbones. But it wasn't just her striking features that pulled me in. It was that her hazel eyes seemed alive and intelligent, as if she saw something other people didn't.

She had a combination of beauty and confidence that made me forget I was supposed to be the one commanding the room. Instead, I felt more nervous than ever. I thought, *Buddy, you've been doing comedy mainly because someone told you women appreciate a sense of humor. Well, there's a particularly lovely woman right there. Don't mess this up!*

I knew I had to find some way to talk to her. She even seemed familiar in some way. It was suddenly hard to focus on the setlist I had scribbled down. I kept sneaking glances at her. She wasn't sitting next to a guy, but this was Vermont, so that told me very little. Still, she wasn't holding hands with anyone, which was a start. I stepped onto the stage, while feeling that the stakes couldn't possibly be higher. As if to increase my level of risk, my first bit involved not just punchlines, but acting out full on yoga poses as well.

"Does anyone here know how awkward it is to be the only one laughing out loud in a yoga class? Unfortunately, I do. See, there's a pose in yoga called the Warrior, and what you do is you lunge forward, belly exposed, and put both hands over your head . . . Now, I don't know who your war is against, but it doesn't matter anyway because you'll be killed instantly.

"Warrior Two is equally baffling, and Warrior Three does not disappoint either. In that one, you stick one foot up behind you . . . And you stretch your neck forward like a human airplane . . . And then you'd better get airborne fast because you are in the perfect position for a beheading.

"But the pose known as Reverse Warrior gives me a flicker of hope! You lunge forward and reach your front arm behind you, and then you look backwards over your shoulder to somewhere behind you . . . This one is accurately named. It's exactly the reverse of what a warrior should be doing."

It finally clicked where I'd seen this woman before. She worked at the front desk of a yoga studio in Burlington that I'd visited a couple of times. I froze for half a second, my arms still outstretched above my head, then broke character and said, to her and straight into the microphone, "Oh, my God, I know where I know you from! You work at the yoga studio that I'm making fun of right now."

I was busted, and the audience roared, but inside I was thrilled for a different reason: I was actually talking to her. The joke, and the entire set, went well. I was proud to have made a pretty woman laugh, and I took note of the fact that she had a great laugh.

She came up afterward and introduced herself as Lindsey. "I remember you from the yoga studio. You were usually late," she said with a playful smile. She said she occasionally worked at the yoga desk in exchange for free classes—her real job was teaching career skills to high school students. I blurted, "I teach financial literacy to high school students!" She smiled. "How have we not heard of each other?"

I felt a spark the entire time she spoke to me, then felt it extinguish when her boyfriend stepped forward with a handshake that said, "Back off." They hadn't been sitting next to each other

CHAPTER 24: THE BIG PICTURE

for some reason, and I was disappointed. But something in me hoped there was more ahead than just this chance encounter.

• • •

The fact that this beautiful woman had a boyfriend was a pretty major speed bump. Our work was similar, though, and Lindsey soon reached out to explore potential collaboration on an upcoming school event she was organizing. The event went well, and we partnered on other events, too. We ended up becoming work colleagues and then friends. We got to know each other in a relaxed way that didn't necessarily involve trying to impress each other (well, we may have tried a little bit) and that had a shared goal—helping students with their futures.

One day, Lindsey mentioned that the reason she wasn't sitting next to her boyfriend during that comedy show was that they had actually been arguing right before it. Once I talked to her from the stage, he suddenly became her loving boyfriend again.

Our friendly relationship continued in this manner for a long time before things fell into place, and we were both single. When we admitted we liked each other and started dating, we already knew each other so well that we could be completely ourselves.

There's a little unintended pressure on the partner of a "professionally funny person" to be funny, too. Lindsey never had a problem with that. She made me laugh in every conversation we had. The compliment I've still never managed to land is that Lindsey has "Chris Farley energy." By this, I am referring strictly to her dance moves, her penchant for funny voices and . . . Oh, never mind, I still can't make it work. But when it comes to her particular comedic genius, it's the best compliment I've got.

Her humor was one of the many reasons I knew, way sooner than I was ready to admit, that Lindsey was my person. Besides being funny and beautiful, she was smart, kind, hardworking, one of the most generous people I had ever met, and she had never had a day of church in her life. She also had a small car and a large dog. There was a lot to like.

After a long period of hiding behind humor and avoiding real vulnerability, Lindsey made me want to be seen—not as the guy with jokes but as the person underneath them.

One day, I tentatively shared with Lindsey that I had started saving money to leave my job someday and pursue speaking as my own business. Emphasis on "someday." For me, this was intimidating, uncharted territory. For Lindsey, there was no doubt—just math. She asked how much I needed to save and how many months that would take. Then she opened up a calendar and said, "We can pick out the date for your first day of working for yourself!"

Lindsey cared about me, and she also challenged me, pulled me outside my comfort zone, and saw potential in me even when I didn't see it in myself. It was Lindsey who taught me that the people who challenge us believe in us.

People who live with depression are often trapped in the present, in a pattern of daily survival. The future is a big unknown, a nice thought we don't have time for because we're too busy dealing with *right now*. This is why it amazed me to have met Lindsey at a place called "The Big Picture." Thanks to her, I was finally starting to see one. For the first time in a long

CHAPTER 24: THE BIG PICTURE

time, I could imagine a future—not just having to survive it but potentially embracing it. I felt cautiously ready to discover what it had in store for me.

Comedy had shown me that I could be courageous. To build a bigger life—one that included love, purpose, and adventures along the way—I'd need to carry that bravery offstage as well.

CHAPTER 25
ONE MINUTE LESS AFRAID

While I was growing up, my mom kept a photo of me on the family fridge. In it, I was standing next to a swimming pool, looking absolutely miserable. This picture said a lot about my mom's sense of humor. It also said something very specific about me.

Even back then, I had an unusual and intense phobia. I was deathly afraid of being attacked by sharks, in *any* kind of water—lakes, rivers, even good-sized pools. Whenever I got into a pool, I envisioned a shark about to attack me. This made me a very fast swimmer.

It was a true phobia in that it was both overwhelmingly intense and completely irrational. Yes, I knew that sharks don't live in freshwater. Yes, I knew that sharks and chlorine don't mix. I agree, this fear was irrational. *And yet . . . there's a first for everything.*

Even as I got older, the phobia remained. I tried exposure therapy by watching Shark Week. It didn't help. I started watching shark movies, and since visual effects had only improved since *Jaws*, I realized I was adding trauma instead of addressing it.

But now that I'd experienced upticks in courage with public speaking and performing, this unaddressed phobia started to really bother me. Fear shrinks our lives if we let it, and even though this fear had always felt unbeatable, I decided to try. It was time for a courageous step. So, I signed up for a scuba dive course . . . in Lake Champlain.

Okay, so it was a courageous *half*-step. Lake Champlain definitely does not have sharks. But it is dark and deep. I'd swum in it many times, and no matter how many times I hadn't been attacked by a shark, I had absolutely no difficulty visualizing being suddenly devoured by one.

That is why I found myself sitting in a pungent basement classroom, about to begin my scuba dive certification course. The class started, and there was very little time to worry about sharks, because I was so busy learning the many things I needed to do to avoid dying. I learned how to monitor my remaining oxygen, clear water from a leaking mask, and communicate with others using only hand signals. The emphasis was always on staying calm.

On day two, we were paired up with our dive buddies. Mine was Tonya, the wife of a divemaster. I was bummed for Tonya. She didn't know it yet, but I was the short-straw dive buddy. I was certain my future held a panic attack.

Way too soon, I found myself in the van with the others, driving to the site of our first dive. I kicked myself. *This is my comedy class all over again—not nearly enough preamble. We're getting right into it.*

CHAPTER 25: ONE MINUTE LESS AFRAID

We donned our dive fins, a mask, an oxygen tank, a buoyancy vest, and a weight belt, and before I knew it, we were wading out into the water. As soon as we got beyond where I could touch the bottom, I vividly pictured sharks swimming right at me. Every second, every sound, my head spun, and my hands shook.

I pretended everything was fine, but I was starting to seriously panic. I needed something to focus on, so I looked over at Tonya.

To my surprise, Tonya was going through . . . something. She was floating on her back, seemingly unable to snorkel or descend, just looking into the sky and breathing fast. She was completely quiet as she blinked rapidly at the sky.

That was not how I had seen things going. Tonya stole my move. *I* was going to black out and become my dive buddy's responsibility, not the other way around.

"What's going on, Tonya?" I asked.

She answered in panicked breaths, "I'm so mad at myself. My husband is going to be so disappointed in me. I can't do this. I'm sorry I'm slowing you down. I think I have to go back."

I looked ahead and saw how far away the others were. It was up to me. I don't know if you will ever have to improvise a motivational speech to a catatonic complete stranger, but it will not go perfectly.

I began with, "Tonya, do you do yoga? Because you should. I mean, not now, obviously." I laughed awkwardly, and she didn't join in. I pretended that taking two yoga classes had turned me into a guru. "If you have a thought that's overwhelming you, just focus on your breath. The key is to just breathe. In. Out. In. Out. And what did we learn was the key to scuba?"

I saw a flicker of a smile, just for a second. She didn't look at me, but she answered. "Just breathe."

"Exactly. Just breathe."

I'd temporarily distracted her, so I shared another thing I'd learned, thanks to my two-class guest pass. "How about we try something? What if you take the thought that's bothering you right now and imagine you're writing it on a piece of paper? Got it? Now you're going to tie that piece of paper to the leg of a bird. I forgot to say there's a bird. Oh, and I forgot to say that there's also a window. Now imagine you're opening the window so the bird flies away with your note . . . which is that thought, um, from earlier."

It definitely sounded less stupid when Yogi Kevin said it. *If only I had a little gong.*

I abandoned that approach and tried a little reverse psychology. "You know what? We don't even have to dive; we can just float here. It's a beautiful day. And I don't know about you, Tonya, but I am totally loving how it feels to pee in this wetsuit."

Tonya laughed. There it was. A stupid joke achieved what my off-the-cuff mindfulness retreat couldn't. *Well, if it's jokes you want, I have more . . .*

"Tonya, did you know that, growing up, I was afraid of sharks in any kind of water, even in swimming pools?"

Tonya laughed at this, just like everyone laughed at this.

But then I said something I hadn't planned on saying. "I'm not a brave person. I think I've mentioned that I give speeches for a living. I used to be terrified of public speaking. I knew I had to get past it, but I didn't know how. So, one day, I told myself that every minute I spent in front of an audience, every

CHAPTER 25: ONE MINUTE LESS AFRAID

minute I spent doing the scary thing, I would be one minute less afraid. I just had to do this minute."

Tonya was starting to swim now. I had been smiling, breathing, and building Tonya up for several minutes, and suddenly I realized that I had completely forgotten about my own panic. I felt great, and not just from peeing in the wetsuit.

I concluded, "If you want, Tonya, we can just do this minute."

Then something terrible happened. My speech had completely succeeded in restoring Tonya's confidence. She pulled her mask into place, exhaled, and smiled at me like the married-to-a-divemaster woman she was and gave me the hand signal to descend, which was a thumbs-down sign.

I thought, *Thumbs down is about right. Why did I give such a good motivational speech?* Because now, Tonya was leading me.

I quickly adjusted my own mask and secured my respirator, and then we slipped effortlessly down into a whole other world. The turbulent surface of the water gave way to complete calm. The water created refracted stripes of sunlight all around us. We were surrounded by mesmerizing fish, each one detailed and unique. All we could hear was the sound of our own breath. Walking from the beach to the water in the heavy gear had been nearly backbreaking, but here we were, weightless.

At some point, I looked up at the surface, and it was 25 feet above me. For the first time in my life, I was in water and I was totally calm.

• • •

By the end of the course, we had spent about 40 hours in the water. That's 2,400 minutes of courage. By the end, I couldn't believe how much fun I was having. I graduated from the course and was officially PADI Dive-Certified.

Also, I was cured of my phobia!

Or at least, so I thought. Six months later, Lindsey and I took a trip to Bali, and for my birthday, she booked me a scuba diving tour. I plastered on a smile and thanked her. The class felt too long ago. Some of the fear had returned.

For some reason, I watched a diver's POV video on YouTube, shot in that exact diving area. It showed an eight-foot shark hovering around a piece of coral. *From years ago, right? Nope, yesterday. Awesome.* This wasn't a swimming pool; these were actual, shark-inhabited waters. It was also beautiful—truly the blue world, and I wanted to see it.

As the day of the dive inched closer, upsetting thoughts flickered into my mind.

I will be rushed to an Indonesian hospital, missing both hands. Unless I bleed to death in the Indian Ocean first.

If I even get that far! What if I have a panic attack and am unable to jump out of the boat and they bring me back to the shore completely dry?

Each thought brought on a wave of fear and anticipated embarrassment until I remembered that my brain was not my friend in this situation. For the next few days until my dive, I simply didn't think about it at all. I planned on distracting myself from the thoughts all the way up until I was actually in the water.

When each thought arose, I asked myself, *Is that helpful? No? Then try not thinking about it. Just breathe instead. In. Out. In. Out.*

On the morning of my dive, I got into a cab driven by a jovial, Balinese man named Nyoman. I soon learned that he'd

CHAPTER 25: ONE MINUTE LESS AFRAID

rebranded himself as "Norman," which he thought sounded cooler and more exotic. For most of the drive to the dive company's location, he offered running commentary on his favorite types of fish to eat, along with extensive detail on how to prepare them. It at least helped me avoid thinking about where I was going.

Soon after we arrived, we were in the boat and leaving the harbor. I tried not to scan the surface for fins and, instead, focus on the roughly eight seconds of equipment training I was offered. Next thing I knew, my dive guide and I were rolling over the side into the water. We immediately descended to the ocean floor, and I was in awe.

I saw turtles, sea horses, needlefish (which look like kitchen knives with eyes), Moorish idols (like Gill in *Finding Nemo*), and a shrimp that took one look at us and scuttled away fearfully, leaving a path of poop behind it as it went. *Been there, buddy.* The coral reef was vibrant, intricate, and vast. I even saw the same piece of coral where the shark had been hanging out, but there was nothing there. It was an ideal experience. And the icing on the cake: my guide sneezed underwater. It's a visual you never forget.

Finally, I looked up from the ocean floor, and the surface of the water was more than 65 feet above me. Once again, I was completely calm.

I thought back to being a little kid and panicking because I didn't want to get into the pool with my family. I wished I could tell my younger self, "You are not going to believe what happens when you push through this fear. And it's going to be way easier than you might think! All you have to do is to take your fears and tie them to the leg of a bird . . . and there's a window . . . never mind. That isn't going to work, but here's what will: Focus on your breath. Find a buddy. Feel the fear and act anyway. Because every minute you face a fear, you are one minute less afraid."

I realized this all happened because of a method, not a miracle. I didn't do what I did because I was unusually brave. I took this plunge *because* it scared the crap out of me, and I had reached a point where I figured stepping forward was better than hanging back.

I wasn't sure how often I'd actually go scuba diving in the future (since I lived inland), but that didn't matter much, because I'd already experienced more wonder and awe from this adventure than I could have imagined. This success reinforced the power of the simple formula I'd pieced together for building courage. Just do one minute outside your comfort zone, then another, until your comfort zone is bigger than you ever thought possible.

You just have to do this minute.

CHAPTER 26
THE COMPLICATED ART OF FINANCIAL COMPASSION

I was standing in the middle of a large circle of teenage parents, about to give my financial presentation, and this time, it felt very different.

At this point, my grant-funded work as a financial literacy guest presenter had taken me to numerous high schools in Vermont, and I had become adept at both connecting with people and teaching personal finance. I felt competent at what seemed to be important work. I had become passionate about it as well, because I was applying the same financial advice in my own life and seeing excellent results. I felt as though I was living my very own American Dream.

Now my job had led me here, where I was feeling oddly unprepared. First, this talk wasn't at a traditional high school. Instead, it was at an alternative GED program for teen moms on fixed incomes, or, as it's more commonly called, welfare.

Second, I couldn't teach them anything unless I could get their attention.

The young women seemed perfectly happy to chat with each other at full volume while I talked. It wasn't hostile; it was how they liked to listen. They frequently interrupted to react out loud and elbow each other. "*She* should listen to this. She's broke!" The accused party would fire back, "Oh, like *you* live in a palace!" Each of my points functioned as a prompt for another lively in-group discussion. I knew that if I wanted to educate them, I would need to engage them.

I tried telling a funny story, but I took too long to get to the point. Midway, one young woman loudly asked another, "Why is he talking about this?" The second student shushed her and replied, louder than I'd have liked, "I think he's trying to be funny." She then turned to me with a look that said, *You're welcome. Please continue.* It was a withering assault on my ego, but my defender meant well, so I smiled and shifted gears with an icebreaker question. "Let's go around and answer a question. If you unexpectedly got $100, what would you spend it on?"

According to everything I'd ever heard about welfare recipients, they should have listed such items as cigarettes and lottery tickets. But the three most common answers were rent, gas, and baby formula. In my effort to set up a lesson on Wants versus Needs, they responded with a Need, a Need, and a Need for someone else. I felt my prepared lesson crumble in my hands.

Having to manage every penny, with so little margin for error, had made these young women unusually *good* at managing money. When they did spend, it wasn't only for themselves. Often, it was to provide for the people who depended on them.

CHAPTER 26: THE COMPLICATED ART OF FINANCIAL COMPASSION

I was caught off guard, and a thought flashed across my brain. *What exactly am I doing here?*

Glancing around, I quickly realized the problem. I was the only male in the room, the only non-parent, and the only person who hadn't experienced poverty firsthand. I was also the only one standing, looking down at the mothers who sat in a circle around me. *There's the issue: I am the center of attention. Literally.*

So, I did something unplanned. I added a chair to the circle and sat down. I said, "I can tell you all have good ideas, and I bet we can learn from each other. So, I'm going to sit with you, and we'll just have a conversation." The chatter died down. A few of them looked genuinely surprised.

It was a chance to use the lesson I had learned long ago from my beloved Grandma Edmay: The most interesting thing about you is your interest in others. Sure enough, my genuine curiosity about them quickly earned more of their attention than my prepared material had.

I asked them question after question and learned a lot. The more they shared, the more fascinated I became. I learned that most of them were bullied by their peers for being young and pregnant, which was a big part of why they had dropped out of school and enrolled there. I heard how impossibly expensive childcare was for them and how grateful they were to find the program they were in. The more we talked, the more my middle-class stereotypes about them proved ridiculous, paper-thin, and insulting. Many of these 16-, 17-, and 18-year-olds were as wise or wiser than their peers at traditional schools where I had spoken. Besides being more frugal, they were also more financially charitable than I expected. They were generous in another way, too—they tolerated me, even though it had been obvious from the moment I arrived that I didn't see them for who they were. I was starting to.

Then I asked the group, "What have you learned about managing money from the adults in your life?" As one, in perfect synchronicity, they laughed. Hard. The notion that they had learned good financial habits from the adults in their lives was hilarious to them. As they laughed, my heart hurt.

As Marian Wright Edelman famously put it, "You can't be what you can't see." To thrive, we must have a network—as small as a parent or friend or as large as a community—to elevate us and connect us to opportunities. These women didn't have the same connections that others did. Furthermore, some of them faced downward pressure from their communities to conform to what was considered loyal, which included not moving away or making certain changes to improve their situation.

As I walked back to my car, I let the experience soak in. I had finally gotten a close-up view of a group of people after years of observing them from a great distance, and this had allowed me to see them for who they truly were. I had been judging people like them my whole life based on what amounted to poverty propaganda. These women had taught me much more than I had taught them.

Back at the office, an older co-worker, who knew what audience I had just presented to, asked, "So, did you talk some sense into them?" A few hours earlier, I might have had more patience for his tone and accompanying sneer, but not now. I told him that they were smarter, kinder, and more relatable than I had thought. He shrugged it off. He was entrenched in his belief that they were freeloaders who used his taxes to pay for their toys, and he couldn't hear what I was trying to say.

Of course, even I wasn't really sure what I was trying to say. It made me wonder, *Where did I get the certainty that working hard will take us to the top? And where did I get the audacity to think I knew everything about those at the bottom?*

In her TED talk, activist, author, and researcher Mia Birdsong addressed the propaganda that is too often spread about people experiencing poverty this way:

> I'm tired of the story we tell that hard work leads to success, because that story allows those of us who "make it" to believe we deserve it, and by implication, those who don't "make it" don't deserve it. [...] For every story I hear demonizing low-income single mothers or absentee fathers, which is how people might think of my parents, I've got 50 that tell a different story about the same people, showing up every day and doing their best. [...] Those negative stories allow us to not really see who people really are, because they don't paint a full picture.[20]

Her words echoed what I had just witnessed with the teen moms. The reality of their lives was far more nuanced than the stories I'd been told. It was a rupture that cracked my belief and shook my confidence. My goal for this job had just shifted beyond making people smile while I contributed a nice, light-hearted message. My work had become a responsibility.

Finance is a class that few of us take, but all of us need. For many of the people in whatever audience I was addressing, my presentation was the first exposure to the topic of personal finance that they had ever had. Financial educators often describe the challenge with an expression: "They don't know what they don't know." It turns out that "they" aren't the only ones. I had just walked into a room full of people and discovered that most of what I knew about them was based on assumptions. *I also don't know what I don't know.*

• • •

When the federal grant that had funded my short-term position ran out, I used the money I had been saving to start my own business as a professional speaker. I pitched myself to colleges and companies, and many hired me to speak on financial literacy to their audiences. Over the next few years, I traveled to almost every state and had countless conversations with people about their economic challenges, fears, and dreams. Everywhere I went, people told me about the same obstacles—debt that grew faster than their paychecks, health care they couldn't afford, wages that refused to rise, skyrocketing tuition costs, and the constant grind to keep up with the ever-increasing costs of vehicles, food, and rent.

To make matters worse, those obstacles were accompanied by messages that, although implied, were extremely clear. "Your financial problems are entirely your fault. You should have known better. If you admit to making that financial mistake, people will judge you. Asking for help will make you look weak, and nobody will help you anyway. Everyone else understands this stuff; why can't you? You're just bad with money, and you always will be."

These messages are dangerous simplifications and are more myth than fact. But they are so familiar that they *feel* true. We were all raised hearing them, we have internalized them, and

CHAPTER 26: THE COMPLICATED ART OF FINANCIAL COMPASSION

we repeat them to ourselves. The shame they so easily create keeps people silent and prevents them from seeing how similar their financial challenges are to those of others.

For example, at a college in Ohio, a young woman pulled me aside after a talk. Her father had worked two jobs for twenty years, yet her family had lost their house after a series of medical bills put them underwater. She said, "I'd always been taught if I just worked hard enough, things would work out. But my dad works harder than anyone I know." Her words made me believe, even more, that people need a society that looks out for them, especially when they remain one setback away from ruin even while they're doing everything right.

I met folks from every possible income bracket and background, from millionaire investors to marginalized families. It was strikingly evident that just because some of them lacked cash, that didn't mean they lacked character. For many, the crisis of poverty was happening *to* them, not because of them. This was evident and easy to see.

What I didn't see was enough *compassion* in our attitudes toward personal finance. For most of us, it has become all too easy to judge others for spending money on such things as cars or shoes, without pausing to ask why they do. For some, those items represent forms of wealth—maybe owning real estate or being debt-free—that wage and opportunity gaps have made unattainable for them.

I remember sitting in a cafeteria with a group of community-college students when one of them teased another for buying new sneakers. "Man, you're broke, why waste your money?" The young man shrugged and said, "Because when I walk in wearing these, people don't see broke. They see *me*."

His words hit home harder than any economics statistic ever had.

I sat there for a moment, watching him straighten his shoulders while a few of the others nodded their heads in agreement. That's when an important concept clicked into place for me. Financial compassion isn't soft or sentimental. It's equal parts justified anger at the system and justified kindness toward each other—and ourselves.

The deeper I went, the more convinced I became that financial education should be about more than numbers, and that understanding systemic barriers should be just as crucial as teaching personal responsibility. I read every book I could find, expanding beyond personal finance into books on inequality, economics, class, race, privilege, and more. It helped evolve my thinking, but at times it felt like I was trapped in a painful library. My demographics had created advantages I hadn't accounted for in the opportunities I received. I had never faced the challenges that many in my audiences lived with daily.

My life was easier by comparison, but it wasn't easy. I had begun experiencing health issues and the increased financial strain they brought with them. Managing my mental health was an ongoing non-negotiable, and it required constant, costly effort. I had also developed chronic lower back pain that I could not resolve, despite exorbitant MRIs and endless specialist visits. I reached the point where paying $600 for a doctor not to make eye contact with me and leave the room in under five minutes no longer even angered me. I just felt numb.

My experiences were shaping me as a consumer, as a person, and as an educator. In an environment where many of the professional services with the word "care" in them seemed expensive and indifferent, I decided to bring whatever care I could into my conversations about money. I couldn't change society, but I could certainly change how I approached being a speaker. I often reflected on the presentation I gave to those teen moms—the one that fortunately turned into a conversation instead. That day, my decision to extend curiosity and acceptance allowed them to open up and trust me. Perhaps socioeconomics had drawn us to the same room, but it was empathy that had created the connection between us and sparked a meaningful conversation.

Drawing on my journalism experience, I focused on listening and being non-judgmental. I asked questions and sought to understand. I began exploring ways to create an interactive presentation that avoided blame or shame, one that was safe enough for people to share money mistakes and lessons with each other.

At my next opportunity, which was during a training for financial educators, I asked, "Who in here has learned something about money the hard way?" A woman named Jessica, who looked to be around 30, tentatively raised her hand.

"When I was a teenager," she said, "I opened my first credit card, with my parents as co-signers. I didn't know what I was doing, and I ended up wrecking my credit. I wrecked their credit, too." The room was totally silent, because this was a difficult story to hear and, no doubt, a difficult one for her to tell. I knew this was a key moment.

I turned to the group and asked, "Will you raise your hand if you relate to Jessica's story in some way, and you appreciate her courage in being so real with us?" Every hand in the room went up.

Jessica emailed me a couple of days later and said, "All those hand-raises and head-nods made me realize I wasn't alone in my experience and that I'd been carrying shame about it for years. But now I know I can let it go. I made a mistake, that's all it was. And a mistake isn't a statement on who I am. It's simply a lesson I can teach."

She and her parents had never discussed this incident. I could see how financial mistakes can create tension in important relationships, disrupting the close bonds people depend on because of shame and fear of resentment—two weighty emotions that strain even the strongest connections and support systems when it comes to one's mental health.

After that, I asked about hard-learned money lessons in almost every speech. Someone would inevitably share something vulnerable, and it resonated with everyone. In that moment of courageous honesty, I got to smile at them and say, "You might not have noticed this, but as you were telling your story, people around you were nodding. Thanks for being real."

Then I got to see this happen in a much bigger room. At a conference with hundreds of employees, I asked them to write down, anonymously, of course, a financial mistake they had made. As I read them aloud—"I ruined my credit in college," "I hid debt from my spouse"—the atmosphere in the room changed noticeably. People looked around and realized they weren't alone. The shame gave way to nods and, with some of the more ridiculous examples, shared laughter. Their collective exhale reminded me that compassion doesn't just change individuals, it changes whole groups.

I gradually came to feel, once again, that I was in the right place and was the right person for the job. I had realized the full measure of compassion. It isn't entirely real when it flows in only one direction; it needs to go outward toward others and go inward toward myself, too.

I had grown a lot as a speaker. I still believed that good financial habits could make a big difference. I also understood that financial success for a majority of people, not just a few, depends on a balanced mix of personal responsibility *and* systemic fairness. I wasn't sure how we as a society could get there, but I knew that financial compassion was a key ingredient, and a complicated art worth getting better at.

CHAPTER 27
WE WERE ALL 11

Of all the stories I could have told, I didn't expect the one about clown makeup, rejection, and a sixth-grade social blunder to go global.

As I've mentioned, telling 200 strangers about my almost comically late loss of virginity had qualified me for a spot in an upcoming GrandSLAM competition against nine other StorySLAM winners.

When the night of the GrandSLAM arrived, I stood in front of about a thousand people and told what had become one of my absolute favorite stories: the time I outed myself as a Christian clown, and sixth-grade Michelle stood up for me.

The audience's reaction was magical, and the judges agreed. I won and became a Moth GrandSLAM Champion. The downside? A thousand people found out I had been a Christian clown.

It turned out Michelle's story hadn't finished reaching people.

A few months later, I got a call from Jenifer Hixson, a senior director and story producer for The Moth in New York, who had attended the GrandSLAM. After we caught up, Jenifer said, "We've chosen your story for the next episode of *The Moth Radio Hour*. It'll play nationally on NPR."

On the day it aired, my inboxes filled up with kind messages from strangers. Messages like: "Tears streaming down my face in my kitchen while I listen to Colin Ryan's story on The Moth." "An amazing reminder to stand up for someone and be their hero when they need you." And more.

An elementary school teacher emailed me to say she had played the story for her class and had them draw a picture to illustrate it. The attached drawing depicted a diminutive, helpless me being defended by a tall, confident Michelle. I thought, *Honestly, that's spot-on. They nailed the power dynamic. And in crayon, no less.*

Soon after, I received a thoughtful message from a designer in Massachusetts. He wanted to know if he could use his favorite line from my story in an art piece for an upcoming show. "Where would you like to travel? Wherever a book takes me." I said yes and was delighted when I saw the finished piece, which featured the quote artfully arranged across a collection of old books.

The more I read, the more I thought, *Instead of laughing at me, people are . . . thanking me?* I had expected some chuckles and little else. I didn't expect students, teachers, artists, and many others to tell me it meant something to them. I was deeply moved by all of this and assumed that was the end of the hoopla. It had been a great ride, after all. A few months later, I received another call from Jenifer Hixson. "Great news. I'm including your story in an upcoming collaboration we're doing. It'll be part of a story collection in *Reader's Digest*." That collection ended up as the cover feature, which bore the title "The Best Stories in America."

It was quite surreal. To be featured in a magazine I had grown up reading, accompanied by such a stunning superlative, was something I never could have expected.

Later, a retired CEO sent me a picture of my story framed and hanging on a wall in his house. He said he had read it at least thirty times, and it choked him up every time. It resonated with his hope to raise sons who are curious, who don't judge, and who can help spread more empathy in the world.

Still, I knew I had officially "made it" when my neighbor, whom I'd only talked to once or twice, yelled across the street to me, "Great job on the story in *Reader's Digest*." That's how I found out what he reads while he's pooping.

• • •

So, yeah, now *millions* of people across the world know that I had been a Christian clown. Somehow this simple story about a moment that always mattered to *me* seemed to matter to many, many other people, too.

Sharing that story led me to two meaningful interactions.

The first was after I performed the story at a show. A woman approached me, gave me a kind look, and said, "I loved your clown story."

Instead of just accepting the compliment (never a strong suit of mine), I quickly deflected by saying, "Thank you, but I'm surprised that people relate to this story. It's such a specific thing to have been a Christian clown as a kid."

She smiled knowingly and said, "Maybe so. But, Colin, we were all 11."

It was as if a puzzle piece had just clicked into place. The stories I had thought were only about me were also about the people listening. More people than I would have expected were able to easily relate to them. Even if they couldn't relate to the circumstances of my experience, they could connect to the emotions involved. This meant that the same elements that made a story personal also made it universal. That's a paradox, of course, but I know it's true. Because we were all 11.

In that moment, I honored my younger self. I had been a bit of a peculiar kid, to be sure, but I was also interesting in a way I couldn't yet see. I didn't realize it at the time because, on that day in that classroom, I had been completely authentic and almost universally rejected.

But the truth lay in that word "almost." I wasn't universally rejected that day. Not by everyone. I had an ally who came and stood beside me. Since I had glossed over this, I had walked away from that day in desperate need of others' approval. My mantra became the very definition of impostor syndrome: *Tell me what you want me to be, and I'll be that.*

Now I understood something more important: When you muster the courage to be your authentic self, some people won't get it, but some will, and those people will come and stand beside you.

The second interaction that meant a lot was when I found and reconnected with Michelle Beaver, decades after we were sixth graders together. I told her about the impact the story had had, and it meant a lot to her to know that she'd done something good. It turned out she was going through a lot of trauma at that time in her life—something I never knew. And yet, she had helped me immensely back then, despite her own challenges. Now, somehow, I was helping her too.

When I played the video of the story performance for her, she began to cry. It meant a lot to her to know someone remembered that small moment when she had tried to do the right thing. And it meant even more to her to know that the story had helped many people find the courage to follow her example.

I think that would make me cry, too.

Knowing Michelle and telling this story publicly taught me that being yourself is courageous and that courage is contagious. Being yourself gives the people around you the courage to be themselves, too. Now, I was part of that spiderweb of honesty. I had told Michelle's story and, in the process, shared my authentic self with countless people. I had told millions of strangers that I was a Christian clown, and I didn't mind at all.

CHAPTER 28
THE BLURT, THE BAT, AND BEING SEEN

Lindsey was quickly becoming my favorite person in the world. But I had a concern. Although I thoroughly enjoyed getting to know her better, I had serious doubts about the flip side of that coin—Lindsey getting to know *me* better.

In the early stages of dating, I could put on a show. I could be charming for long enough to seem at least mildly sophisticated until I could go home and unwind. I would think, *Oh, thank god, I can be my awkward self again. And finally fart.*

As I got more serious with Lindsey, she slowly saw more and more of who I was. I knew she would eventually see all of me. (Heh heh.) It was exciting to no longer be going through life alone, but I was nervous, too. She was already seeing more of my awkward, unscripted self than I would have liked. Sure, she might witness my best and proudest moments. She would also see me in the moments when I'd rather be invisible.

The first indication that she'd glimpsed the unrehearsed me occurred when she informed me that I was a sleep talker. This wasn't good news. I can be a blurter, which creates a situation in which *both* of us hear something for the first time. All day long, I worked hard to suppress this, but apparently at night my brain was betraying me. One morning, Lindsey said, "I need to ask you about something you said in your sleep last night."

"What did I say?" I asked groggily.

"You said, 'Stop kissing me, Ryan Gosling.'"

It was 8 a.m. My brain was still booting up, but I knew I needed to do better than "Huh?" I was immediately proud of what I came up with: "That sounds like the statement of a man who is trying to be faithful."

We made it through the Ryan Gosling moment, but things were about to get even more real. One night at about three in the morning, we heard a bat in our room.

Lindsey and I were a pretty equitable couple. We bucked stereotypes. She was mechanically inclined, and I was emotionally accessible. Still, in Lindsey's view, removing small, unwanted creatures from the apartment was strictly "man's work."

The bat was on a wall, near the ceiling—a tiny, winged, mouse-sized ball just clinging there. At least, until it was disturbed. I got a stepladder and climbed up with, I'm not proud of this, a metal mesh trash can over my head, like a low-budget Knight of the Round Table.

I got close enough to make a plan and said to Lindsey, "Grab me a bowl so I can trap it." Lindsey ran to the kitchen, came back, and handed me a tupperware bowl. As I took the handoff, I sensed—too late—that something was wrong with this option. As I cupped the bowl over the bat, it dawned on

CHAPTER 28: THE BLURT, THE BAT, AND BEING SEEN

me: *This bowl and this bat are the same size. Also, this bowl is clear!*

Sensing it was trapped, the bat whirled around and unfurled its wings like something straight out of a nightmare. It dove toward my hand with fangs extended (or so I imagined). I instinctively yanked my hand back, dropped the bowl, let out a few curse words, and retreated down the steps so quickly that the wastepaper basket fell off my head. I remained hunkered while the bat flew around the room, madder than ever.

Ladies and gentlemen . . . meet your hero, I thought. *Wow, it would've been great for Lindsey not to have witnessed this moment in my life.*

While I did finally figure out a way to chase the bat out the window, the whole incident—and specifically my putting a trash can on my head—became a funny shared memory for us. But there were other things I was sure we *couldn't* laugh about, things I desperately tried to keep hidden. And as our romantic relationship grew, so did my stress and discomfort.

• • •

When Lindsey and I first met, I was onstage, in my element, at the peak of my confidence. In our early months together, I was frequently performing onstage. This enabled me to ensure that Lindsey saw less of the Real Me than she saw of the Best Me.

The Real Me was the depressed, awkward version of myself that I felt like in everyday life, in the moments when I wasn't performing or giving a talk. As a depressive, I hid this version underneath the Best Me, who showed little signs of awkwardness or depression, other than what I turned into comedy onstage. It was a persona or alter ego that I had created in order to fit in and be likable.

Being much closer to Lindsey meant that, without realizing it, I was now performing offstage too. I did well at first, but over time, I found it more challenging to hide the fact that I was affected by depression. The lesson I'd learned back in my auditions for Dakota Joe re-emerged: Acting is not my strong suit.

On the days when my depression spiked, Lindsey could tell something was wrong. I had "depression brain," which meant I was foggy, confused, hard on myself, and slow to respond because I was rehearsing what I would say before I said it. Lindsey had never experienced having a partner with depression before, and she demonstrated only concern and interest in learning more about it and how she could help me through it.

We continued that way, falling more and more in love, while my depression made only occasional appearances and remained mostly in the background, until the day that Robin Williams died.

The popular and, as it turned out, mistaken explanation for his death by suicide was that Williams was a person who wrestled with the invisible weight of depression. It was striking to most people that one of the funniest people imaginable had faced depression severe enough to cause him to take his own life. It would later be revealed, as a result of an autopsy, that Williams actually had an undiagnosed brain disease known as Lewy body dementia. It was this, not depression, that led him to suicide.

However, the idea that depression caused Williams's death was widely accepted. In my opinion, this was, at least partly, because it resonated with many people, including me, who hold

CHAPTER 28: THE BLURT, THE BAT, AND BEING SEEN

a certain belief about comedy and comedians: At the root of humor is often intense sadness.

Robin Williams's death hit me hard. I first saw *Mrs. Doubtfire* as an adolescent, and witnessing a father's vulnerability and unwavering love for his kids during a difficult divorce meant a lot to me. It made him an unofficial "movie dad" of mine. But now I saw something of myself in him; we both performed to mask sadness. An article I found, written by David Wong the day after Williams died, explains why this can happen. Addressing comedians, he says, "[At a young age] you learned that being funny builds a perfect, impenetrable wall around you—a buffer that keeps anyone from getting too close and realizing how much you suck." Further into the article, Wong goes on to say that "you wind up creating a second, false you—a clown that can go out and represent you, outside the barrier. The clown draws all of the attention in order to prevent anyone from poking away at the barrier and finding the real person behind it." As he points out, the safety comes with a cost. "If people hate the clown, who cares? That's not the real you. So you're protected. But the side effect is that if people love the clown . . . well, *you* know the truth. You know how different it'd be if they met the *real* you."[21]

As a kid with asthma and a serious case of feeling like an outsider, I had been connecting through humor many times a day, every day, as far back as I could remember. The approval I got once I started doing stand-up comedy only reinforced this pattern. With most people, I hid behind the funny, confident version of myself. I couldn't do that with Lindsey.

I myself had dated someone with a mental illness in the past, and I knew how draining it could be for the other person in the relationship. It had been overwhelming to keep her worrisome behavior a secret and to feel that I was her only lifeline, all while having no idea what I was doing. I didn't want to put Lindsey in a position where she had to blur the lines between intimacy and therapeutic care. Unfortunately, I was quickly realizing that I had no clue how to keep this part of me separate from her.

Because I was now sitting across the breakfast table from her, on a beautiful morning, talking about my intense emotional response to Robin Williams's suicide, and my long history with depression. I found myself assuring her, for the first time, that I wasn't a danger to myself. I had avoided reaching this level of intimacy in the past because I assumed any partner would want only Best Me, not Real Me. Surely *this* would give Lindsey pause.

She never wavered in her commitment. Lindsey taught me that a relationship is like a mirror held up by someone else. The mirror reflects your true self, flaws and all. You might not like what you see, but the other person does. As they hold up that mirror, it's as if they are saying, "I can love this version of you. Can you?"

* * *

In Lindsey, I had found an ally in my battle against depression, but she was a person who loved me, not a professional mental health counselor. The safety I felt when I was around her was a godsend, but it also planted the seed for something difficult.

Lindsey's belief in me was intoxicating. When I was around her, I felt that anything was possible. She gave such great advice

CHAPTER 28: THE BLURT, THE BAT, AND BEING SEEN

that I constantly wanted more of it. Neither of us noticed at first that her confidence in me wasn't building my own—it was replacing it.

I started seeking her opinion on every decision, from what pants to wear to which friendships I should pursue. Without realizing it, I had lost faith in my own judgment. I'd fallen into a pattern of obsessive checking and reassurance-seeking. *[Note from the future: Years later, I'd learn that this kind of behavior can show up in many mental health struggles and is a hallmark of Obsessive Compulsive Disorder (OCD).]*

In other words, the more I asked Lindsey for reassurance, the more I needed to keep asking for it. It was as if I was saying to her, "reassure me again . . ." while failing to recognize the endless loop embedded in those words.

A relationship can feel like "two people against the world," but sometimes, it needs one (or a few) more in the fight—professionals who can help. The partner of someone facing mental health challenges carries an invisible weight. They offer love and support in a role they were never trained for, even as they're present every step of the way, directly impacted, and doing their best. Their presence matters deeply. But they shouldn't have to, and can't adequately, do it alone.

Over the years, I frequently gushed about my relationship with Lindsey, pointing out that, as I pursued my unconventional business, Lindsey believed in me even when I didn't believe in myself. At the time, I didn't realize this wasn't entirely a good thing. Her belief in me would never be enough if I didn't believe in myself, too. It wouldn't sustain me if I had to borrow it from someone else. I was going to have to learn how to build it from within.

CHAPTER 29
SOCIAL ANXIETY ON A JUMBOTRON

I was in the middle of giving a speech about how one could live a bold and happy life when I had a sudden realization. *Well, how about that . . . there is such a thing as a depressed motivational speaker. I'm the proof.*

I had recently branched out from financial speaking into a new area for me: motivational speaking. Somewhere in my subconscious, I had assumed having a job in the "inspiration business" would make me depression-proof. Clearly, that was not the case, which came as an unwelcome shock.

As I addressed the audience, who appeared to be having a good time, I found myself feeling jealous. I could barely hear what I was saying over my own critical inner monologue.

I had experienced depression while onstage during my comedy days, when self-loathing wasn't just par for the course in our community of comedians, it was practically a job requirement. This, however, was something else entirely and much more difficult to manage. For the first time, two speeches were happening simultaneously. One was cheerful, upbeat, and passionate. That was what the audience heard. The other was a running litany of self-critical assessments, doubts, and panicked speculations about what the audience might be thinking. That was heard only by me.

No one could tell, because I knew my stuff well enough not to lose my place. I'd had lots of practice hiding my depression beneath confident body language, but the contrast between the two speeches was quite striking. Out loud, I said, "If you practice this advice I'm offering, I know you'll have the kind of life you want." At the exact same time, I thought, *You're so full of shit.*

The irony of the situation intensified the disconnect. While I was giving a speech to middle-school students about standing up to bullies, I was losing a fight with the bully in my brain.

For most of my career, the stage had been a place of freedom. It often still was. But when depression and anxiety reared their heads, it became difficult to trust that things would turn out well. Dread would creep in as I visualized the next speech—not as a fulfilling opportunity, but as the ultimate exposure. I would look at the next gig on my calendar and think, *This time, I won't be able to hide it.* This *speech will probably end up being my* last *speech.*

After the anti-bullying speech was over, I was packing up my things when a heavier question settled in. *If this is how much effort it takes to get through a low-pressure talk for middle schoolers, what happens when the stakes are much higher?* I was about to find out.

• • •

CHAPTER 29: SOCIAL ANXIETY ON A JUMBOTRON

A few weeks later, I got a call from a booking agency looking to hire me for a new gig, the national conference for the National FFA Organization (the national leadership conference for students in agricultural education.)[22] It would be in Indianapolis at the end of October—about six months away—and the lineup of speakers would be the long-distance swimmer/world record holder Diana Nyad, global survival celebrity Bear Grylls, and me. A classic trio. Additionally, the event would be held at the stadium where the Indiana Pacers play, with an expected attendance of 18,000 students and adults.

I wondered briefly if the agency meant to call a more famous Colin but, of course, said yes. If there is a "major league" in speaking, this is it. This was a career-defining opportunity, and I love a good adventure. I was reflecting on what it might be like to stand in front of such a massive audience when I was struck by another thought. The bigger the crowd, the more likely it was that the spotlight would find the parts of me I tried to hide. Somewhere inside, a self-confident voice clicked off, and a quieter, anxious voice clicked on.

I was now fully aware that being hired to inspire others didn't magically make my inner critic disappear. I kept wondering, *If I can't live by what I preach, who am I to tell others how to live?* If I had a close enough friend among the speakers I knew, I might have confided in them and learned that this type of internal struggle is a pretty relatable one. But the social lives of professional speakers can easily shrink to hotel lobbies, conference green rooms, and email inboxes. In the midst of my entrepreneurial hustle, mine surely had.

Around that time, I met Tom. Tom was a former MMA fighter turned anti-bullying speaker. (Yes, you read that right.)

He was relentlessly upbeat—always full of happiness and motivation. Yet, sometimes his cheerfulness felt like evidence against me; every conversation ended with a reminder from him that life was, basically, incredible. During my dips of depression, I couldn't help but compare myself to him, and I'd find myself wanting what he seemed to have.

Once, he called me while out on a late-morning walk. *He's heading to the gym,* I assumed. *Probably for the second time.* In the midst of his update about a young person he was currently mentoring, he said, "Hold on, I'm just going to run across the street and hold a door open for this lovely old lady." I thought, *I haven't even changed out of my PJs yet.*

When good things happened in my business, my brain offered one tidy explanation: luck. The successful gigs, the positive reviews, the emails from people who said I'd helped them—all of it translated into "flukes." My sense of unworthiness colored everything.

Onstage, though, things were different. Sometimes I'd hear that inner criticism, but most of the time, I didn't. Instead, I'd feel free, in control, fully present, if only for those precious minutes. It reminded me of something I'd heard about actors with depression: the stage becomes a sanctuary.[23] Their dread arrived not before the show began, but before the final curtain call, because that meant that soon they'd have to leave the predictable world of the set and return to the complexities of everyday life. I could relate. During the last section of a speech, I'd glance at the clock behind the audience, wishing it would move more slowly so I could stay in performance mode instead of having to go back to feeling like crap.

• • •

CHAPTER 29: SOCIAL ANXIETY ON A JUMBOTRON

When October arrived, I had already begun feeling burned out from traveling and speaking, as well as exhausted by my constant rollercoaster of emotions. Even the sanctuary of the stage couldn't shield me. Now it was the month of the big speech, and I sensed trouble. I was stuck in a depression that absolutely would not lift, and I couldn't find a way to calm my racing thoughts.

I was awash in the same stress-inducing anxiety that had struck me so unexpectedly during my anti-bullying speech. Although I understood that depression and anxiety are closely related and can feed on each other, I was more familiar with the heaviness of depression and not as practiced in dealing with this rapid, unstoppable overthinking. It kept growing.

Typically, sitting down and assembling my presentation for a speaking event would turn my worrying into confidence as I focused on what I wanted to say. I'd get excited as I made a few quick adjustments to the nice-looking slides that had worked well with previous audiences. This time it had the opposite effect. I soon found myself repeatedly changing my slides—adjusting font sizes, subtly altering background hues (and then reverting them), and obsessing over making already concise phrases one or two words shorter.

I wasn't actually improving anything; I was obsessively tinkering as a ritual to keep my panic at bay. Each click was avoidance—a small, repetitive task that brought a brittle illusion of control. No matter how much time I spent "improving" my slides, each one felt like a billboard announcing what everyone must be thinking, *This guy isn't supposed to be here.*

Nothing else was helping either, including taking my antidepressants and getting exercise. My sleep started to resemble what it was like during my novel-writing days: nonexistent. I was up all night with spiraling thoughts, consumed by a vivid sense that my career was about to come to an end. It didn't exactly help to know that the audience would be larger than the population of the town I lived in during high school.

Before I knew it, the event was three days away. Desperate, I visited my doctor and got my first-ever prescription for anxiety medication. The day before I would fly to Indianapolis and give the speech, the pharmacy called to say they had filled my prescription. I drove there but arrived three minutes after they had closed.

I stood in a panic outside the darkened building for a long time. As I drove home, all I could think was, *I have no medical support. I am going to stand in front of these people and tell them how to have a big life, and I am falling apart.*

When I got home and tried to select what to wear in front of 18,000 people, I found that I couldn't breathe. Lindsey came home a little while later and found me sitting on the edge of the bed, unable to make eye contact, with all my dress clothes strewn across the floor. My eyes were darting back and forth, searching for some explanation of what was happening to me. I was dizzy, exhausted, and in full panic. All I knew was that I was having some kind of episode.

Lindsey sat beside me, put her hand on my back, and asked what was wrong. I closed my eyes, and all I could say was, "It's not supposed to be this way. I can't help anyone have a better life. My speech is a lie, and I'm a fraud."

I stopped talking then, but I had two more awful thoughts that I chose to keep to myself. The first was, *I can't go to Indianapolis because I can't hide what is happening to me, but not going will be the end of my career.* The second was, *How could I have screwed* up this badly and let Lindsey see me this way? Will this moment be the end of us?

I was convinced that, thanks to one catastrophic mistake of emotional mismanagement, I was about to lose the two things that were most important to me simultaneously.

But then, in one of the worst moments of my life, Lindsey remained. I didn't have to go through it alone. She didn't say a lot, but she sat beside me, held space for me, and once I had calmed down, helped me pick something to wear.

It felt like she was holding up that mirror again, and even though I recoiled at the reflection, she was still telling me, "I dare you to see and love the same person I do." That's what Lindsey did for me, and it's one of the many reasons she's my favorite person.

The next morning, I flew to Indianapolis. That night, I delivered the speech pretty much flawlessly. No one knew what was going on with me. This was an accomplishment because, during my speech, my face was on two giant video screens above the audience. Have you ever experienced barely-controlled anxiety while being on multiple Jumbotrons for 30 minutes? I don't recommend it.

On the other hand, due to the magic of stage lighting, talking to 18,000 people was not as scary as I had thought it would be. From the stage, I could see only about 300 people, although I knew that outside that light were, well, quite a few more. The laughs were huge and extended. The adrenaline was out of this world. They received me well, and I was so glad I got to do it.

A few times, I had trouble remembering my place because of my depression-brain, but I managed to stick to my script for the most part. I veered off into the unplanned only once, and it was to say something strategically vague, but honest, about my current situation.

I said, "Here's the thing: Everyone you know is a success and a mess. In some way, they are killing it, and in some way, they feel like a kid in grown-ups' clothes. So when you have that feeling, it's not a disqualifier. It's a signal to lean in, to keep going, because the toughest parts of the challenge you're in now will be the best parts of the story you'll tell about it later."

It was what I needed to hear, too.

When I got back to my hotel room, I was utterly spent and numb, but I had gotten through the talk successfully. I noticed the live feed of the video was already up on the FFA website, so I watched some of my speech. Even I couldn't tell anything was wrong.

• • •

I had been sure that my speech to a stadium's worth of people would be one of the most remarkable experiences in my professional and personal life. While the speech was a big moment in my career, it wasn't the best memory I'd have about that week. That distinction belonged to Lindsey and her unwavering presence as she sat beside me, encouraging me, believing in me, and not going anywhere.

I flew home and immediately filled my prescription. I felt my depression and anxiety staking their claim over me, overtaking my new life and chasing away all the good things. *What is it going to take for me to win this battle?*

I took inventory, and I could see that I'd experienced many things that society touts as solutions. I'd tried practicing

CHAPTER 29: SOCIAL ANXIETY ON A JUMBOTRON

religion, getting therapy, performing comedy, being my own boss, making great money... I'd even tried getting lots and lots of applause. Some had helped, and some hadn't, but nothing had helped enough. *What was I missing? What else could I try? What else could possibly be driving this thing?*

I no longer had a choice. I knew I couldn't pretend anymore. I had to figure this out. If I couldn't solve this, I wouldn't just lose a career. I'd lose the love of my favorite person.

CHAPTER 30
BREAKTHROUGHS AT THE BOTTOM

When I looked back on my years as a speaker, I could see that my mental health highs and lows had become more erratic and pronounced around the time I started my own speaking business. Those first six months were an extended rude awakening.

Like a lot of people, I wasn't really prepared for what it would be like to be self-employed and own my own business. After an exciting beginning, the couple of gigs I'd lined up came and went, and then work slowed to a standstill. The dream became alarmingly real. Working for myself had turned into working *by* myself. Every day, I would sit alone at my desk/dinner table, stare at my laptop, and try to ignore how lonely it felt.

My work stress and financial worries were through the roof, yet I knew I couldn't complain about this because, to anyone else, I was living the dream. No boss! No commute! No pants! Also, no income, and no idea what I was doing.

Now *I* was my boss, and as bosses go, I was not exactly consistent. Sometimes, in the middle of a workday, I would say to myself, "You know what, buddy? Take the day off. Watch all the *Die Hard* movies. You deserve it. We'll get 'em tomorrow." And I would think, *Man, what a cool boss!* But then at the end of the day, that same cool boss would add, "Yeah . . . you're not getting paid." My cool boss was also a confusing boss.

Cocooned in the silent emptiness of my apartment, I realized that, while I was good at speaking, there were about seven other things—either skills I hadn't mastered or tasks I tended to put off—that stood directly between me and getting paid to speak. They included negotiating, marketing, reading contracts, paying taxes, and managing my time. The last was the toughest to deal with, given that it involved the extremely challenging task of *not* watching multiple movies on a Wednesday. Speaking trips were magical, reinvigorating experiences, but sometimes months would pass between them.

Mostly, I would sit in my apartment alone, trying to update my website and build my email list, while frequently losing my mind in front of my dog. "Jake, I don't know what I'm doing wrong here." Jake would wag his tail. "I don't know what that means," I would protest. He'd look at me in a way that made mind-reading easy. *It's very simple. It means take me for a walk.*

But when we returned from that walk, things got complicated all over again. I was living my version of what author Seth Godin calls "the Dip."[24] The term refers to the period of struggle and difficulty that occurs between starting a business and making a success of it. Imagine you set off to climb to a mountaintop, and not long into your hike, you are surprised to discover that you must go down into a valley to reach the base

CHAPTER 30: BREAKTHROUGHS AT THE BOTTOM

before you start your ascent. You're going lower, not higher, which you definitely hadn't anticipated.

There is no way to know how long this part will last. Perseverance may lead to success, but quitting almost certainly won't, at least in that business. Since paid speaking was how I planned to support myself financially, the stakes were high. Thanks to my desperate Google searches on the subject, I began receiving targeted social media ads from business coaches. One of them seemed pretty good, and I ignored my hesitations and paid him $5,000 to help me for the next year. He turned out to be exactly the wrong coach for me. He was a confident, handsome guy from California with great hair who didn't want to talk about emotions. A little too cool for my comfort.

We spoke only once a month, and he opened each call by asking if I'd completed the aggressive cold-calling and email-marketing goals he'd set for me. I knew if I said no, he'd end the call and I wouldn't get my money back. I really wanted to say no, though. In fact, what I wanted to say, but couldn't seem to, was "Of course, I didn't! How am I supposed to market myself when I don't believe in myself? I'm pretty sure Reebok's marketing team can't call in sick with the excuse 'We're just not feeling confident today.' But apparently, I have no problem doing that. I know the stakes are high! I also know I can't do this part of my job!"

What I did say was, "Yes, I made the calls." It was a fib—a convenient cover story. Okay, no, it wasn't. It was a ridiculous lie. As soon as I hung up, I felt worse. The next call, I did it again. By the third call with this coach, I was painfully aware that I was paying an obscene amount of money to lie to a stranger about smart business actions I wasn't taking. *Wow, I am in the Dip.*

In an effort to get out of my head and focus on my business, I started seeing a new therapist. And went 0 for 2. He was no Sam, to say the least. In fact, he turned out to be exactly the wrong therapist for me. When I confessed to him that making great money (which, on the occasions that I actually got speaking engagements, was the case) had somehow *increased* my stress around my finances and my self-worth, he just shrugged and said, "It doesn't matter if you have seven dollars or seven million dollars. If you can't accept that you are worthy as you are, then no amount of money is going to change that."

Huh? I thought. *Technically, you're right, but are you at all familiar with America? The message that I'm only as worthy as my net worth is kind of everywhere.* I nodded, as if what he'd said was in any way helpful.

Listening to him dispassionately dump "the Answers" in my direction felt strange. His advice was correct without being the least bit useful. During our exchanges, I would frequently feel stupid. Once again, I found myself telling lies and making payments to an unhelpful guide. I would nod and tell him that I got it, even though I didn't, and the pretending made me feel more alone than ever. *Ugh, I am still in the Dip.*

At this point, my negative moods were dominating the calendar. Literally. I took out a calendar and started putting frowny faces on the weeks, then months, during which I had been depressed and anxious more often than not. When I realized I had been more sad than happy for *nine* out of the last twelve months, it became clear: *This is not working.*

Then, a minor miracle. One day, I stumbled upon an excellent life coach. Michael taught me about mindfulness, thought

CHAPTER 30: BREAKTHROUGHS AT THE BOTTOM

work, and the practice of gratitude. He was unlike my other experts. He listened. He asked questions. He spoke kindly. Most noticeably, he trusted me to find the answers for myself.

Our conversations helped me learn an essential idea—that my thoughts are just thoughts, not truths. He reminded me that no matter what self-critical thought I had, I had every right to *respond* to it. This allowed me to defend myself against my internal enemies.

I was struck by how familiar this idea sounded, then remembered I had learned it already—during my work, years earlier, with Sam. So much of this journey seemed to be learning valuable ideas, then forgetting them, then learning them again. (And again).

At first I judged myself: *I already learned this and forgot it? Now I'm re-learning it all over again?* But then I realized that lessons about mental health aren't things I could learn once and check off a list. They were truths I had to slowly integrate over time. So what if I needed to hear something eleven times before it sank in? Each encounter was progress. With each one, I was closer than I'd been before.

I noticed that I was starting to get a bit better—more stable and confident. At least enough that I could start marketing myself again, which gradually led to an increase in work. Slowly, ever so slowly, I started climbing out of the Dip.

• • •

Inspired by my excellent coach (and perhaps equally inspired by my not-so-great one), I decided to pursue my own coaching certification. As I worked my way through a six-month

Executive Coaching program, I was pleasantly surprised to find that the exercises and reflections intended to help my clients in the future were also helping me in the present.

One of my key *aha!* moments occurred when I learned that, while many clients have a "surface agenda" (something tangible they want or a milestone they want to reach), they often also have a "deeper agenda" (something they're not even aware they truly need).

In considering my own case, I realized why the concept of a "deeper agenda" was a revelation. My wrong coach and my wrong therapist hadn't asked me nearly enough questions. They had jumped too quickly into telling me how to achieve my surface agendas without providing any insight into how I might discover what was underneath them.

I'd had a lot of surface agendas in my life: to fit in at school, to have strong faith, to be liked and admired in college, to lose my virginity, to pursue stand-up comedy, to run a business, to meet women, to make good money, to endure my most intense periods of depression and anxiety.

In every single one of these quests, even when I achieved my goal, I still felt unfulfilled on some level. So, if these were my surface agendas, what were my deeper agendas? How could I even begin to figure that out? One key exercise that helped with this was identifying my "Inner Critic."

The Inner Critic is a voice we hear only in our minds. I learned it was important to recognize my Inner Critic's voice, figure out where it came from, and learn to counter its criticisms. Mine turned out to be, like other people's, overly harsh and always on the job. To identify when mine first began, I reflected back to my childhood. As a kid, at some point after my parents split up,

CHAPTER 30: BREAKTHROUGHS AT THE BOTTOM

I had started blaming myself for everything bad or painful that happened. I'd invented my own Inner Critic.

Over time, I'd strengthened him to the point where the voice I often heard, in my darkest moments, was one of contempt. I grabbed a pen and wrote down some of his most repeated catchphrases about me. "You're a worthless idiot . . . You screw everything up . . . I f***ing hate you." Seeing these things on paper was upsetting, and then saying them out loud was even more so, but doing this made it clear to me how unfair and downright toxic these statements were.

While doing this difficult inner work, I realized something. During the painful months I spent in the Dip, I hadn't actually been going lower. I had been going *deeper*—deeper than I wanted to go. Deep enough to figure out what I was like when I was scared, desperate, and truly vulnerable.

Down there, at what felt like the bottom, my Inner Critic would show up and take center stage. He had years of practice tearing me down, and his aim was devastatingly accurate because he knew exactly what would hurt me the most. In a sinister display of brilliance, he would phrase his hurtful comments in the first person, making it sound like they were coming from me: "*I'm* a worthless idiot . . . *I* screw everything up . . . *I* hate *myself.*"

I knew instantly that no one deserves to be spoken to that way. My Inner Critic wasn't helping me—he was sabotaging me, interrupting any good thing in order to tear me down. Once again, I recognized him for what he was: my inner heckler. The Heckler in my Head, who I'd thought had moved on to bother someone else, was very much still with me. He had shapeshifted into a different form, and it had taken me a long time to recognize him again, because he'd started using different phrases and capitalizing on new experiences to hurl abuse at me.

This recognition helped me recall another defensive weapon I had forgotten about. From doing stand-up comedy, I had learned how to handle a heckler. It wasn't easy, but it was effective: Shut them down, not with contempt but by being smarter than they are.

This was my Deeper Agenda. Whenever I found myself at what felt like the bottom, I needed to challenge myself to think of one thing I could do to be kind to myself. And gradually, that's what I learned to do. This practice of being kind to myself, fragile at first but becoming stronger through repetition, started to give me a new sense of control. I was finally using my creativity as a weapon against my depression instead of against myself.

From there, every better decision I made was an act of kindness and a small, helpful win. Believe me, these wins were *small*: drinking water, exercising for five minutes, calling a friend, taking medication, replying to an email, going for a walk, accepting a compliment . . . These were all forms of kindness I could give to myself, and they helped me experience more of the self-acceptance I really needed.

It was when I was at my lowest and most vulnerable that I learned how to accept myself.

• • •

One of my most common reactions to depressive episodes was to withdraw from others. The voice in my mind would encourage this by saying, "No one wants to see me like this. I should stay away from people, otherwise they'll think I'm weird, a burden, exhausting to be around." It felt safer to stay home and stop returning texts and calls.

As comedian Gary Gulman says so perfectly in his HBO special *The Great Depresh*, "If you are suffering from a mental illness, I promise you, you are not alone. Wait, you are alone. But only because you didn't leave the house today."[25]

Gary is right. (He's more than right—he's also a hero of mine.) Even though those real-world interactions with people felt uncomfortable, they actually helped, while staying home made me feel cut off from the world. But then I got another nudge in the form of the movie *I Love You, Man* (once again, a comedy that somehow felt more like a tragic documentary about my life). There's a moment in the movie when Paul Rudd's character realizes he doesn't have any male friends. Not even one. I thought, *Uh oh. That's me.*

I wasn't the only one in this situation—loneliness among American adults has surged over the past several decades, including a rise in outright friendlessness, with as many as 15% of men reporting in 2021 that they had no close friends. This number is five times higher than it was in 1990.[26]

I'd always wanted solid male friendships but found it difficult to create them, because I didn't enjoy the kind where we watched sports without making eye contact and spoke only about safe, external, non-emotional topics. I wanted male friends I could be genuine with. So, I made it a goal to reverse my tendency to isolate and, instead, to put myself out there at more social events. I eventually met Chris.

Chris and I quickly found we could have genuine conversations that covered not only our circumstances and hobbies but also our emotions, insecurities, and goals for our lives. This became the template for what I was looking for, and I found it again when I met Joe, a fellow speaker who personally understood both the cool and the isolating aspects of our shared profession and was totally real about both. And then I met Steve at a storytelling event. In a surprise twist, Steve was a pastor, albeit one who didn't shy away from curse words.

Developing these friendships was helpful, but I knew I needed something else, too. A loss I couldn't deny after I stopped attending church was how good it had been at creating community: weekly gatherings, check-ins, shared meals. I didn't miss the doctrine, but I missed *that*. In my effort to recreate that kind of community, I tried coworking spaces, book clubs, and language groups. And one day, I surprised myself. I visited Steve's church.

Walking in, I felt a mix of nostalgia and discomfort, and I was surprised by how powerful this sensation was. I was also optimistic for one very specific reason: when I'd looked up the driving directions on Google Maps, I saw this church had a series of *one-star reviews* from people who were absolutely furious that the church accepted gay people and had women pastors. That was all the encouragement I needed. As a bonus, I could be sure that the people who left those reviews would not be there.

Seeing Steve's church welcome people excluded from my old churches was meaningful. I found out that, a few years earlier, this church had publicly affirmed the LGBTQIA+ community and lost nearly *half* its congregation. For the same reason, it earned my respect, and I kept attending.

It turned out to be good medicine for me. There would, however, prove to be one downside. I would routinely look around and wonder, *Do they not know Dakota Joe is in their midst? Does no one want their Bible signed?*

Gradually, I picked up a few more close friends, and that was plenty. I had found the meaningful relationships I needed. I nurtured them by focusing on being a good friend. I modeled vulnerability and encouraged it in return. I sat with my new friends' tough emotions. I told them I was glad I knew them, that they were easy to root for. I held space for them, just as many others in my past had held space for me.

The key to maintaining these friendships was so simple, I couldn't believe I'd never thought of it before. At the end of each hangout or call, we'd schedule the next one. This simple ritual eliminated the lag of "Let's catch up again sometime" and became a moment of mutual appreciation and commitment. It was as if we were saying, "I want us to hang out again because you matter to me."

Through it all, I still had periods of depression. But now, I had phone numbers. When I was low on energy, tongue-tied, and feeling awkward, I had people who liked me anyway. Now, when I heard statistics on male loneliness, I knew they no longer applied to me, or to my friends either. We were no longer alone.

• • •

Over time, these breakthroughs of inner kindness and solid friendships helped me do something I had been attempting unsuccessfully for a long time: they helped me raise the *height* of my lowest points. Now *that* is an honest, "Depressed Motivational Speaker" message if I've ever given one! It's not about dodging low points completely, but by, in small but real ways, making those low points higher.

In my experience, finding more happiness has little to do with unicorns and rainbows and platitudes. It certainly isn't about being amped-up or grinning ear-to-ear every single day. I believe a key to more consistent happiness is to build a higher, stronger floor so that *when* you fall, it prevents you from crashing through to where you feel even lower. Happiness is raising the height of your lows. You can't completely eliminate the Dip, but you can at least fill it in a bit.

CHAPTER 31
DIAGNOSED, AT LAST

The mental health diagnosis that would finally explain my entire adult life came with a shocking twist: I *wasn't* a person with anxiety and depression. Or at least, not technically.

For years, depression had been a cloudy lens, a gray veil that distorted everything and drained the color from life. Now, for the first time, that veil was lifting. But hope felt fragile, and I didn't want to lose it.

I thought to myself, *I'm so close. This is my life I'm talking about. After all the things I've tried that haven't helped, I finally feel like I'm on the right track—and I need to keep asking questions.* It wasn't just about surviving anymore. I felt momentum building as I worked toward well-being, and I sensed there was more at stake than just getting through each day. I wanted to be ready for the next chapter of my life, whatever it might bring.

I was diagnosed with Major Depressive Disorder in my late 20s, and I received a diagnosis of Generalized Anxiety Disorder not long after that. Ever since then, I had been taking antidepressants daily, anxiety medication when needed, and just sort of surviving. There had been some good stretches of happiness in there, but if something major and unexpected happened, or my good habits slipped for just a few days in a row, I would fall back into what felt like a state of numb defeat. This continuous precariousness made me wonder, *Is this mental wellness? Is this as good as I can hope for?*

I had no way of knowing that the cycle of highs and lows, accompanied by a distorted self-image and deep insecurity, was not simply the result of concurrent depression and anxiety. I was about to figure out the actual conditions that were driving them.

During a conversation with one of my sisters, Leigh, in which she leaned heavily on both her degree in Child Psychology and her deep knowledge of me, she suggested that I might have OCD (Obsessive Compulsive Disorder). In listening to her describe it, I became curious about whether this condition might be affecting me. I scheduled a doctor visit, and one completed screening questionnaire later, it was confirmed as my new diagnosis.

OCD is the fourth most common mental health disorder. Still, most people who experience it wait years to get help. For those like me, this is because they don't even know they have it. In his memoir, *The Man Who Couldn't Stop: OCD and the True Story of a Life Lost in Thought*, psychologist David Adam, who was diagnosed with OCD himself, explains some key reasons OCD can be missed as a diagnosis.

> "Mental health professionals refer to OCD as a secret disease and a silent epidemic. The number of people who report obsessions and compulsions to doctors is

CHAPTER 31: DIAGNOSED, AT LAST

routinely much lower than the studies of their prevalence would suggest. A lot of people with OCD choose to suffer in silence. Their thoughts are their dirty little secret. They believe they are freaks, and their silence has allowed compulsive actions to come to define their condition."[27]

I was deeply embarrassed by my overanxious mind, but I didn't even know it was OCD. For me, movies and TV had effectively linked OCD to things such as repetitive tapping and extreme tidiness. OCD does not always include the performance of rituals—it can be marked by rumination and worst-case scenario thinking and manifest as subtle *mental* compulsions rather than physical ones.

Adam points out how the act of seeking reassurance from others prevents reassurance seekers from learning to manage their own uncertainty and creates a vicious cycle. In his words, "One of the many cruel ironies of OCD is that the compulsions—the solutions that obsessed people reach for—make the situation worse . . ." Later, he notes, "An intrusive thought silenced with a compulsion comes back. It comes back hard."

Another reason OCD is missed as a diagnosis is that it can show up in odd behaviors and patterns that can be hard to explain, and it can, in specific ways, simply look like anxiety and depression.

I felt seen when Adam explained the severity of the disorder by saying, "OCD dissolves perspective. It magnifies small risks, warps probabilities, and takes statistical chance as prediction, rather than as a sign of how unlikely things are."

In light of this information, some of the issues that complicated my mental health challenges and impacted my closest relationships, including my relationship with Lindsey, started to make sense. For starters, a key treatment for OCD is different from those used for an anxiety disorder. It's called Exposure and Response Prevention (ERP) therapy. In this type of therapy, the patient is gradually exposed to situations designed to trigger their obsessions in a safe environment, while learning how to resist responding with compulsions. (I can accurately report that this is exactly as not-fun as it sounds.)

I found a therapist, Jayda, who was trained in ERP therapy. When I logged on for my first session, I thought, *Hmm . . . my first therapist was several years older than me. Now my therapist is several years younger. A decade of therapy, illustrated.* During our first session, Jayda and I dissected a recent meltdown I'd had as our focal example of my compulsions related to self-doubt and insecurity.

The previous day, I had been writing a work proposal when I became flooded by a panic-inducing thought. *If I don't phrase this proposal perfectly, I won't get hired. And then I'll run out of money and lose my house, and my life will fall apart. And my dogs will lose respect for me.*

(Okay, that last part isn't true. My dogs think I'm CEO material.)

As I began to spiral, I had no choice but to drag my poor partner into the situation. I asked Lindsey to review my proposal, and then I kept asking her until I'd had her consider and approve of every word, phrase, and sentence I used. She tried to be patient, but the more I sought her reassurance, the more helpless I felt. I was horribly embarrassed to put her in this position, but I felt unable to move forward on my own. I was even more embarrassed when, after Lindsey finally helped me finish it and stepped away, I continued to worry it wasn't good enough and never actually clicked Send.

Jayda asked me to picture this stressful scene, focus on what I feared would go wrong, and let those ideas flood through me. "Don't fight it," she said. "Just sit with it." I thought, *I hate this with a passion. This feels awful.* But I did as she instructed, and I focused on the thoughts that had upset me. My chest tightened, my palms got clammy, and my heart pounded. I felt cornered. The feeling was almost physically painful, but I kept it at the front of my mind until I was nearly overwhelmed by the intensity of my discomfort. I sat with it and stayed in the discomfort. Gradually, the fear started to lose its intensity. My body began to relax, and my brain became calmer.

I relayed this to Jayda, and she said, "Now don't force it, but pay attention and wait for your next thought about the situation to arrive."

I waited for what felt like an eternity (probably ten seconds) before a thought arrived. It was, *Sure, your proposal might not be perfect. And you might lose out on the opportunity because of it. But nobody can know if a proposal will be successful until they send it and find out. So just submit it.*

It felt as though this thought came from my real self—a place of resourcefulness—rather than from my panic. (This is how it *felt* anyway—I'm not an expert in brain science.) As I recognized the simple truth in these words, I also noticed that my brain had gotten bored because I hadn't taken the bait. I felt calm and composed, and as soon as the session ended, I submitted the proposal.

It occurred to me how similar this technique was to the gentle "Okay" that I had first learned to offer myself whenever I started to spiral into anxiety. This was like that, but with a strong connection to the body as well. I had already been learning a form of it, and now I was getting even better at it. When an anxiety-inducing thought came to my brain, I wouldn't try to block it, solve it, debate it, or defend myself against it. I would simply sit with it instead.

We worked on numerous other examples, and they all played out in similar ways. Uneasiness → panic → a decision to coexist with the panic → gradual calm → productive action.

The more I accepted that my reassurance could, and should, come from myself, the more I developed the ability to distinguish between wanting other people's support or their perspective (healthy) and wanting their permission or reassurance (unhealthy). Over time, I improved at providing my own reassurance, and it had profound benefits on my relationship with Lindsey, on running my business, and on my mental health. Ultimately, learning to give myself permission in life freed me from needing to get it from someone else.

With a diagnosis of OCD and a strong plan for how to manage my version of it, I was now creating confidence rather than outsourcing it. This didn't happen because I stood on a stage and got strangers to clap for me. It wasn't because I won awards or achieved milestones. It occurred because of the work I did to achieve quieter and longer-sought inner victories.

. . .

After this progress, Jayda brought to my attention that there is a second condition that affects people with OCD so often that it is considered a co-morbidity: ADHD (Attention Deficit

CHAPTER 31: DIAGNOSED, AT LAST

Hyperactivity Disorder). This neurodevelopmental disorder is characterized by difficulty paying attention, excessive activity, and impulsive behaviors. While it can affect people of all ages, it's most commonly diagnosed in children.

As a child, I had never been able to sit still and was constantly talking in class. I spent a great deal of time either in detention or with my desk moved away from the other kids, if only to get me to stop talking for a few blessed minutes. (I must have been insufferable.) An actual quote from my third-grade report card reads, "Colin and I have discussed his talkativeness, which continues to be a problem." My mom was my fervent ally, but she didn't have mental health training. She and I believed my hyperactivity was caused by all the asthma medication I was on. It may have been, in part. But it was also because I had undiagnosed ADHD.

This second diagnosis explained my recent problems in working with business coaches. I was a neurodivergent person seeking and getting neurotypical advice. My coaches always said, "Pick one niche, audience, and topic, and market that every day until you make six figures." My response to such advice was to feel like shit, because I knew I couldn't do it. I'd try for a few weeks, then grow bored and want to start something else and then something else, until the combined weight of all my interests created so much stress that I started fantasizing about quitting altogether.

Research shows that people with ADHD have a higher-than-average need for dopamine, a "feel good" brain chemical that is triggered by novelty and creative experimentation rather than by doing the smart, sensible thing. Because I'd had no way of knowing that my brain was different, I had always judged myself for not following the "right advice." Now I realized that those coaches had been giving the right advice to the wrong person.

Jessica McCabe is a YouTuber and author who is diagnosed with ADHD. In her book *How to ADHD,* she offers this glimpse into what neurodivergent people's experience can be like when they attempt to stick with the plans they make. "For most of my life, my relationship with schedules has looked like this: Set up a schedule. Fail to follow the schedule. Repeat steps 1 and 2."

At another point in her book, McCabe explains the inner tension that results in a failure to follow traditional advice:

> Those of us with ADHD experience far more failure, criticism, and rejection than our neurotypical peers. When we do a "simple" task—say, making a phone call—we're not just dealing with that task. We're also dealing with an emotional barrier that has been built from past failures. ADHD coach Brendan Mahan calls this barrier the "Wall of Awful." The more we've struggled with a task in the past, the higher we build that wall. So, we don't just need motivation to complete the task; we need motivation to climb the emotional wall in front of it.[28]

As a business owner, I needed to establish and follow a daily structure. But the effort required to improve my focus (and resist the tendency to start new projects instead of finishing old ones) made progress nearly impossible.

I started approaching my business through an ADHD-informed lens, and found I could create forward momentum by

CHAPTER 31: DIAGNOSED, AT LAST

using a concept called "well-designed actions" that I'd learned in the coaching course I took. Instead of setting a vague goal, such as "Do more marketing," I would set a specific and measurable one, such as "This Wednesday morning, between 10 a.m. and 11 a.m., at my coworking space (rather than my house, which is full of tempting distractions), I'm going to make two phone calls and send two emails."

That very Wednesday, I sat down at the coworking space with my laptop open and my phone beside me. I stared at it for five minutes, tempted to reorganize my desktop, redesign my website, or learn how to play piano instead. My stomach knotted, and my brain screamed for me to do *anything else*. Finally, I picked up the phone and dialed the first number. By the time I finished, my heart was pounding, but I had done it. The next call felt easier, as did the one after that.

Essentially, I learned how to create structure by breaking it down into its components. This didn't cure my dopamine cravings or eliminate focus issues, but it greatly increased my overall productivity. *[Note from the future: It also comes in handy should one want to write a book.]*

• • •

These weren't quick fixes, but together, the lessons from ERP therapy for OCD and the structured actions I had learned to manage ADHD began to build something I had rarely experienced before: real momentum toward mental wellness. It wasn't just that I was more productive or calmer or able to focus. It was that these tools were working in concert, creating a foundation I could rely on.

As I combined my growing ability to focus and create structure with the other practices I had learned, I discovered I had been in good spirits for more days in a row than I had been in a long, long time.

I kept up these good habits, and that streak of days became six months. Six months of mostly happy days. Then, a year! I had achieved a year of mental wellness. For the first time in my life, I was able to talk about anxiety and depression in the past tense. I knew I would always have these mental health conditions. But I also knew how to thrive despite them.

I had become more "successful at depression" than ever before. I knew what to do whenever my mind started to spin out, making isolation begin to seem appealing. I could respond in a helpful way rather than by intensifying the problem. As I grew more adept at being kind to myself through good habits, mental health diligence, and leaning on community, I developed the capacity for greater productivity, motivation, joy, creativity, and clarity than I could ever have expected.

The gray veil of depression was gone, and more often than not, it remained that way. This progress was just in time, too. Because I would soon experience a day in my life I wanted to remember, in total clarity, for as long as possible. That day would be momentous for two reasons.

First, it would be only the second time in my life that I would see my mother and father in the same physical space.

Second, it would be my wedding day. Wait, let me rephrase. Our wedding day. Lindsey would be there, too.

CHAPTER 32
A PHOTO OF US

One weekend, Lindsey and I were in the kitchen of our apartment making breakfast. It was a common experience for us—making jokes, feeling entirely at ease around each other, and growing closer. I suddenly felt my heart swell as I thought, *Not only is she my person, I'm her person, too.* Without even planning to, I took a knee in the middle of our kitchen and proposed to her.

For a second, I became concerned about how non-creative my proposal was. I released zero doves. I hadn't hidden a ring inside a waffle. I didn't even make sure it was being livestreamed on all social media platforms. I just did what was in my heart, and I was overjoyed when she said, "Yes."

Two months later, Lindsey and I went to Edinburgh, Scotland. I was excited to show her the place I had lived after college, and show off my hard-earned proficiency at understanding "Scottish." We walked up Arthur's Seat, the ancient volcanic hill overlooking the entire city, now covered with lush green grass. I took in the view. The sky was vividly blue, and it was a perfect day. I looked back at Lindsey, and she was down on one knee, proposing to me.

Damn. She totally won at proposing. (I also said yes.)

When we returned, we set a date and started inviting people to our wedding. That's when it hit me. We were inviting my mom and my dad to be in the same room with each other—and with me—on one of the most important days of our relationship.

At 35 years old, I had only one memory of my parents ever being together in the same physical space. It was at my high school graduation, and it was remarkably brief and predictably tense. They exchanged terse hellos from a noticeable distance. They were two ships in the night. Each ship then hosted its own graduation dinner for me, continuing my theme of two separate celebrations for special occasions. Overall, the experience was uncomfortable for me and, almost certainly, for them, too.

As we got closer to the wedding date, I began to feel a growing sense of dread. Who was going to say something that could never be unsaid? Who was going to throw a glass of wine in whose face? I was excited to be getting married, but I was increasingly anxious about how this parental reunion would go.

The day of the wedding, I met my dad and stepmother in the room they had booked on the top floor of the venue—an elegant and historic bed-and-breakfast with a classic-looking reception area just large enough for a small wedding.

My dad walked down the stairs with me to the room where I was going to get married. Three floors. We walked in silence, but also in solidarity.

CHAPTER 32: A PHOTO OF US

When we entered the room, I watched as my mom saw my dad, and he saw her. My heart stopped for a second as they walked toward each other and . . . immediately started talking and laughing. They seemed to be, to borrow one of my mom's favorite phrases, getting along famously. I, on the other hand, felt a little bit like my head was going to fall off. I mean, what was even happening right now? It was such an unexpected, emotional moment.

Very soon, I had another reason to be emotional—watching Lindsey as she walked toward me. She was the most beautiful sight imaginable, and I knew I would never forget her loving expression in this moment.

The officiant was our close friend John, who was a yoga instructor. As we stood facing him, we both took note that he was wearing a shirt tucked into black jeans and a bolo tie—the tuxedo of yoga instructors. It was only his second wedding, but it was our first, and in our opinion, he really nailed it. After all, we did end up married.

During the reception that followed, my parents each gave a toast. My mom's speech, which resembled an affectionate comedy roast, absolutely killed. She had constructed it around five words that described me, following the letters of my name. I already knew how it would begin. "The 'C' stands for 'Colly,'" she said, sharing my dreaded childhood nickname with everybody, to uproarious laughter. Then this: "The 'O' stands for 'Oily,'" after which she recounted the time when I was nine or ten years old and came out of the bathroom, announcing, "Look, Mom, I put hair gel in my hair!" Only I hadn't done that—I'd put baby oil in my hair. She was quick to prevent me from sitting down anywhere and ruining any couch cushions.

It looked like I was wearing the Soul-Glo hair product from the movie *Coming to America*.

Then my dad stood up, and after a few humorous comments of his own, he turned to look at my stepfather with an emotional expression on his face. "I want to say, 'Thank you' to you, Phil. I've never thanked you before, and I should have. Thank you for raising Colin." And then the two men, who had hardly ever communicated with each other, hugged. There wasn't a dry eye in the house.

After the speeches were over, my mom came up to me. She said, "I'm so proud of you. And I just wanted to tell you that I reached out to your dad recently. I asked him to forgive me for my role in our relationship not working out."

This was classic Jackie—honest, humble to a fault, and vulnerable in the strongest possible way. She embodied what it meant to believe in the power of forgiveness.

That's when my dad approached us. He put his arms around both me and my mom, and we hugged. Then he looked at me for a moment and said, "We're good."

This was classic Tim—impressively succinct and endlessly ambiguous. *Two words? That's it?* But my dad wasn't done. He gestured to the wedding photographer, who came over and took our photo. One of hundreds of photos she took that day, except that photo was my family photo.

My dad was smiling. My mom was smiling. I was on the verge of crying. I ruined my picture!

I like to think that my dad was smiling because, just like in the movies he loved, this moment represented how, sometimes, things finally come together in a killer ending. My mom was smiling because, just like in the faith that meant so much

CHAPTER 32: A PHOTO OF US

to her, this moment was all about second chances and new beginnings. I was crying because, well, I do that sometimes, especially when it's a moment I had hoped for my entire life.

Lindsey joined our embrace, and then the other wedding guests followed suit and surrounded us in a full wedding party group hug! (This is part of my argument for having a small wedding.) It made the moment even closer to perfection than it already was.

Suddenly, I recalled the story I had told myself as a child: *My mom is on the East Coast with her family, and she is enough. My dad is on the West Coast with his family, and he is enough. I'm somewhere in the middle, and I'm just not enough.* That story had prevented me from realizing that my family had never stopped existing. Maybe they didn't look like other families, but they had turned into two groups of people who loved me.

In that moment, I knew that I was enough.

* * *

In the days that followed, I frequently pulled up that family photo. In it, I saw my parents—two of the people I cared about most—in a new way. On one of the most important days of my life, my father and my mother carried themselves with poise and generosity. They showed up for me. That day, their actions said, "We're proud of the man you've become. We've always been proud of you. We've always been a family—*your* family."

Right when I needed them the most, my very own unreliable narrators could not have been more reliable. I was proud of them. I could also tell that I was becoming a more reliable narrator, too.

As a kid, I had assigned myself a lot of hurtful labels, and they contributed to my feeling passive and powerless. X-factor. Outsider. Weird kid. Unaccompanied. Not holy enough. Kid from a broken home. Weak lungs. Sad for no reason. As an adult, I'd simply kept doing it. Coward. Virgin. Failed writer. Religious backslider. Depressed speaker. Unlovable partner.

But of all of them, the only label that really mattered was Unreliable Narrator.

My stories had grown in power until I lost track of the fact that I had created them in the first place. Uncontested, they became the monsters in my mind, the hecklers in my head, the bullies in my brain. The call had been coming from inside the house the whole time. I just didn't know it.

Now I do. I've come to believe that few things are as powerful as the stories we tell ourselves, because the stories we tell ourselves are the stories we live out. But we can change the hurtful, limiting stories we tell ourselves, and whenever possible, we should.

For a long time, I had a secret sentence: *If you really knew me, you'd reject me.* That sentence didn't match reality. In key moments, when I revealed my most vulnerable, authentic self, I wasn't rejected. I was accepted. Many people had shown up for me. Together, we proved my secret sentence wasn't true. With their help, I had written a more accurate sentence, one that no longer needed to be hidden at all: "When you really know me, you'll *relate* to me."

CHAPTER 33
AUTHORLAND

The cover's colors were richer than they were on my screen, and from its pages rose the unmistakable scent of paper and ink. It felt real in a way no PDF ever could. I was standing by my mailbox and holding the first-ever copy of my book, *A Comedic Guide to Money*, and the moment was even better than I'd hoped it would be.

I'd just achieved my lifelong dream of being a published author.

I thought back over the experience of writing it, and what I needed to do next became crystal clear. I vowed, with absolute conviction, "I will *never* write another book *ever, ever, ever again.*"

I had started writing it a few years into my speaking career, with the hopes of encapsulating what I had learned about personal finance from traveling the country and speaking to thousands of people about money. I hoped the book could change how people thought about and managed money, opening up new possibilities in their lives. I also knew that by publishing this book, I'd have finally arrived at the magical place I'd dreamed of—a place I called "Authorland."

Authorland was an exclusive club and a mythical realm. Those fortunate enough to get there sold countless books and earned lots of money. Their work was quoted during casual conversations. They regularly hosted live book readings for hushed, sometimes even worshipful, audiences.

Of course, once I arrived in Authorland, there would be many requests for interviews, during which I would be asked, "So tell us, what's the secret to writing a book?" As my writing project progressed, I realized that I had an answer. I would say, "Writing a book is like rowing a cruise ship by yourself. *Technically,* it is possible. But it's the hardest thing in the world to get started, and it feels amazing each time you give up. And everyone around you is having a better time than you are."

During the first two years, there were lots of times I opted to feel amazing. Writing a book was too big a challenge, while taking days off was easy. Then I stumbled upon some helpful advice from an unlikely source.

Don Shula, one of the most successful coaches in NFL history, once said, "It's the *start* that stops most people." He had verifiably excellent insight into what it takes to get motivated, and it was the advice I needed. The very next morning, I decided to start (again), and this time, never stop. No matter what. The next morning, and every morning after that, I started the day by writing for a minimum of thirty minutes. I could write for more if I wanted to, but never less. And I couldn't skip a day. Protecting the streak became its own motivation.

This worked. I found myself getting into a rhythm. Days

CHAPTER 33: AUTHORLAND

started adding up, and so did my page count. I was on my way. And then, I became obsessed. It was all I thought about. I worked at my job all day, wrote for hours in the evening, and started leaving bed around 2 a.m. to write until dawn. Rinse and repeat.

I wasn't setting an alarm. I woke up because I was constantly shaping and reshaping sentences in my head. I was totally consumed by the drive to finish what I'd started. In a sense, this was the epitome of hustle culture. #RiseandGrind and #WorkWhileYourCompetitionSleeps and #SomethingaboutLions. But I had never been a fan of hustle culture. And to be honest, some other hashtags needed to be included: #ImFreakingOutMyPartner and #ImFreakingMyselfOutToo because #ImLosingALotOfWeight.

One day Lindsey informed me, as politely as she could, that I was starting to look like a skeleton.

A sexy skeleton? I wondered hopefully. Not sure what else to do, I tried to eat more and sleep a bit more, and I kept writing.

When I'd finished the complete draft, my editor informed me I had written something like a hundred pages more than I had needed to. I may have gotten a little carried away. So, the work continued. Cutting so much content took several more months, but eventually, the day arrived. After four quick, breezy, totally effortless years, my book was published. I had reached Authorland.

It started off being every bit as good as I had imagined. When the mail truck delivered that first printed copy (and I tore open the packaging and smelled the book like a lunatic), I stood there beaming. This was a moment I had dreamed of my whole life.

After the quick vow to never ever write a book again, I called out elatedly to the mail carrier as he headed back to his truck, "Hey! I just wrote this book!"

He turned back to me, smiled, and said with a surprising amount of thoughtfulness, "Wow, man. Good for you!" It was so genuine I briefly wondered if we should hug, but he was already driving away.

At my first speaking event as an author, I was asked to stay and sign copies of my book. The morning of the speech, I practiced my signature on every single page of the hotel room notepad, signing it about fifty times, so I could convincingly appear to have done this before. Writing brief personal messages in each purchased book felt wonderful.

A few months later, the momentum began to dwindle. Sales dropped off, and reality set in. I faced a grim realization: I wrote a book, and no one cared. Or, more accurately, no one knew. Unless I told them. I marketed it for a while, but then I got discouraged and felt myself fall, once more, into a depression.

A troubling thought plagued me. I'd finally gotten "there" only to discover there was no "there." There was no magical place where all my problems were solved and my life felt complete. Authorland hadn't turned out to be as good as I'd hoped. Or maybe *I* hadn't turned out to be as good as I'd hoped. I was the same, only now with a book.

This time, I was conscious of my oncoming depression, and I responded strategically with the better habits I had learned. They weren't helping. Despite my best efforts, the depression took hold of me, and it was a powerful one. I slept constantly, but I never felt revived. It felt like the first real test on the other side of my breakthroughs, and I was failing it.

CHAPTER 33: AUTHORLAND

I exiled myself to the spare bedroom and watched TV shows, trying to think as little as possible about anything real. Lindsey was now dealing with something very different from a non-sleeping partner—one who couldn't get out of bed.

I was distant from her and intensely disappointed in myself. I was still trapped inside that person who sometimes managed his depression and, at other times, was managed *by* it. I had been so sure I'd finally figured things out. Yet, somehow, I was back where I started.

• • •

It was this exact thought that I was "back where I started" that triggered a memory from my screenwriting class back in film school. I remembered that my teacher, Kris, loved to wax poetic about an idea he called "Page 90."

In a feature-length screenplay, page number 90 roughly corresponds to a key moment in the story that happens late in the movie. It's when the main character suffers a crushing setback and is left feeling further from their goal than ever before. Suddenly, everything seems hopeless. This part is very sad, and it's probably also raining.

Kris pointed out that Page 90 isn't the end of the movie. Instead, it's one of the most pivotal beats in the story's arc, because this moment of hitting a metaphorical wall is the moment that causes the protagonist to grow the most. It also, most often, occurs just *before* the climax. The character has to experience this moment in order to actually succeed. When viewed this way, a low point is not merely an interminable slog. It's a testing ground and the ideal setting for an unexpected revelation.

I looked around me and thought, *Man, I really hope this is my Page 90 scene.* Visually, my surroundings were spot on. I was lying in bed in a darkened room, around noon, doomscrolling through social media, comparing myself to friends and peers whose lives seemed absolutely incredible by comparison. It was definitely metaphorically raining.

That's when I saw a post from a friend from back in high school, and what he wrote took me by complete surprise:

> Most of you are aware that I've been dealing with depression for much of my adult life. I just found out that I'm not actually depressed in the clinical sense. Instead, I've been diagnosed with Bipolar II . . . I was never aware that bipolar disorders don't necessarily require a full-on manic episode. Bipolar II is characterized by cycling between hypomanic episodes [less severe than full-on manic episodes] and major depressive episodes . . . I never realized my hypomanic episodes were abnormal. I always thought those were when I was actually in a normal state of mind.[29]

I was stunned. I recognized myself in his description. I, too, had experienced times when I was incredibly happy, productive, and "up." But since I spent most of my time struggling with sadness, I thought these short interludes were anomalies or, perhaps, times when I was feeling normal. The possibility of being bipolar had never even occurred to me.

But then there had been my recent experience of staying up night after night, writing the book and not sleeping. It had not been the first time, but it had certainly been the most dramatic iteration. The memory was still vivid. I had transformed into a happy, human version of a hummingbird. Every new idea I had was the most inspiring thing ever. My speech was rapid, my heart pounded, and my body felt full of rocket fuel. I didn't need sleep or coffee. I got a lot done.

It was like I had a performance-enhancing mental illness. *Yay?*

Of course, if anyone were to get jealous, I'd want them to know I also overthought everything and could be extremely draining to be around.

The more I read about this disorder, the more it resonated with me. Bipolar II (also referred to as Bipolar 2) is frequently misdiagnosed, partly because people who have it are *depressed* a majority of the time, and partly because their manic episodes bear little resemblance to those depicted in movies. Bipolar 2 is the under-the-radar Bipolar. It's the non-Kanye version. Its ups and downs don't involve interrupting celebrities or running for president.

For those who have Bipolar 2, getting correctly diagnosed is crucial. The disorder often emerges in a person's mid-twenties and can become progressively more severe if left untreated. This is most likely what had happened to me. Its triggers and treatment are different from those for depression, as are the medications. In my case, switching from an antidepressant to a mood stabilizer resulted in improvements. I began tracking which ends of the cycle I was in at any given time. It became clear that my main trigger for switching into a hypomanic state was interrupted sleep.

If I got three bad nights of sleep in a row, I would enter into mania. (I thought of it as the "M Zone.") Watching movies on my phone at bedtime was no longer an option. I had to protect my sleep until I dropped out of the M Zone and no longer felt turbocharged. In her book *Welcome to the Jungle,* Hilary Smith stresses the significance of sleep when dealing with bipolar issues:

> Straight up: sleep can make or break you. Reduced sleep is both a trigger for and a symptom of mania and hypomania, and insomnia is also an unfortunate feature of depression. It can't be stressed enough: get plenty of sleep, and get it around the same time each night.[30]

By observing my new medical advice, things leveled off for me, and a state of gentle happiness returned and stayed. I began to sense that I would be all right. My crushing Page 90-level episode hadn't been the end of my story. It was the first big test of my ability to recover from a mental health challenge, and I hadn't failed the test after all. I had passed. Not with flying colors, mind you. But I had passed, nonetheless. My post-book depression wasn't just pointless pain; it was the scene in which I took note of my surroundings and changed them up a bit. I let a little more sunlight in.

I also had to laugh when I realized that those consecutive weeks of five-hour-long, predawn writing jags hadn't happened because #LionsNeverSleep or because I had an "unstoppable grind set." They'd happened because I was in an extended manic episode while diligently taking the wrong medication. There's a hashtag for you.

Now, I had the tools I needed. I knew to be kind to myself. I knew not to isolate. In other words, I finally knew how to thrive

CHAPTER 33: AUTHORLAND

with depression and anxiety. Well, at least mostly. My despair had blossomed into beautiful, unexpected, and life-changing proof that the breakthroughs I'd experienced at the bottom were the real thing.

Around this time, reviews began to appear from people who said that reading my personal finance book had helped them. Their positive comments and gratitude showed me that thinking no one cared was inaccurate. This changed how I felt about all the effort involved. Writing that book might have felt like rowing a cruise ship, but from the first time I grasped the metaphorical paddle, it had been worth it.

I had to lose something pretty important to me along the way, though: my belief in Authorland. While I remained alive, there would be no blissfully comfortable spot where life would feel complete and problem-free. But I felt strangely okay with that.

I also knew, deep down, that someday I would probably break that promise I had made to myself. I *would* write another book. Not any time soon, of course. Someday I'd write a book about the goals I pursued and challenges I faced throughout my life—and how they led me to the one thing I'd been searching for all along: to learn to love myself.

After what I went through, I know this: Authorland isn't the miracle. Rowing is.

CHAPTER 34
RELIABLE

We were standing in the middle of a crowded subway station in downtown Beijing, the only tourists in sight, and I was projecting as much confidence as possible. Projecting it, not feeling it.

After a month in Thailand and Bali, Lindsey and I were near the very end of our vacation travels and would soon be on our last flight home. We'd timed it to have a 12-hour layover in Beijing, with a very specific goal in mind: to see the Great Wall of China and make it back to the airport in time for our flight.

The closest access point was roughly 45 miles outside of the city—easily reachable if you hire one of the expensive private cabs in town. But we'd been spending money for a month straight, and our budget was practically begging us to find a cheaper option.

That's when I had an idea. Well, borrowed an idea. Someone had posted on TripAdvisor, claiming they had taken a city bus, followed by a short taxi ride, and gotten to the Great Wall for about a tenth of the cost of a private cab. It had sounded great until the reality of the plan sank in. Few, if any, of the people we'd meet would speak English, all the signs would be in Mandarin, and we wouldn't have time to buy data plans for our phones.

My brain had years of practice as a prediction machine for worst-case scenarios. But I'd been training myself to make my anxiousness function more like radar, detecting potential mishaps without treating them as unavoidable disasters. So, I focused on preparation, visualizing the trip minute by minute, rehearsing subway routes, downloading maps, and even saving photos of every sign we'd have to use.

We aced our first challenge and got off at the right subway stop, which was named "东直门外站." Easy! Actually, it kind of was. Because I was looking for "Christmas tree, parked helicopter, goal posts, a different kind of Christmas tree, and two men riding one unicycle."

We navigated through the crowd and down the long tunnel that led to the bus station, where we spotted the 916 Express bus. (I knew it was the Express because after "916" it had "快." Or, to me, "A man being punched by another man wearing a hula hoop.")

We got in line, and a stern-looking man looked at me for a few seconds and then said in a loud, gruff voice, "Tsien!"

I had no idea what that meant, so I gave him a thumbs-up, as if to say, "You and me both, buddy."

Once again, he yelled "Tsien!" at me. I thought, *I really only had the thumbs-up thing. I don't know what to say now. Could he be saying "Chin"? Do I have something on my face?*

He approached me and placed a hand against my chest to prevent me from getting on the bus. Simultaneously, the

CHAPTER 34: RELIABLE

people behind me started leaning against my back because they wanted to get on. Pinned in place—and the tallest person there by over a foot—I could feel the tension of the moment rising. The awkwardness in the air was so palpable I felt like I was absorbing it from all directions. Like radiation. My tolerance for this sort of thing was usually high, but this was edging toward nuclear levels of embarrassment.

Things had just officially gone awry. I had an unstoppable force behind me and an immovable object in front of me. The immovable object was currently yelling at me. The man gestured angrily at the yen I held in my hands. Something about it was oddly important to him, so I just held it out, presenting it to him as if to say, "Here is . . . money."

With a huff, the man snatched two of the red bills from my hand, fished into his own pocket, and handed some of the combined yen to the driver. He turned back and shoved our tickets into my hand, and only then did I catch on. He hadn't been yelling at me to scold me—he'd been trying to save me from overpaying. The bus didn't give change, and all that shouting had actually been his own strange way of doing me a favor.

I was flooded with relief. (The man was not interested in my high five.)

We got on the bus, and I thought, *This plan isn't going quite as great as I'd hoped. Roughly 20 people have already gotten mad at me.* Of course, when I looked at it through a historical lens, this wasn't that unusual. When we were traveling, people did seem to often yell at me. We took our seats as the bus lurched forward and were soon barreling down the highway. I quickly began poring over my notes for what was to come. I glanced over at my travel partner, who was having a different experience. Lindsey was asleep. On a bus, tearing through the Chinese countryside, with no idea what sign to look for next, Lindsey was asleep! How was this possible? I'll tell you. Lindsey trusted me, just as she always had.

In this moment, I wondered if that trust was a bit misplaced. I was way out of my depth here. I began to second-guess myself, and a wave of anxiety hit. As the familiar spiral of self-doubt and panoramic panic began to emerge, it felt unbearable. I wanted to relieve this discomfort by getting reassured.

But I didn't wake up Lindsey. I didn't need to, because I reassured myself instead. I told myself I could be okay with moving forward, guided solely by a mental map that rendered only a few feet in front of me at a time.

So, I let her sleep peacefully and focused on what I did know. We were on the right bus, and in roughly 75 minutes, we'd get off to catch a taxi. All we had to do was wait for the sign to say, "怀柔北大街." Or "Microphone, up arrow, very thick Christmas tree, broken ladder, figure skater, and yet another Christmas tree except this one is sticking out of the roof of a house."

Gradually the bus, like the landscape, got emptier. We'd started in a major urban area, but now we were somewhere quite rural, desolate, and mountainous. Finally, I saw it: *Microphone. Up arrow . . . Figure skater! This is it!*

I pulled the cord, and we got off in the absolute middle of nowhere. It was cold! Especially for two people who had just spent a month in Bali. A man a few hundred feet away saw us, stubbed out a cigarette, and pointed to his car. We got in. What could possibly go wrong?

He drove us the remaining few miles to the Great Wall, then parked on a side street and used a translation app on his phone

CHAPTER 34: RELIABLE

to tell me he would wait for us if we gave him half the money. This seemed reasonable enough, and this time I glanced at the picture of various yen I'd saved on my phone before I gave him two red ones and a green one.

That's when, for the second time that day, a man began yelling at me. I had no idea what he was saying, but it was clear that he wanted more money.

The car quickly took on a "someone's-being-robbed" energy. We needed our remaining money for the bus back to the airport, so I shook my head. Again, he gestured for more, growing more upset by the second. The tension in the car was climbing rapidly. Finally, I looked once more at the money I'd placed in his hand, and I realized I had given him a blue-green one instead of a green one. This time, I had underpaid.

He had been yelling at me so I wouldn't short-change him—because if I had, he'd have driven off and left us there. Quite rightly! I immediately replaced the wrong bill with the correct one, and when the man broke into a smile, so did I.

The relief that flooded the car quickly gave way to shared laughter. He and I had both thought we were getting ripped off by a stranger, only to find out we were each trying to do the right thing. I asked his name, and then Zhang asked mine. After we mangled each other's names, we smiled and shook hands. Lindsey and I stepped out of the car and finally took in the sight of the Great Wall. It was beyond impressive.

After a cable car ride to the top, we stood on stones that had been placed there 1,500 years earlier. The views were stunningly beautiful. Hardly a cloud in the bright-blue sky or another person on the wall. Because it was an afternoon at the end of November, the frigid weather and the coming dusk meant the walls were much emptier than usual. With almost no one else there, our selfies were all keepers. The unrestricted views of the Wall, which extended for miles in each direction, seemingly to the horizon, were breathtaking. There had been no way to fully imagine the scope and the scale of this wonder of the world until that moment.

As I looked in the direction of Beijing, miles away from us now, a thought flickered in my mind. *All day I've been focused on how I might mess up, yet I got us here. This is my proof: I can trust myself.*

When we finally came down, we found our driver (who greeted us with a warmth typically reserved for old friends), and he drove us back to the bus stop in the middle of nowhere. We said goodbye and stood there in the dark until our bus came around the corner and picked us up. We had cut it pretty close, but as the lights of Beijing finally appeared up ahead, I knew we would make it. The trip had gone perfectly. Well, minus the yelling.

This risky undertaking, which once would've paralyzed me, had been *fun*. I got more than just a breathtaking view. I got an adventure to remember.

There had been plenty of moments that could have sent me into a spiral. Once, they would have, but not now. All day long, despite my worries, the path kept opening up ahead of us. That wasn't due only to luck. Everything about this excursion went successfully . . . because of me.

As we faced one unknown after another, while feeling vulnerable and exposed, we had trusted ourselves. We had trusted *me*. This wasn't a leap for Lindsey, and now I could see that it wasn't so much of a leap for me either. Lindsey had shown me

CHAPTER 34: RELIABLE

many times that she could carry us when needed. I could carry us, too. It was the only kind of romantic relationship I ever wanted—one in which we were friends and lovers and equals.

Somewhere amidst the subway, the bus, and the Wall, I realized that trusting myself doesn't demand certainty—only enough faith to leave the familiar behind. Trust is taking action when certainty is nowhere to be seen.

As we gratefully collapsed at our gate, I thought of three reasons I handle the unexpected well.

First: I love people. I value humor, kindness, and curiosity, just as my gran did. That makes it possible for me to find common ground and connect with a lot of the people I meet.

Second: I absorb awkwardness. In fact, if someone in any group I'm in happens to break some unspoken rule and finds themselves being yelled at, they can just aim that irate stranger at me, and I'll get yelled at instead. I don't mind.

Third: I feel fear but act anyway. I anticipate risks others might miss, but I no longer get paralyzed by them. I simply make a plan. I am much more resourceful and reliable than I tend to give myself credit for.

These reasons apply to more than just traveling. They are the reasons that Lindsey trusts me, and they are why I trust myself, too.

Facing the unknown is a lot easier when you're the one you'd most want beside you.

EPILOGUE
EPIC, TINY VICTORIES

It's taken me years to truly grasp the idea that dealing with mental health challenges doesn't mean I'm flawed or broken. It doesn't define me, and I'm not alone. If you face similar challenges, this is true for you as well. You've likely wrestled with the same question I did: *Why can't I function like most of the people around me?* I stayed persistent in my search for the answer, which is how I discovered what works for *me*.

One of the answers I needed involved diagnosis, which, in my case, had several layers. But I did get it, and here it is: I don't experience depression and anxiety because something is wrong with me; I experience depression and anxiety because I have Bipolar II, OCD, and ADHD. (And probably some complex PTSD too, but this list is long enough for now.)

I also needed to see that all my disconnected efforts were actually progress toward some kind of healing. Once I did, I could expand the scattered collection of skills, habits, strengths, and insights I'd pieced together over the years. That collection was, in reality, something more: a series of interlocking pieces. Those pieces began snapping into place, forming an unexpectedly sturdy foundation—a foundation I had earned.

I'm not pretending everything is all fixed and settled and behind me now. During the two years it took to write this book (I'm getting faster . . . sort of!), I experienced a few periods of significant depression. I'll never not be a depressive. However, I can bounce back from episodes of depression and anxiety more quickly and confidently than ever before.

It took me a long time to realize that developing a strong and kind relationship with yourself rarely happens through big, dramatic breakthroughs. The successes are usually small, but they are definitely still successes.

Look at it this way. When you're confronted with a huge challenge, aim for one small, smart action to take rather than doing nothing. You won't get anywhere by aiming for the moon, but you can get everywhere by getting out of bed.

I have a feeling that once you achieve a few tiny victories, you'll see, like I have, that none of them were insignificant. They are all epic. Every single one matters, and it matters a lot. Gather the courage to take a small step, ask others for support when needed, and keep repeating the process until you've built some momentum. It becomes easier from there.

Now that we've reached the end, let me share one final epic, tiny victory with you: writing my second book was *nothing* like my first. Yes, the effort was still immense, and I felt the grip of perfectionism more than I'd have liked to. But there were remarkably few sleepless nights, anxious spirals, and waves of impostor syndrome to battle against. In their place, I found myself rediscovering something unexpected in my time spent writing: joy.

I hope I made you laugh a few times. I hope I reminded you that you're not alone. But most of all, I hope you sensed what will be possible when you fully embrace the truth: You are a success, and you are a mess, and you are enough.

ACKNOWLEDGEMENTS

This book would not have been possible without the wisdom, humor, and insight of the artists and experts whose work helped shape my thinking and inform my writing. My deepest gratitude goes to the creators of the books, essays, comedy specials, and stories that guided me along the way:

Alice Greczyn, for *Wayward*.
Andrew Niccol (screenwriter) and Peter Weir (director), for *The Truman Show*.
Craig Pierce (screenwriter) and Baz Luhrmann (director), for *Strictly Ballroom*.
David Adam, for *The Man Who Couldn't Stop: OCD and the True Story of a Life Lost in Thought*.
Debby Irving, for *Waking Up White: Finding Myself in the Story of Race*.
Donald Miller, for *Blue Like Jazz: Nonreligious Thoughts on Christian Spirituality* and *A Million Miles in a Thousand Years: What I Learned While Editing My Life*.

Edward Hallowell and John Ratey, for *Driven to Distraction: Recognizing and Coping with Attention Deficit Disorder.*

Elizabeth Dunn and Michael Norton, for *Happy Money: The Science of Happier Spending.*

Gary Gulman (writer and performer), for *The Great Depresh.*

Hannah Gadsby (writer and performer), for *Nanette.*

Helaine Olen, for *Pound Foolish: Exposing the Dark Side of the Personal Finance Industry.*

Hilary Smith, for *Welcome to the Jungle: Everything You Wanted to Know About Bipolar but Were Too Freaked Out to Ask.*

Jean Kilbourne, for *Can't Buy My Love: How Advertising Changes the Way We Think and Feel.*

Jessica McCabe, for *How to ADHD: An Insider's Guide to Working with Your Brain (Not Against It).*

John Moe, for *The Hilarious World of Depression.*

Jonathan Gottschall, for *The Storytelling Animal.*

Joseph Campbell, for *The Hero with a Thousand Faces.*

Linda Kay Klein, for *Pure: Inside the Evangelical Movement That Shamed a Generation of Young Women and How I Broke Free.*

Linda Tirado, for *Hand to Mouth: Living in Bootstrap America*

Mark and Dan, for *The How-To Heretic* podcast.

Mike Birbiglia, for *Sleepwalk with Me.*

Nikos Kazantzakis, for *The Last Temptation of Christ.*

Sarah Wilson, for *First, We Make the Beast Beautiful: A New Journey Through Anxiety*

Seth Andrews, for *Deconverted: A Journey from Religion to Reason.*

Stephen King (author) and Frank Darabont (screenwriter and director), for *The Shawshank Redemption.*

ACKNOWLEDGEMENT

The Apostle Paul, for *Philemon*. (Admittedly, less so now.)
Trevor Noah, for *Born a Crime*.
Valerie Young, for *The Secret Thoughts of Successful Women and Men: Why Capable People Suffer from Impostor Syndrome and How to Thrive In Spite of It*.
Will Storr, for *The Science of Storytelling*.

Lastly, as a writer, I think I am legally required to thank Anne Lamott for *Bird by Bird*.

To these authors, creators, and storytellers, your work made this book possible. Thank you for reminding me that we are never alone in our questions or in our journey.

Mountains of heartfelt gratitude go to my friend, fellow author, and the editor of this book, Jan Gleiter. Jan, this is a better book because of your tireless commitment and insights. You were more than an editor—you were a thought-partner, a cheerleader, a translator, and a friend. Your comments on each chapter made me laugh out loud, better understand the art of grammar, and learn to write like a writer rather than a public speaker. To quote one of my favorites of your many *bon mots*, "It's okay to sound informal, Colin, as long as you don't sound illiterate when you're being informal." Or another "You may have acted like a bonehead in this moment, but at least you were a relatable bonehead." Or my favorite, "Yet another piece of proof that you and I are an unbeatable team." You provided the frankness, the encouragement, and the tough medicine required to help these stories become what I hoped they could be. I hope you enjoyed the milk chocolate with toffee and almonds.

ABOUT THE AUTHOR

Colin Ryan is on a mission to connect meaningful ideas to the audiences who need to hear them. As a humorous financial and mental health speaker, Colin's fusion of stand-up comedy, storytelling, and interactive discussion has drawn national attention, putting him on stage in all 50 states, speaking at companies, conferences, and universities. He has been named one of America's Top Ten Personal Finance Speakers, is a Certified Executive Coach, and has presented to more than one million people.

His storytelling performances have been featured on PBS, NPR, The Moth Radio Hour, World Channel, and more. *Reader's Digest* featured his story, "Saved by the Belle," in its "Best Stories in America" collection. Colin is the author of two books: *A Comedic Guide to Money: The Skills You Need to Build the Life You Want* and *Epic Tiny Victories*.

Colin brings his lived experience with mental health, resilience, and recovery to organizations and communities seeking to break stigma and foster authentic conversations. To learn more about his speaking work, visit www.colinryanspeaks.com.

Colin spends his downtime plunking piano keys, learning languages, woodworking, traveling, and watching movies. He is a brother, son, uncle, and friend, but he is most proud to be Lindsey's husband and Remy and Enzo's dog dad.

ABOUT THE EDITOR

Jan Gleiter is the author of *Lie Down with Dogs*—winner of the St. Martin's Malice Domestic Contest for the Best First Traditional Mystery Novel—and more than thirty books for readers of all ages. A versatile storyteller, her work spans mystery, fiction, biographies for children, and educational materials that bring language and history to life.

Jan has introduced young readers to historical figures such as Jane Addams, Booker T. Washington, and Sacagawea in her acclaimed biography series with Kathleen Thompson. Her other titles include *A House by the Side of the Road*, *Words to Go: Words to Know*, *Paul Bunyan and Babe the Blue Ox*, *This Is a Test*—and many more.

Jan lives in Chicago, where she continues to write, edit, and develop educational materials for students nationwide.

• • •

A note from Colin . . . In mid-2024, Lindsey and I volunteered to help a friend of a friend prepare an old Craftsman house for sale after her sister's passing. That's how we met Jan and her husband, Paul.

When Jan heard I was writing a book, she immediately offered to edit it. I thought it was just a polite gesture—but within days, she returned the prologue marked with funny and insightful notes. Since I write the way I speak on stage—which is to say, in a way that would make a grammarian of Jan's caliber wince—she responded with patient, humorous grammar mini-lessons that made me laugh and learn along the way.

This book is much better thanks to Jan. But more than that, I gained a friend. I remember the day I called Jan, not to talk about the book, but just to chat. She told me a great story about the time a fan approached her and, in an excited voice (right within earshot of a famous author who, for some reason, wouldn't give Jan the time of day), asked, "Oh my goodness, are you *the* Jan Gleiter?" She was—and is—and from that day forward, I've always thought of her as The Jan Gleiter.

Jan, I apologize for not letting you edit this section—hopefully I didn't make too many mistakes. XOXO.

EASY WAYS TO SHARE THIS BOOK

I was talking to a friend recently, and he mentioned struggling with a fear of failure in his career. So I sent him a copy of this book and encouraged him to read the chapter where I failed in front of a comedy audience and learned something helpful on the other side. A student mentioned she was living with a health condition, so I recommended the chapter on growing up with asthma and using humor as one of my tools to manage it. In both cases, the stories resonated with them, and that is exactly what I hoped for when writing this book.

Each chapter in this book is a stand-alone story that addresses universal experiences and everyday challenges, which means you can recommend specific chapters based on what someone you know is going through. Here's a guide for matching chapters to experiences. You could simply say, "Hey, you mentioned [experience or challenge]. Chapter [X] in *Epic Tiny Victories* deals with that—I thought it might be helpful."

Here are some common experiences/challenges and the chapters that explore them:

ADHD
Ch. 31: "Diagnosed, at Last" (Some potential indicators of ADHD, what it can feel like, and an example of how one might respond to its unique challenges.)

Anxiety
Ch. 5: "It Ain't Easy Being Wheezy" (Dealing with chronic health issues—using comedy to manage anxiety.)
Ch. 11: "Pamplona Took My Breath Away" (The emergence of anxiety and catastrophizing beyond what's manageable.)
Ch. 25: "One Minute Less Afraid" (Tackling irrational fears and phobias in a practical way.)
Ch. 29: "Social Anxiety on a Jumbotron" (Anxiety at its peak during a high-stakes challenge.)

Belonging / Feeling Like an Outsider
Ch. 2: "Unaccompanied" (Feeling like you don't belong or dealing with something above your maturity level or age.)
Ch. 6: "Saved by the Belle" (Longing to disappear after humiliation.)
Ch. 27: "We Were All 11" (Everyone can relate to feeling like an outsider.)

Bipolar Disorder
Ch. 33: "Authorland" (A frequently misdiagnosed disorder that can present as depression, along with bursts of

high productivity, and worsen if left untreated; some of its unique triggers and how to manage them.)

Courage

Ch. 2: "Unaccompanied" (Performing courage even when you're afraid.)

Ch. 10: "Scotland Needs Subtitles" (Believing in yourself when others might not.)

Ch. 18: "From My Seat to the Stage" (Being courageous, even in mundane ways, can still be exciting and significant to your growth.)

Ch. 25: "One Minute Less Afraid" (Overcoming irrational fears by pushing through them.)

Ch. 34: "Reliable" (Becoming the person you'd want by your side.)

Depression

Ch. 1: "A Successful Depressive" (Hitting your breaking point and learning a life-saving technique.)

Ch. 13: "A Tourist in Other People's Passions" (Battling paralyzing depression while trying to make ends meet.)

Ch. 28: "The Blurt, the Bat, and Being Seen" (When your partner discovers your depression.)

Ch. 29: "Social Anxiety on a Jumbotron" (Depression intensifying even as you give motivational speeches.)

Ch. 30: "Breakthroughs at the Bottom" (How freelance isolation can foster depression.)

Ch. 33: "Authorland" (Post-achievement depression and discovering a new mental health diagnosis.)

Divorce
- Ch. 2: "Unaccompanied" (Flying solo between divorced parents and not belonging to either of your two families.)
- Ch. 3: "Unreliable Narrators" (Blaming yourself for your parents' divorce and not measuring up to impossibly high standards.)
- Ch. 32: "A Photo of Us" (When a nontraditional family reunites at a wedding and puts each other first.)

External Validation / Self-worth
- Ch. 13: "A Tourist in Other People's Passions" (A job can make you feel important; external validation doesn't have the power to define your self-worth.)
- Ch. 30: "Breakthroughs at the Bottom" (Knowing you are worthy as you are isn't enough—you have to learn how to believe it and internalize it.)
- Ch. 29: "Social Anxiety on a Jumbotron" (Even having 18,000 people clap for you doesn't mean much if you don't have your own approval.)

Faith Crisis / Leaving Religion
- Ch. 7: "Holy(ish)" (Trying to meet impossible religious standards.)
- Ch. 12: "Accidental Movie Star" (A funny take on making art for a religious purpose.)
- Ch. 15: "Late to the Party" (Making decisions that don't align with religious beliefs but are true to who you are.)
- Ch. 16: "Ruptures" (Losing your religion but finding yourself.)

Fear of Failure / Rejection
Ch. 4: "The F-I-A-S-C-O" (Losing when you thought you won; finding the lesson in a rejection or failure.)

Ch. 17: "An Audience of One" (Being so afraid of rejection that your life gets smaller.)

Ch. 18: "From My Seat to the Stage" (Facing your fear head-on through stand-up comedy.)

Ch. 19: "The Setup and the Punch" (An ode to failing spectacularly; discovering you're tougher than you thought.)

Ch. 21: "Finding Life Funny" (Reframing embarrassing moments as material.)

Impostor Syndrome
Ch. 9: "Once Upon a Huffy in Hollywood" (Losing your nerve when opportunity knocks.)

Ch. 29: "Social Anxiety on a Jumbotron" (Giving a motivational speech while falling apart inside.)

Ch. 30: "Breakthroughs at the Bottom" (Recognizing that someone's surface goal often masks a deeper need.)

Inner Critic / Negative Self-Talk
Ch. 3: "Unreliable Narrators" (Blaming yourself for things that aren't your fault.)

Ch. 23: "The Heckler in My Head" (Dealing with your harshest critic—yourself.)

Ch. 30: "Breakthroughs at the Bottom" (Learning to be kind to yourself.)

Ch. 32: "A Photo of Us" (Realizing you've been the unreliable narrator of your own story.)

Isolation / Loneliness / Community
    Ch. 2: "Unaccompanied" (Learning to build confidence by talking with people.)
    Ch. 5: "It Ain't Easy Being Wheezy" (Discovering the power of laughter to connect with others.)
    Ch. 8: "Mayor of Campus" (Craving universal approval and sacrificing authenticity to get it; realizing that popularity can be isolating.)
    Ch. 13: "A Tourist in Other People's Passions" (Meeting unique characters while struggling with isolation.)
    Ch. 22: "Story Therapy" (Discovering that most people have a greater capacity to relate than you might think.)
    Ch. 30: "Breakthroughs at the Bottom" (How isolation inherent in freelance life can foster depression; learning how to make friends as an adult.)

OCD
    Ch. 28: "The Blurt, the Bat, and Being Seen" (Undiagnosed OCD in the form of constant reassurance-seeking.)
    Ch. 31: "Diagnosed, at Last" (Learning that OCD can consist of compulsions that are mental rather than physical and getting real techniques to fight it.)

Personal Transformation
    Ch. 32: "A Photo of Us" (Realizing you've finally accepted that you're lovable.)
    Ch. 33: "Authorland" (It can be common to experience depression *after* reaching a significant milestone; it's okay to accept that the work is never done.)
    Ch. 34: "Reliable" (Proving your capabilities to yourself;

using challenges as tools rather than barriers.)

Physical Pain / Chronic Illness
    Ch. 5: "It Ain't Easy Being Wheezy" (Illness ruling your childhood.)
    Ch. 11: "Pamplona Took My Breath Away" (Surviving an all-night asthma attack.)
    Ch. 26: "The Complicated Art of Financial Compassion" (Navigating a seemingly indifferent health care system.)

Purpose & Impact
    Ch. 13: "A Tourist in Other People's Passions" (Wondering if you'll ever find your passion.)
    Ch. 20: "I Somehow Invent My Own Job" (Finding work that's truly meaningful.)
    Ch. 26: "The Complicated Art of Financial Compassion" (Waking up to your privilege and showing vulnerability.)

Pursuing Dreams / Personal Fulfillment
    Ch. 17: "An Audience of One" (Being afraid your life is smaller than it should be.)
    Ch. 18: "From My Seat to the Stage" (Showing yourself what you're capable of.)
    Ch. 33: "Authorland" (Pursuing your dream despite mental health crises; how achieving one can sometimes feel bittersweet.)

Relationships & Vulnerability
    Ch. 24: "The Big Picture" (How a relationship can help you see an interesting future rather than just surviving.)

Ch. 28: "The Blurt, the Bat, and Being Seen" (Letting your partner see the real you—depression and all.)

Ch. 32: "A Photo of Us" (Accepting that you are lovable.)

Storytelling & Humor as Healing

Ch. 21: "Finding Life Funny" (Viewing struggle as funny in order to feel differently about depression and awkwardness.)

Ch. 22: "Story Therapy" (How storytelling can provide a way to change the meaning of bad memories.)

Ch. 27: "We Were All 11" (Discovering your embarrassing moments are actually things people will respond to with empathy.)

Therapy & Mental Health Treatment

Ch. 1: "A Successful Depressive" (Gathering courage to see a therapist for the first time.)

Ch. 14: "My Secret Sentence" (How therapy can be transformative—a love letter to therapy.)

Ch. 30: "Breakthroughs at the Bottom" (You can still find the right coach or therapist after trying ones that don't work for you.)

Ch. 31: "Diagnosed, at Last" (Getting the correct diagnosis after years of misunderstanding.)

PHOTO GALLERY

You can see an entertaining gallery of images that correspond with these stories by visiting www.epictinyvictories.com.

ENDNOTES

1 Jack Zavada, "TULIP Acronym: Calvinism Explained in 5 Simple Points," *Learn Religions,* May 17, 2024, accessed September 2, 2025, https://www.learnreligions.com/five-point-calvinism-700356.

2 "Sin against the Holy Spirit," in *New Catholic Encyclopedia,* 2nd ed., vol. 13 (Detroit: Gale, 2003), reproduced in Encyclopedia.com, accessed August 29, 2025, https://www.encyclopedia.com/religion/encyclopedias-almanacs-transcripts-and-maps/sin-against-holy-spirit | *Author's Note: The "Unforgivable Sin" is technically a reference to blasphemy—rejecting God—but the term itself felt vague and unsettling. In my Christian circles it was variously described as "a hardening of the heart" or "impenitence" or "sinning against the Holy Spirit," all of which left it difficult to easily comprehend. As a young person, this ambiguity led me to worry that almost any misstep against biblical counsel or church teaching could qualify as the Unforgivable Sin. I even wondered, half-jokingly, whether something like dancing might count.*

3 Michael Foust, "Study: Abstinence Pledges Help Delay Premarital Sex," *Baptist Press,* March 19, 2004, https://www.baptistpress.com/resource-library/news/study-abstinence-pledges-help-delay-premarital-sex/. | *Author's Note: In evangelical circles, many teens in the 1990s took "virginity pledges," promising publicly to abstain from sexual intercourse until*

marriage. Later research suggests that, while those pledges did delay sex on average, as many as 88% of pledgers did have sex before marriage. Although I could not track down a primary study with that exact figure, the broader scholarly consensus affirms that a majority of pledge-takers not only did engage in pre-marital sex, they were also less likely to use contraception when they did.

4 National Center for Biotechnology Information. (n.d.). *Bookshelf.* National Library of Medicine, National Institutes of Health. Retrieved November 28, 2024, from https://www.ncbi.nlm.nih.gov/books/NBK315/

5 Wilson, S. (2018). *First, We Make the Beast Beautiful: A New Journey Through Anxiety.* First U.S. edition. New York, NY, Dey Street, an imprint of William Morrow.

6 Pease, Kryssy. "Baron Vaughn and His Inadvisable All Cheerio Diet" Audio podcast. The Hilarious World of Depression. January 30, 2017. Web. https://www.hilariousworld.org/episode/2017/01/30/episode-8-]baron-vaughn-and-his-inadvisable-all-cheerio-diet

7 Moe, J. (2020). *The Hilarious World of Depression.* St. Martin's Press.

8 Gottlieb, L. (2019). *Maybe You Should Talk to Someone: A Therapist, HER Therapist, and Our Lives Revealed.* Houghton Mifflin Harcourt.

9 Harris, Joshua. *I Kissed Dating Goodbye: A New Attitude Toward Relationships and Romance.* Colorado Springs, CO: Multnomah Books, 1997. | *Author's note: The author of this book, Joshua Harris, (who, it bears repeating, was only 22 when he wrote it) would later publicly apologize for his book, renounce its message, pull it from the shelves, and make a documentary investigating the damage it had done. Unfortunately, many people already had the trauma, divorces, and heartache that resulted from taking its message to heart.*

10 *2 Timothy 1:7,* New King James Version. (1982). Thomas Nelson.

11 Hanson, S. B. (2022, July 17). *My Misunderstood Story of Losing Faith:*

For Christians I Love. Medium. Retrieved November 28, 2024 from https://medium.com/christianish/my-deconstruction-story-a-letter-to-christians-i-love-8baaa16711f1

12 Weir, P. (Director). (1998). *The Truman Show* [Film]. Paramount Pictures.

13 *Author's Note: While writing this book, I queried a Facebook group of deconverted Evangelicals regarding what fears in their childhood were normalized by the adults and teachers in their church. They quickly responded with well over 100 examples.*

14 Holmes, P. (2016). *Pete Holmes: Faces and Sounds* [TV special]. HBO.

15 Kierkegaard, S. (1843). *Either/Or* (H. Hong & E. Hong, Eds. & Trans., 1987). Princeton University Press.

16 Campbell, J., & Osbon, D. K. (Eds.). (1991). *Reflections on the Art of Living: A Joseph Campbell Companion* (pp. 8, 24). HarperCollins.

17 Pat Lynch, email message to author, June 1, 2010.

18 Siegel, D. J. (1999). *The Developing Mind: Toward a Neurobiology of Interpersonal Experience*. New York, NY: Guilford Press.

19 Brown, B. (2021). *Atlas of the Heart: Mapping Meaningful Connection and the Language of Human Experience*. Random House.

20 Birdsong, M. (n.d.). The Story We Tell about Poverty Isn't True [Video]. TED Conferences. https://www.ted.com/talks/mia_birdsong_the_story_we_tell_about_poverty_isn_t_true

21 Wong, D. (2014, August 12). *Robin Williams and Why Funny People Kill Themselves*. Cracked.com. https://www.cracked.com/quick-fixes/robin-williams-why-funny-people-kill-themselves/

22 National FFA Organization. *FFA | Preparing Members for Leadership and Career Success*. Accessed October 10, 2025. https://www.ffa.org/.

23 Moe, J. (Host). (2017, January 2). Episode #4: Dick Cavett Tells Tales of Hollywood's Secret Shame [Audio podcast episode]. In *The Hilarious World of Depression*. American Public Media.

24 Seth Godin, *The Dip: A Little Book That Teaches You When to Quit (and When to Stick)* (New York: Portfolio, 2007).

25 Gulman, G. (Performer). (2019, October 5). *The Great Depresh* [TV special]. HBO.

26 Daniel A. Cox, *The State of American Friendship: Change, Challenges, and Loss. Findings from the May 2021 American Perspectives Survey* (Survey Center on American Life, June 8, 2021), accessed August 29, 2025, Americans Survey Center.

27 Adam, D. (2014). *The Man Who Couldn't Stop: OCD and the True Story of a Life Lost in Thought.* Sarah Crichton Books/Farrar, Straus and Giroux.

28 McCabe, J. (2024). *How to ADHD: An Insider's Guide to Working with Your Brain (Not Against It).* Harmony/Rodale/Convergent.

29 Name withheld, Facebook post, 2018.

30 Smith, H. (2010). *Welcome to the Jungle: Everything You Wanted to Know about Bipolar but Were Too Freaked Out to Ask.* Conari Press.

www.ingramcontent.com/pod-product-compliance
Lightning Source LLC
Chambersburg PA
CBHW052012070526
44584CB00016B/1713